Wine for Women

LESLIE SBROCCO

WILLIAM MORROW
An Imprint of HarperCollins*Publishers*

Wine for Women

A Guide to Buying, Pairing, and Sharing Wine

HarperCollins books may be purchased for educational, business,
or sales promotional use. For information please write: Special
Markets Department, HarperCollins Publishers Inc., 10 East 53rd
Street, New York, NY 10022.

FIRST EDITION

Book design and Illustrations by Shubhani Sarkar

Printed on acid-free paper

Library of Congress Cataloging-in-Publication Data

Sbrocco, Leslie, 1963-
    Wine for women: a guide to buying, pairing, and sharing
wine/Leslie Sbrocco.
        p. cm.
    Includes index.
    ISBN 0-06-052332-8 (hc)
    1. Wine and wine making.   I. Title.

TP548.S385 2003
641.2'2—dc21

                                                        2003052743

03 04 05 06 07 WBC/QW 10 9 8 7 6 5 4 3 2 1

I dedicate this book to Leonard, my love and partner in life; to my sweet and smart daughter, Grace; to my joyous son, Dominic; to Beverly, my inspiring mother and guiding light; to my irreplaceable "second" mom, Rita; and to the rest of the fantastic, eclectic Hartley/Sbrocco family. I love you all.

Contents

Acknowledgments

WHILE WRITING A BOOK IS A SOLITARY PROCESS, THE FINAL RESULT IS a collaborative effort. I want to thank those people who helped bring my creation into this world.

The first is Harriet Bell, my editor extraordinaire. After meeting Harriet, I felt an immediate connection because of her warm smile and humor. She believed in my book from the beginning and mentored me through the journey of a first-time author with encouragement and patience. I remember a pivotal point early on. After nervously sending Harriet the initial draft of several chapters for feedback, I received a message that read "This is going to be one fabulous book!" A printed-out version of that e-mail posted above my computer inspired me to do my best.

This book wouldn't have taken off without my talented literary agent, Judith Riven. She saw the potential of my diamond-in-the-rough idea and helped me polish it into a book proposal that got published more quickly than I could have imagined.

An instrumental part of this whole project was Gail Spangler, my business partner and friend. Her editing input, gentle but persistent prodding, and honesty made this book immeasurably stronger. She is the best partner imaginable and together we're a team ready to tackle the world.

Kathryn Jessup, my young food researcher and culinary sounding board, was a tremendous asset in assisting with the development and testing of a number of the recipes. She spent countless hours in my kitchen with me sipping, swirling, sautéing, and searing her way into my heart. London-based wine researcher Matthew Day, who helped in the book's initial phases, is another rising star whose byline will soon be known by many.

Thanks to the terrific team at HarperCollins, including my copy-editor Chris Benton for her insightful questions and positive comments, the production, editorial, and design departments that made my book come to life, the sales force that helped bring it to the store shelves, and to Katie Connery, Kristen Green, and Kate Stark.

When it came to reading the book for factual accuracy, numerous people had their hands on this manuscript, but the most important was my buddy and colleague Marco Cappelli. As one of California's top winemakers who has trained in Europe and Australia, his wine knowledge is vast, yet he understands how to communicate it in human terms.

A good portion of this book is a thinly veiled travel journal. It translates my journeys through many of the world's wine regions into what I hope is a useful guide for readers. Numerous people have assisted in making my globe-trotting easier, including David Strada and the New Zealand Wine Growers, Steve Burns and his team at the Washington Wine Commission, the staff of Sopexa/Food & Wines from France, the Loire Valley Wine Bureau, the German Wine Information Bureau, and the Australian Wine Bureau, to name just a few.

When I needed answers to my research questions, I turned to Gladys Horiuchi of the Wine Institute, John Gillespie and Jennifer Pagano of the Wine Market Council, and Christian Miller of Motto, Kryla, Fisher. I also relied on the responsive staffs of top importers and a handful of national retailers.

In terms of information gathering and fact checking, my thanks goes to the top-notch public relations professionals who assisted me when I had urgent phone calls and e-mails. Their work was greatly appreciated by this sometimes frazzled author.

Most important, I want to acknowledge the hundreds of winemakers and winery owners that I have met and interviewed over the years. I can't possibly list them all, but you'll read about many of them in the pages that follow. The majority of my wine education came from these "teachers," who generously shared time traipsing through vineyards, sipping through cellars, and toasting at tables. They have taught me so much on the technical side, while balancing that with a burning passion for wine.

My career has been nurtured by numerous people who gave me a chance to shine. I am a better writer/person because of my colleagues (many I consider dear friends), whom I've had the pleasure of working with: Linda Murphy, Norm Roby, Sara Hare, Peter Hirschfeld, Jean Jacote, Tim McDonald, Bob Cappuccino, Jay Soloff, Jack Bittner, Evan Goldstein, W. R. Tish, Bruce Kyse, Jeff Moriarty, Lynn Forbes, Kathleen Buckley, Jim Hammett, Oz Clarke, Frank Prial, Doug Frost, Victor Fisher, Burton Anderson, Adrian Webster, Dan Saltzstein, Kristen Bieler, and Judith Knudsen. All have left an imprint on my first book.

Finally, thank you to my friends and family for putting up with months of "no Leslie again" while I was holed up in my office day and night or traveling to a far-off place. Your support and love mean everything.

Wine for Women

Introduction: Why a Wine Book for Women?

I
F YOU'RE READING THIS, MY GUESS IS YOU ENJOY WINE. WHETHER YOU
indulge regularly or only occasionally, reaching for a glass is a welcome pleasure. From cocktail hour to the dinner table, wine signals celebration, recreation, and relaxation.

I think we can all agree, however, that wine can be a mystery. You
know you like it, but often don't quite know why. *Wine for Women* is
here to answer your questions and empower you to squeeze more
enjoyment from each bottle you drink and dollar you spend.

Need help making smart buying decisions or just want to be more
confident navigating a wine list? This book is for you. If you're a time-
challenged cook who enjoys wine with meals, this book is also for you.
Interested in creative, entertaining ideas to share wine with family and
friends? You're in the right place.

Penned with passion for wine, my practical guide is ideal for busy
women who love to eat and drink well. Depending upon what you
want to learn, you can either skim for tips or dive for details. While I
offer serious wine information, my book doesn't take itself too seriously. Remember, wine is fun!

Are "Men from Bordeaux and Women from Burgundy"?

You may be asking "Why a wine book for women?" Is the battle of the sexes now played out over dueling glasses of Chardonnay and Cabernet? Hardly. The point of this book is not to create a vinous male/female divide but rather to highlight wine information that is relevant to most women's daily lives. (Men reading this book—congrats for being secure enough with your feminine side to pick it up.)

As the majority of wine buyers and drinkers in this country, women comprise the largest slice of the enological pie. According to the non-profit Wine Market Council, women now account for nearly 64 percent of all wine consumers. "Women are the very key to the future of the industry," says John Gillespie, the organization's president. I agree, which is why I've written this book.

The female skew shouldn't come as a surprise when you consider that women are generally the household shoppers. As national wine buyer for the retail chain Cost Plus World Markets, Mark Albrecht knows the power of the female consumer. "Eighty percent of our customers are women. I find they're very adventurous when it comes to wine and enjoy exploring bottles from all over the world."

A recent study conducted for California's Canyon Road Winery concluded that women are more involved with wine than men. Of the more than one thousand wine drinkers surveyed, more women than men drink wine at restaurants, by itself as a cocktail, and in celebratory situations. Wine for women is not a status symbol or collector's item; it's about enjoying life with family and friends one bottle at a time.

What Women Want to Know: Buying, Pairing, and Sharing

During my career as a wine writer and speaker, I would often be approached by women who wanted to know more. The idea of a wine book for women crystallized in my mind but I needed to understand what, if anything, would make the female perspective on the subject unique.

After compiling research done by others and conducting my own interviews and surveys, I discovered the majority of women are less focused on wine ratings, vintage charts, and acquiring bottles.

Forget the notion that women sip white while men slurp red (women actually drink more red than white these days). It is not about what's in the bottle but how we approach what's in the bottle. Women tend to be interested in personal recommendations, food ideas, and helpful tips on finding wines that simply taste good.

As a result, you'll find chapters organized into sections I've called THE BIG THREE: BUYING, PAIRING, and SHARING. This is what we do with wine—head to the store and buy something to drink that night, take it home to serve with dinner, and uncork it with our family and friends.

- **Buying** sections are focused on how to buy wine by taste and style, and highlight wine regions as they correlate to what you might actually see on store shelves, hence the focus on wine labels.
- **Pairing** sections offer practical, everyday advice on enjoying wine and food together. They come complete with shopping lists and Design-a-Dinner suggestions for people with busy lives, or for those who want easy meal ideas.
- **Sharing** sections address common questions about storing and serving wine, giving wine as gifts, and entertaining with wine from casual picnics and brunch gatherings to once-in-a-lifetime celebrations.

Wine is an intimidating subject, but it doesn't have to be. When I first started learning about wine I was afraid to open my mouth if I couldn't correctly pronounce the name of a wine or region. But my desire to explore overtook any embarrassment and I simply asked lots of questions and pointed to the bottle I wanted. The wine doesn't care, right? Now, even when I can't say something perfectly, it doesn't matter. I buy it, try it, and remember it for the next time.

That's the beauty of wine information, which I think of as building blocks. Each time you learn something new, it's like placing one block on top of another. Over time, you build up layers of knowledge and confidence. If you walk away remembering just one thing each time you open this book or taste a new bottle, you've succeeded and so have I.

My Personal Passion

Learning about wine is a factual process, yet it is also very personal. After years of living among vineyards and traveling to the world's top wine regions, this book reflects my love of the grape. It highlights my favorite winemakers, countries, and individual wines in a way that will hopefully help you enjoy wine more.

Wine has always been a part of my life, but it didn't become a true obsession until I moved to the San Francisco Bay area after college. While working in television during the day, my interest in and knowledge of wine was growing in leaps and bounds by night. I took wine classes, started tasting groups, and read wine books voraciously. Soon, my avocation became my vocation as I began writing about wine for a living.

It started when I joined forces with a local television station to produce a wine program. Then, the Internet, an emerging medium at the time, intervened and I transferred my skills to creating wine web sites. Working for companies such as Microsoft and the *New York Times*, I have spent nearly a decade covering the wine world from a multimedia perspective, writing and talking about faces and places behind the bottles and tasting thousands of wines annually.

Between making my own wine, judging at some of the country's largest wine competitions, leading seminars, and writing for various publications, I am lucky enough to experience the joys of wine every day. I still love wine as much as I did when I took my first sip. My hope is that others will feel the same and wine will find its natural home on more American tables.

Wine on Every Table

In Europe, regional wine and food are natural complements. Over centuries the two have developed together, creating an intertwined culinary identity: Burgundy with escargot and *boeuf à la Bourguignonne*, Bordeaux with duck and spring lamb, and Chianti with grilled meats, beans, and rustic bread.

By comparison, America's food traditions are young, and we measure our wine history in decades, not centuries. While we mature as a gastronomic nation, embracing and developing our wine regions and local cuisines, wine is slowly weaving its way into the fabric of our culinary culture. As we create rich, multilayered customs revolving around the table, women will continue to play a large role in bringing wine to daily life.

Wine for Women is a celebration of wine, food, and fun. I hope you learn, explore, and, most of all, have a good time. Cheers.

Building the Essential
Wine Wardrobe

'M GOING TO TALK ABOUT SHOPPING. NOT ALL WOMEN LOVE TO SHOP, just like all men don't get pumped up by watching sports, but most of my female friends do enjoy hitting the stores every once in a while.

From finding the perfect-fitting jeans to getting a classic suit on sale, assembling the basics of a wardrobe is enjoyable. Other than buying a bathing suit, shopping can be fun and relaxing. It is called retail therapy for a reason.

But shopping for wine used to make my palms sweaty and my head hurt. No wonder, with questions like these swirling around in my brain:

"I need to buy a bottle of wine as a gift. What should I get?"

"I wonder if that white on sale is any good."

"I'm serving steak tonight. What was the name of that red wine I liked so much?"

If you've ever felt this way, you are not alone. Most of the questions put to me as a wine expert have to do with buying the "right" bottle. The good news is there are no right or wrong choices. The trick is arming yourself with knowledge to find the wines that appeal to you.

Reading this book, you'll discover how easy and fun it can be to assemble what I call the essential wine wardrobe. Instead of retail therapy you'll be introduced to the joys of vino therapy.

Step One: What Wine Is Called

THE GRAPE STORY

The first step toward making informed buying decisions is to understand what wine is called and what it tastes like.

Most of us are familiar with wines such as Chardonnay, Merlot, and Cabernet Sauvignon. These wines are called *varietals*, which means they're named after their predominant grape variety. Think of apple varieties. From McIntosh to Golden Delicious and Granny Smith, each one looks and tastes different. The same is true of grapes. From sassy Sauvignon Blanc to pretty Pinot Noir and zesty Zinfandel, grape varieties have their own recognizable aromas, flavors, and sense of style.

THE NAME GAME

In the New World countries like America, Chile, New Zealand, and Australia, wines are named after their grape varieties, such as Chardonnay, Merlot, and Cabernet Sauvignon. It's not, however, the only name game in town.

In Old World European countries such as France, Spain, Portugal, and Italy, wines are usually named for their region of origin. Think of Bordeaux, Burgundy, and Champagne. These are simply regions in France. Rioja is a place in Spain, and Chianti is an Italian wine region. In the Old World, winemakers discovered through centuries of trial and error that certain grape varieties grow well in certain places. This is just like a garden where tomatoes do well in a sunny spot, but hydrangeas prefer some shade.

Through a sort of survival of the fittest, generation after generation of winemakers honed in on the best grape varieties for their particular soil and climate. Eventually governmental organizations intervened, and now in most Old World countries only certain grape varieties are legally allowed to be planted in particular regions. In Burgundy, Pinot Noir is officially the primary grape variety used to make top red wines. We don't order a bottle of Pinot Noir from Burgundy; we simply say "I would like a red Burgundy."

Imagine if we had the same sort of regulations in this country.

Cabernet Sauvignon might be the only red grape variety allowed to be planted in Napa Valley because it thrives there, while Chardonnay grapes might be the only ones legally grown in California's Sonoma County, where they shine. In this scenario, if you wanted a Cabernet or Chardonnay from northern California, you would simply buy a red Napa or a white Sonoma.

In each chapter you'll learn the connection between grape variety and place. This knowledge will be a springboard to exploring a world of wines. You'll discover that Chardonnay is the grape variety that produces the white wines of France's Chablis region, so if you like California Chardonnay, you might want to branch out and try Chablis.

Knowing what wines are called helps in making educated buying decisions because you can actually make sense of the label, but it's also the basis for understanding what wines taste like.

Step Two: Connecting Place to Taste

LEARNING HELPFUL LABEL LINKS

When you walk into a store, you're faced with buying wine in one of three ways: by price, by producer, and/or by label.

Even if you know how much you want to spend, you might not remember the name of the winery your friend told you about. Or, what if you can't locate the particular bottle you enjoyed at a restaurant?

You can buy the wine with the most appealing label (we all do this), or you can use the label as a guide to discovering what the wine might taste like. How? By looking for the place where the wine comes from, which is marked on the label:

GRGICH HILLS

Napa Valley
CHARDONNAY
2000

PRODUCED AND BOTTLED BY
GRGICH HILLS CELLAR, RUTHERFORD, CA

FOR EXAMPLE:
NAPA VALLEY,
CALIFORNIA, OR

BAROSSA
VALLEY,
AUSTRALIA, OR

BORDEAUX,
FRANCE

The same grape variety grown in different countries or regions expresses itself individually in the glass. Learning the Name Game will help you make the correlation between grape and place, but memorizing a few of my favorite wine-growing regions through the Label Links takes you one step further by empowering you to begin associating place with taste.

Associating place with taste offers a quick way to buy wine armed simply with the knowledge of certain wine regions. Rather than focusing on soon-forgotten facts and figures, I talk about the regions from a personal perspective to give you a snapshot of the place and how it relates to what is in the bottle.

My highlighted list of regions is by no means exhaustive but offers a way to begin exploring the connection between place and taste. Try a few of my recommendations for yourself and then discover your own favorites.

THE STYLE PROFILE

It dawned on me when I was looking for a new pair of pants how much wine is like fashion. We describe both with words such as *stylish, elegant, opulent, fresh, clean,* and *pretty.* Wine and fashion are both artistic expressions—one uses grapes, the other fabric to achieve a final product.

We seek out certain brands/designers because we are partial to their styles. We like the way certain clothes fit, feel, and look. The same is true of wine. We buy a brand/type of wine because we prefer its style—or the way it smells, tastes, and feels.

Just like fashion, where the material and designer dictate the final style of a garment, a wine's individual style is the end result of a combination of factors:

WHAT (grape variety)
WHERE (place grapes are grown)   ▷   **STYLE PROFILE**
WHO (producer/winemaker)

THE WHAT AND THE WHERE

Since Chardonnay grapes taste different from Sauvignon Blanc grapes, for example, a wine's style is influenced first by the grape variety used to make the wine. But, because grapes take on unique characteristics depending on their environment, the final taste is also affected by where those grapes were grown. A region's climate (arguably the most important factor in New World countries), soil, and topography play crucial roles in determining the character of the grapes and ultimately the finished wine.

Let's take a peek at how this plays out in different bottles of Chardonnay. One is from California's Napa Valley and the other from France's Chablis region in Burgundy.

The warmer areas of the Napa Valley regularly have temperatures that reach into the nineties during the growing season. Chardonnay grapes get very ripe, usually resulting in a richly fruity wine with a medium-full body and fairly high alcohol level.

In contrast, Chablis can be a downright cold place that pushes the envelope for actually getting Chardonnay grapes fully ripe. When grown in this cool climate, the grapes generally produce lighter, elegant wines with a crisp fruit character. Think of biting into a ripe pineapple (Napa version) versus a tangy lemon (Chablis). Chardonnay from Chablis is also distinctive because the soil the grapes are planted in is comprised of chalky, limestone clay, which imparts a unique minerallike character to the wine.

See what I mean? The same grape, two places, and the end result is two uniquely different wines.

As wine-growing areas become smaller and smaller, the connection between place and taste becomes more intense. For example, if the grapes for a bottle of wine all come from one small vineyard versus an

---

The Buzz on... *Terroir*

In France the importance of place is paramount when it comes to wine. The French name their best wines after regions, not grape varieties, right? Though there is no direct English translation, the French term *terroir* refers to the way climate, soil, and grape variety interact in each place to create a unique, specific taste in the wine.

entire region, it follows that the wine will taste more distinctive—and usually cost more, too.

THE WHO

The third piece of the style profile after grape variety and growing region has to do with human hands. Nature has done its job, and now it's the winemakers' turn. From the vineyards to the cellar, the decisions they make play a large role in determining the final taste of the wine.

Take the use of oak, for example. Many Napa Valley winemakers age their Chardonnay in heavily toasted oak barrels to impart a spicy, vanilla, oaky character. Most Chablis winemakers, on the other hand, don't let their Chardonnays see any time in new oak barrels so that the wines retain the freshness of the fruit. Each makes a decision that affects the ultimate style of the wine.

The Buzz on...Oak and Wine

Oak barrels are used in fermenting and aging wine because oak is a watertight yet porous material. Oak—more than any other wood—has inherent characteristics, such as vanilla and spicy notes, that complement wine. (French oak is generally used in winemaking because it's a mild yet flavorful wood, but oak from American forests is popular as well.) Barrel makers also augment oak's natural spiciness by "toasting" the inside of the barrel over an open fire. When wine rests inside a toasted oak barrel, it picks up complex aromas and flavors of vanilla, butter, and spice. New oak barrels impart the most oak character because as barrels age, the "toastiness" wears off and they become neutral vessels. Winemakers can choose highly toasted new barrels or old ones with essentially no oak essence to achieve a desired taste in the final wine.

A MATTER OF STYLE

Style can mean many things, from the basic types of wine such as sweet, sparkling, and fortified to the overall style of a region.

You'll often hear a wine described as "Burgundian style" or "Bordeaux-like," which means even though the wines aren't made in Burgundy or Bordeaux, they are reminiscent of wines made in those regions. There are "Old World" styles and "New World" styles, too. An individual winery may also have a particular style. One producer may strive for a lighter, elegant style, while another makes all its wines in a full, blockbuster style. Within a grape variety various styles can also be expressed, from juicy, soft Cabernet Sauvignon to powerful and tannic versions of Cabernet.

If words like *blockbuster* remind you of the movies, or *elegant* describes Grace Kelly rather than wine, that's fine. In each chapter there's a Lingo Lesson to introduce the words frequently used in describing certain types of wine. Though many of the words I highlight are accepted wine terms, others are personal favorites I use to sort through the maze of wine. There is an infinite number of ways to describe wine, so if my descriptors don't mean anything to you, replace them with ones of your own.

YOUR PERSONAL STYLE

As we've seen, what I call a wine's individual style profile is a combination of impressions (aroma, flavor, taste, and feel) that come from the grape variety, growing region, and winemaker. Wines with similar styles can be grouped together and distinguished from other groups of wines, which makes style a useful tool for finding new bottles to enjoy. If you prefer light-bodied, crisp Chardonnay, branch out and try a dry Riesling or Sauvignon Blanc with a similar style profile.

My sister cringes when I pour big reds with what she calls "back-talking tannins," so I tell her to stay away from heavy reds, such as Cabernet Sauvignon or Syrah, with a style profile that says *tannic*. (Tannins are a chemical compound found in the skins of grapes that often create an astringent sensation in red wines, see pages 138—140 for more on this quality.)

Determining what you like or dislike is vital to learning about wine, and my style profiles will help you do that. Each chapter's buying section culminates with shopping suggestions.

Here I highlight wines from my favorite Label Links regions by price and individual style profiles. Once you have identified wines you like, these guides will open the door to exploring and discovering new bottles to uncork and enjoy. I have grouped them by general price category from bargain sips to luxury sips.

Due to the fact that prices vary wildly from store to store and from one place in the country to another, I offer a price range for each wine. Use these as a guideline only since the cost of the same wine can double depending upon where you purchase it. (Note: I have offered price ranges for wines and wine types in the text of the book, too, but the same rule applies—these are simply guidelines to give you an idea of cost. In the Checkout Counter: Resources at the back of the book I have listed some of my favorite stores and web sites to purchase wine so you really need to shop around to find the best deals.)

I have chosen not to highlight particular vintages, rather to pick wines that perform consistently well from year to year. In addition, I pinpoint particular wines that make good gift choices and party picks to make buying wine for any occasion a breeze.

The Buzz on...Crush Me, Squeeze Me, Make Me Wine

The simplest way to understand the wine-making process is from the perspective of a grape. Let's look at the life of a grape we'll call Brut. During the summer Brut will bask in the sun and grow to be a strapping grape about the size of a marble. In the fall he will reach his optimum sugar content (about 22 to 25 percent) and be harvested. Brut and his bunch will then get tossed into a crusher/stemmer, which gently breaks the skins to release the juice inside. Don't feel sorry for Brut; he has shed the trappings of his former life and is free. He is juice.

All juice, whether from red or white grapes, is pale in color. The deep purplish hue and mouth-puckering tannins attributed to red wines are extracted from contact with the dark skins and seeds. For white wine the juice is immediately drained off the grape skins, thereby preserving the pale color. Once the juice is put into tanks, the winemaker adds yeast, which then begins to eat the sugar in the juice and convert it to alcohol. This is the all-important stage of the wine-making process called *alcoholic fermentation*. When all the sugar has been consumed, the yeast dies and the juice is now wine. After aging in oak barrels or steel tanks, the wine will be bottled and shipped to a store or restaurant near you.

So, the next time you're imbibing, raise your glass and toast to all the Bruts of the world.

pairing

PAIRING FOOD AND WINE CAN CAUSE ANXIETY, BUT it shouldn't. Just as in buying wine there's no right or wrong, only better and worse. I've had steak with Chardonnay and fish with Cabernet, and though neither was my favorite combination, at the end of the meal my glass was empty. The most important thing to remember is that any wine with a meal is better than no wine.

If you want a little more guidance than that, though, these simple guidelines work for me:

○ Match the texture or feel of the food and wine: delicate foods with delicate wines and big foods with big wines. (Think leather pants with a sweater and linen pants with a cotton shirt.) It's not the outdated mantra of red wine with meat and white with fish; it's about the weight of the food and wine in your mouth. A rich, hearty stew needs a robust wine, and a refreshing one pairs perfectly with light vegetable pasta.
○ Highlight complementary aromas and flavors in the wine and food. An earthy Pinot Noir accompanies pork in a mushroom sauce beautifully, while a buttery Chardonnay is ideal with lobster dipped in drawn butter.
○ Think about the wine's acidity, which is the key component in pairing. We'll talk about this in depth later on in the book, but just remember that the refreshing, lively quality of wine comes from its level of acidity. (Why else would we add a squirt of lemon to tea or on top of fish?) Match a bright, zesty red wine like Chianti with an acidic tomato sauce. Or, go for the contrast and use a tangy, high acid wine like Sauvignon Blanc to cut through the fattiness of a rich dish such as fettuccine Alfredo. Remember, in food and wine, as in love, opposites do attract.
○ Consider the concentration or intensity of the aromas and flavors. Piquant Pacific Rim food goes beautifully with a highly aromatic white wine like Gewurztraminer. Both have intense aromas and strong flavors.

○ Finally, think about the sauces in a dish and don't worry too much about the type of meat, as many are interchangeable when pairing wine. Chicken in a cream sauce deserves the same wine as pork in the identical sauce.

Here's the inherent challenge with food and wine pairing: before you even take a bite or uncork a bottle, you need to know the characteristics not only of the food but also of the wine. Food is a slightly easier starting point because most of us are familiar with the feel and taste of salmon and steak, but not as knowledgeable about Verdelho, Verdicchio, or Viognier. Pairing is another place where understanding what makes up a wine's style profile is invaluable.

Certain styles of wine complement particular types of food. A white wine like Sauvignon Blanc with a style profile that is light-bodied, unoaked, and crisp makes shrimp sing, while a medium-bodied, smooth, and juicy Pinot Noir from Oregon is ideal with salmon.

The pairing section of each chapter is based on the idea that wine and food belong together. But who has time to prepare fancy meals every day? Not me. And not many women I know. So I've developed a mix-and-match system for food and wine that is similar to the line of kids' clothing where everything goes together (just match lion-tagged tops with lion-tagged bottoms and so on). With my Design-a-Dinner strategy you can whip up wine-friendly combos in no time.

Forget elaborate recipes for foie gras and truffled salmon or pepper-encrusted ahi on a bed of endive. My suggested dishes use the chicken breasts still in your freezer at 6:00 P.M. As someone who cooks almost every night for my family, I want to prepare a quick meal accompanied by some good wine. Here are some tips for getting dinner on the table in a short amount of time:

Design-a-Dinner

1. **Stock your shelves:** From the "bottoms" (chicken, pasta, meats) to the "tops" (veggies, cheeses, sauces) and "accessories" (herbs, condiments, and spices), shopping lists identify foods that work well with each type of wine.
2. **Get saucy:** Making sauces that act as a bridge between food and wine can be a snap. In each chapter I've included some of my favorites to get you started, such as Creamy Mustard Dressing and Zesty Blueberry Sauce.
3. **Meal ensembles:** These ideas offer ways to mix and match the sauces and "Stock your Shelves" ingredients into fast, delicious meals.

sharing

LEARNING ABOUT BUYING AND PAIRING WINE IS HELP-ful, but only if it makes sharing more fun. So after you've learned about the various wines in each chapter, I'm going to offer ideas for enjoying wine in some real-life situations.

- Lyn is a busy mom with three kids who wants to learn more about wine but doesn't have time to read books or take a class. What should she do?
- Rae Ann wants to host a party for her colleagues and needs help finding wines that will impress for less. Any ideas?
- Bob and Susan are wine lovers on a quest to explore some top wine regions. Where should they begin?
- Bobbie is hosting Thanksgiving dinner for her whole family. What wine choices can she make to please everyone?

○ Melissa is taking her boss and several colleagues to dinner. How should she approach the wine list without breaking into a sweat?

○ Sharon is planning her wedding on a budget. How can she wisely buy wine and still have money left for the cake?

Wine isn't something to fear or revere but to enjoy. Learning the basics of buying and pairing will translate into sharing wine with style and ease.

AISLE 1

White Wine

Chardonnay/White Burgundy
THE "BASIC BLACK" OF WHITE WINE

buying

IF YOU'RE LIKE ME, BLACK IS A WARDROBE STAPLE. Your closet overflows with black purses in various shapes and sizes, pants and jackets from casual to upscale, and most important, that little black dress.

Let's not forget shoes: black flats, heels, and boots in every imaginable style. And if you're like me, you keep buying more black. It's not that bright colors are bad. On the contrary, they're fabulous. But pulling off the cherry-red suit or floral-print pants can take a little doing. Nothing is as slimming, versatile, popular, or easy as black.

Except for the slimming part (although there are only around 100 calories per glass), the same words can be used to describe Chardonnay, which I think of as the basic black of white wines. Chardonnay is simple to sip, goes with many kinds of food, and remains wildly popular.

THE GRAPE STORY

A classic grape variety that was not well known in this country until a few decades ago, Chardonnay has made a name for itself. Today it's the number-one-selling white in America, and "I'll have the Chardonnay" has become a national motto.

Look at any restaurant wine list and count the Chardonnays. Better yet, walk into a retail store where Chardonnays are packed from floor to ceiling, dominating the wine aisles.

Chardonnay is familiar, and that familiarity inspires confidence and comfort. We know it; therefore we love it. But Chardonnay's popularity is due in large part to its versatility. Just like those black pants that come in many fabrics and styles—from casual cotton to sleek silk—Chardonnay can be everything from light and crisp to juicy and soft or buttery and full.

Why is Chardonnay so versatile? It has to do with the grape's personality. Chardonnay was at the head of the line when the grape god handed out easygoing personalities. Not naturally tart and aggressive like Sauvignon Blanc or floral and flirtatious like Gewurztraminer, Chardonnay's mild-mannered fruitiness lends itself to making all kinds of wine.

Chardonnay takes on character and complexity depending on where the grapes are grown and who turns them into wine. Many versions are successful; others are not. With an estimated seven hundred different Chardonnay bottlings on store shelves at any one time, though, how do you sift through the boring to get to the beautiful?

Price is the first thing that comes to mind. Picking a bottle because it costs $10 or $30 is one way to choose a wine, but if you don't like the way the $30 bottle tastes, you are pouring money down the drain. The key to finding Chardonnay in your price range and then enjoying it begins with defining what you like and don't like. Do you prefer Chards that taste a bit tangy like citrus fruits or ones that are more ripe like pineapples? Or a lighter, more delicate Chardonnay versus a fuller, buttery one?

If you're shrugging your shoulders, wondering what in the world I'm talking about, have no fear. Let's take a lingo lesson and start to put words to wine.

Lingo Lesson: Chardonnay

Wine is often intimidating because there's a myth that talking about it requires an advanced degree. Now, granted, some wine geeks appear to be speaking a different language, but they're not. Fluency is just a matter of feeling comfortable communicating about the wine in your glass, much like the food on your plate.

My oldest sister, Lisa, is not in the wine business, yet she is one of the most articulate people I know when it comes to describing wine. I attribute it to her love of cooking. She feels at ease describing aromas, flavors, and textures and is not worried about what other people will think when she talks about wine. Lisa once told a winemaker friend of mine that his wine tasted like chilled asparagus salad. He thought about it a moment and agreed that indeed there was a fresh herbal quality to it.

The beautiful thing about wine is that there are no right or wrong descriptions. With that said, there is a set of generally accepted words that helps people communicate to one another about wine. Some of them pertain to the basic components of wine, which I define as the core words. These include dryness or sweetness, acidity levels, body of the wine (relates to percentage of alcohol), and the tannins present primarily in red wines. We'll address each one of these more in depth in subsequent chapters. The extra-credit words help describe the fruit aromas and overall character of the wines.

Following are the words I use to describe Chardonnay.

Core Words
Dry: Almost every Chardonnay is categorized as a dry white wine, which means the yeast ate the sugar in the grape juice when it was being turned into wine and left little noticeable sweetness. Sometimes people think of Chardonnay as sweet, but that's often the result of ripe fruit flavors and a "sweet" impression that comes from its higher levels of alcohol.

Crisp or smooth acidity: Acid is one of the critical elements in wine, and Chardonnays with higher levels of acidity taste crisp and firm. Smooth Chardonnays have lower levels of acidity and seem softer. The term *flabby* is used to describe wines lacking acidity.

Light-, medium-, or full-bodied: This is the sensation of weight in your mouth when you sip the wine. It's often described as similar to the difference between skim milk, whole milk, and cream, but I liken it to the various impressions you get when you touch chiffon, silk, and velvet. Most Chardonnays fall into the medium- to full-bodied range due to their higher levels of alcohol (usually in the 12 to 14 percent range).

Extra Credit Words
Fruit aromas: Remember, describing wine is very subjective. My peach may be your orange; my plum could be your blackberry. I've offered just a few suggestions to get started. Think of larger groupings such as citrus versus tropical fruit and then see if you can get more specific.

> Tree fruits—apple, pear, fig
> Citrus fruits—lemon, tangerine
> Tropical fruits—pineapple, melon, papaya, mango

Oaky and toasty: When Chardonnay is put into oak barrels, the barrels impart a toasty character to the wine. Winemakers can choose different levels of toast for their barrels and leave the wine in those barrels for a short or long period of time, depending on how much oak flavor they want in the final wine.

Buttery and creamy: Once the grape juice is transformed into wine through alcoholic fermentation, some wines go through a secondary malolactic fermentation (*ML* for short). ML changes the tangy malic acid in the wine—think green apples—to softer lactic acid; think dairy products. *Buttery* in a Chardonnay refers to this effect of malolactic fermentation. If a Chardonnay smells buttery, it will often feel creamy when you drink it.

Vanilla, spice, and nuttiness: If you smell or taste vanilla, butterscotch, spices such as cinnamon and allspice, or toasted nuts, the Chardonnay was stored in oak barrels where it picked up a spicy, almost caramelized character.

Ripe and rich: Consider the flavors of not-quite-ripe strawberries versus plump, juicy red ones or hard green pears compared to lusciously ripe ones. If the grapes get plenty of sunshine and are ripe and juicy, that will transfer to what you taste in the glass.

Having a few key words under your wine belt will help you communicate better about Chardonnay and figure out the tastes and styles you like, but unfortunately, most stores and wineries don't boldly display their wines by taste. Believe it or not, though, labels can tell you something very important about the taste and style of a wine before you pull the cork.

BORN IN THE USA . . . OR FRANCE . . . OR CHILE

Several years ago, when I was hiking through hillside vineyards in the Aconcagua Valley of Chile, a winemaker made a remark that really hit home. As we nibbled on freshly plucked grapes, Tony Coltrin of Seña winery said, "Good wine tastes like a grape, but great wine tastes like a place."

He's so right. I can give you an idea of what basic Chardonnay might taste like, but what about Chardonnay grown in Chablis or Carneros or Casablanca? Each place has a unique combination of sun, soils, and slopes, which makes the grapes grown there taste a certain way.

Luckily that location is on the label, and I think of it as the wine's birthplace. Before we even get to what the winemaker can do when turning grapes into wine (that comes next), the wine's birthplace has the biggest effect on the taste of a bottle of Chardonnay.

The following roundups highlight how wines from some of my favorite regions express themselves in the glass. Just as finding the perfect pair of black pants is simple when you know the style you want, buying wine is easier if you can link words on the label to your preferred style of Chardonnay.

Use these as a guideline to start exploring Chardonnays from different places around the globe. Bon voyage.

leslie's label links
Connecting taste to place makes wine buying easy

CRISP AND JUICY

These wine-growing regions generally have cooler climates and produce Chardonnays with a crisp, bright character, which make them terrific companions at the dinner table. Some wines will be medium in body, others more full, but all will have a vibrant fruit intensity and a nice kick of acidity that invigorates your palate.

Place: Central Coast, California

Taste: Store shelves are lined with Chardonnays labeled "Central Coast," and they are generally crisp and medium-bodied. The grapes used to make these wines can come from anywhere along California's ocean-influenced central coastline, stretching from San Francisco in the north through Monterey and Santa Cruz down to Santa

Barbara. Price is often an indicator of quality when looking at Central Coast bottlings. Affordable versions tend to be refreshing quaffers, while those carrying hefty price tags are more complex and layered.

Place: Monterey, California

Taste: Chardonnays from Monterey often remind me of sweet melons. The region is cool, with the howling winds from the ocean affecting the nearby vineyards. Inland areas are warm, so fruit can ripen fully, but the lovely crisp character shines through in Monterey bottlings.

Place: Russian River Valley, California

Taste: There's an intensity of crisp fruit flavor in Russian River Valley Chardonnay. Think of the most flavorful apple or pear you've ever had and multiply that by ten. These lucky grapes develop such concentration of flavor because

they bask in sunshine during the day but also benefit from low evening temperatures because the appellation, located just an hour and a half north of San Francisco, sidles up to the Pacific Ocean. The warm days allow grapes to ripen, while the cool nights seal in those flavors like a zipped plastic bag.

The Buzz on...Appellations

Wine-growing areas can also be called *appellations,* a French term now used throughout the world. Whether large or small, appellations are officially recognized and regulated geographic wine-growing areas. Depending on the size of the appellation or region, wines develop similar style characteristics—the smaller the region, the more definitive the taste. In the United States we call most of these regions American Viticultural Areas (AVA). The wine must contain at least 85 percent of grapes from the AVA listed on the label, and if it is a varietal wine, such as Merlot or Chardonnay, a minimum of 75 percent of wine must come from that grape variety. Other countries, however, are even more highly regulated in terms of the kinds of grapes planted, how the grapes are grown, and the techniques used to make the wine. We'll talk more about each country's rules in later chapters.

Place: Carneros, California

Taste: Carneros Chardonnay is some of the most renowned in California and sports an exotic citrus quality reminiscent of tangerines. The cool-climate region (often called Los Carneros) straddles  Sonoma and Napa counties and is affected by the chilly waters of the adjacent San Pablo Bay.

Place: Burgundy, France
(Labeled *Bourgogne*)

Taste: These are affordable versions of Chardonnay from a blend of grapes grown in the Burgundy region of France. It is a big region, so bottles labeled sim-  ply *Bourgogne* will express less of a sense of place than wines from its subregions like the ones listed in other Label Links. From a good producer, however, these quaffers should be fresh, light, and lemony.

THE NAME GAME

Chardonnay = white Burgundy

When you see the French growing region of Burgundy, or Bourgogne, on a bottle of white wine, it means the wine is made from Chardonnay grapes. But white Burgundies aren't just fruity Chardonnays from France—they have attitude. Due to the region's unique soils and cool climate, white Burgundies *taste* distinctive: crisp but with a mineral character. The wines get that attitude from the vines. As the vines' roots reach deep into the soil, they can't help transferring a mineral character to the grapes and eventually to the wine.

Drinking white Burgundy can be an exquisite experience, but for every ounce of Burgundian beauty comes a pound of confusion about the region.

Over centuries, due to complex French inheritance laws, families have divided and subdivided land so much that now most growers farm tiny parcels of land. Sometimes each family member has only a few rows. For anyone attempting to learn about wines from Burgundy, it can seem like a jigsaw puzzle with thousands of pieces.

Don't be daunted, however. The Chardonnays are some of the best in the world, and exploring Burgundy to slowly put the pieces of the puzzle together is a rewarding journey.

Did You Know?

You may occasionally see a bottle of white Burgundy with the word *Aligoté* written on it. It is made not from Chardonnay but from the less common Aligoté grape. Try affordable versions from producers such as Louis Latour and Louis Jadot. Small quantities of light-bodied and juicy Aligoté are also popping up from our very own Washington state. Stay tuned . . . it's definitely a white to watch.

Place: Chablis, France

Taste: Crisp and minerally, Chablis is the purest expression of Chardonnay. If you haven't tried real Chablis before, please do. It's as classy as a designer suit. Located at the northern tip of Burgundy, the region is actually closer to the Champagne region than the rest of Burgundy, which means the climate is quite cold. The climate produces wines with a sleek character, but the mineral taste that comes from Chablis' chalky limestone soil is what sets it apart. You can find value wines (less than $15) labeled simply *Chablis* or more intense, expensive premier cru and grand cru versions.

Tasting Tip: One of my favorite producers is Domaine Laroche. From the classic Chablis Saint Martin (around $25) to the pricey Domaine Laroche grand cru bottlings that can cost $60 to $100 per bottle, these are wines worth seeking out.

The Buzz on…Burgundy 101

Burgundy is broken down into five main regions, going from north to south:

1. **Chablis:** A small region at the northern tip of Burgundy that produces some of the most distinctive Chardonnays in the world.
2. **Côte d'Or:** This Golden Slope is what most people refer to when they talk about the source of Burgundy's top wines. A mere thirty miles in length, this little strip of land is broken into two distinctive regions, roughly separated by the city of Beaune:
   ○ The **Côte de Nuits** is north of Beaune and is focused on world-class reds.
   ○ The **Côte de Beaune** lies to the south of Beaune, and although reds are grown there, it is home to the majority of great whites of Burgundy. Within its boundaries lie Meursault, Puligny-Montrachet and Chassagne-Montrachet.
3. **Côte Chalonnaise** is south of the Côte de Beaune, and though it produces good wines in places such as Rully and Montagny, it's the least known region.
4. **Cote Mâconnais** is the place for value Chardonnays such as those labeled Saint-Véran and Mâcon-Villages, but it's recognized as the home of Pouilly-Fuissé wines.
5. **Beaujolais** is a familiar name that's not often associated with Burgundy, but it's the largest growing area of the whole region and lies the farthest south.

Head of the class: Burgundy is not only broken up by regions, but its wines are also classified by the quality of the vineyards (note: price is closely tied to these classifications):

Grand cru on the label means "great growth." It indicates the grapes came from the best vineyards in the Côte d'Or and Chablis. These are expensive (think $80 to hundreds of dollars per bottle), complex and ageworthy.

Premier cru (1 er cru on the label) wines come from grapes generally grown on the upper to middle part of the slopes. Premier Cru vineyards produce wines that are top-notch quality and highly priced but within reach of mere mortals.

Village wines offer the best quality-to-price ratio in white Burgundy with many excellent wines in the $20 to $30 range. Grapes that go into the wine can come from a number of the usually flatter vineyards surrounding the villages after which they're named. For example, look for a label that simply says *Meursault* or *Puligny-Montrachet.*

Regional wines (like Bourgogne and Chablis) are made with a blend of grapes from the whole region and are usually good-value quaffers that can be found for $15 or less.

Place: Pouilly-Fuissé, Burgundy, France

Taste: The best ones sport a medium body
and remind me of biting into a nut-covered
caramel apple but still with a nice zing of
acidity. The grapes that go into these wines
come from a small set of villages in southern Burgundy in the Mâconnais district.

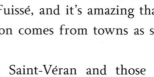

One of them is Pouilly, the other Fuissé, and it's amazing that wine
with such an international reputation comes from towns as small as
Andy Griffith's Mayberry.

Value Tip: Look for wines from Saint-Véran and those labeled
Mâcon-Villages, which I call the smart-buy version of Pouilly-Fuissé.
These Chardonnays, which can often be found for around $10 per
bottle, sport a charmingly soft texture, hints of nuts, and pear notes.

Place: Puligny-Montrachet,
Burgundy, France

Taste: I can say with complete bias that this
is my favorite place for French Chardonnay. There is something so rich and full
yet taut and crisp about a well-aged Puligny

that it combines the best of both ends of the wine spectrum in one
vibrant but luxurious package. Wines labeled *Puligny-Montrachet* sport
an intensity of fruit, medium-full body, and great backbone of acidity. Premier cru vineyards like Les Folatières and grand cru vineyards
such as Bâtard-Montrachet and Montrachet produce Chardonnays of
unmatched opulence, lushness, and tropical flavors, especially when
enjoyed after a few years in the bottle. This indulgence is not cheap,
though, since village-level wines generally start around $30 and esca-
late to several hundred dollars for glorious grand crus. It's worth it,
though.

Look for these places on the label, too . . .

Edna Valley, California
Willamette Valley, Oregon

Marlborough, New Zealand
Casablanca Valley, Chile
Margaret River, Australia

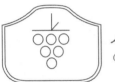

leslie's label links

Connecting taste to place makes wine buying easy

SMOOTH AND RIPE

Bigger and bolder, usually as a result of warmer climates, these Chardonnays can have an inviting smoothness and rich character that remind me of slipping into a well-tailored silk shirt. The flavors are ripe (think pineapple versus lemon) and dripping with a luscious fruit character.

Place: Napa Valley, California

Taste: Napa Valley is synonymous with full-bodied, rich tropical fruit Chardonnay. Though it's a small appellation, only 30 miles long and several miles wide, its reputation is huge. Climatic conditions vary from the cool Carneros district in the south to the downright hot northern reaches of Calistoga, but overall the area serves up sunny, warm California weather, which produces ripe fruit and wines with a lush, fruity character.

Place: Sonoma County, California

Taste: From the warm Alexander Valley appellation in the northern part of the county through ocean-influenced Russian River Valley and down to the cool-climate appellation of Carneros,  Chardonnay grapes reign supreme. One of the state's largest wine-growing regions, Sonoma County produces wines that vary in style but generally have a medium to full body and loads of apple and pear fruit flavors.

Place: Chalk Hill, California

Taste: Chalk Hill is a unique place. As one of the ten appellations within Sonoma County, it is home to some of Sonoma's most full-bodied, rich, and distinctly mineral Chardonnays. Butting up to cool Russian River Valley and the hot Alexander Valley, Chalk Hill's climate is somewhere in between. What makes its Chards different is the chalky, volcanic-mixture soil.

Place: Santa Barbara County, California

Taste: Santa Barbara County is hot. Not climatically but in terms of producing top-notch Chardonnay. Part of the large Central Coast appellation, Chards from here taste like a fresh fruit salad. Though the region is influenced by cooling ocean breezes, Chardonnays marked *Santa Barbara County* often sport a core of zesty acidity with a ripe fruit quality from the southern California sun.

Place: California

Taste: The majority of stash-your-cash Chardonnays will simply use the California appellation on the label. This indicates the wine is a blend of grapes from various parts of the state—some cool areas but most very warm. It's impossible to pin down a style that applies to all these wines, but the best versions have an appealing juicy quality with soft acidity.

Place: Australia

Taste: Just a few years ago Australian Chardonnay was the revved-up Harley of whites because it was so fruit-driven, full, and powerful. The Aussies have modified their approach, however, and many versions now seem restrained and elegant by comparison. Though there are quite a few places in the country with cooler climates, such as Western Australia's Margaret River region, Australia is still a pretty warm place that produces an immense amount of Chardonnay. Much of what is exported to North America comes from two large regions:

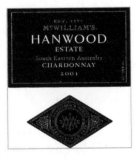

South Eastern Australia

Wines carrying the South Eastern Australia regional moniker include grapes that can come from states such as South Australia, Victoria, New South Wales, and Tasmania. This is a big, big area, and it would be like labeling a bottle of Chardonnay as *Eastern United States* and blending grapes from New York, Ohio, and Virginia. Most bottles fall into the affordable category ($10 or less) and range from medium- to full-bodied with bright fruit and smooth acidity.

South Australia

Wines labeled *South Australia* versus *South Eastern Australia* are made from grapes grown in the state of South Australia, which is the epicen-

ter of the Australian wine business. Its subregions read like a Who's Who of top wine-
growing areas: Barossa Valley, McLaren Vale,
Coonawarra, Clare Valley, and Adelaide Hills, to
name a few. With these wines price is often an
indicator of quality because some versions coming from South Australia will fall into the
affordable quaffing category, but others will be

pricey and collectible. The latter includes one of the country's best
wines, Penfolds "Yattarna" Chardonnay, which is rich, complex, and layered with decadent fruit. A bottle will set you back a hefty $60 to $70.

The Buzz on...Aussie Bins and Blends

Did you ever buy a bottle of Lindemans Bin 65 Chardonnay or Tyrrell's Vat
47 and wondered what *bin* or *vat* meant? This traditional method of naming
wines in Australia simply refers to the vat where the wine was stored before
bottling or the bin where it was kept after bottling. In addition to these numbers, you'll also often see labels on Australian whites that say *Semillon-
Chardonnay.* The Aussies are master blenders and combine grapes from
various regions (hence those labeled South Eastern Australia) to get the best
wine possible, but they also skillfully combine grape varieties. Down-under
blends include Semillon-Chardonnay and reds like Shiraz-Cabernet and
Grenache-Mourvèdre-Shiraz.

Place: Argentina

Taste: Chile somehow garners most of
the press when it comes to South American wines, but for Chardonnay it's
worth traveling over the Andes to
Argentina. Argentina's Chards explode

in the mouth with power-packed ripe fruit and full, voluptuous texture. Interestingly, Argentina is a huge wine-producing nation, but
most of the vino remains in Argentina. That should change in the
next few years, so stay tuned for more from this exciting wine-
producing country.

Value Tip: In Argentina there is a popular white grape called Torrontes, which makes a wine that tastes like a cross between Chardonnay and Sauvignon Blanc. Look for the easy-on-the-wallet version from Santa Julia Winery priced at around $6.

Look for these places on the label, too . . .

Alexander Valley, California

Columbia Valley, Washington

Maipo Valley, Chile

Hunter Valley, Australia

A MATTER OF STYLE

It is an understatement to say wine-making techniques have a big impact on Chardonnay. For instance, one of the ways winemakers can manipulate the taste is to put the wine through malolactic fermentation, which gives a buttery aroma and soft texture. They can also use various kinds of yeast during fermentation to give a little more complexity to the wine. But it's really how oak is used that makes the difference with Chardonnay.

Oak barrels impart those spicy, toasty qualities in wine, which can enhance but also dominate the flavors of Chardonnay. If you like an oaky character, great, but if you don't, you'll be happy to know the pendulum is swinging in favor of using less oak and letting more fruit shine through in Chardonnay. Other than the brilliant folks in New Zealand and Australia who are stamping their Chardonnay labels with the word *unoaked* or *unwooded*, however, it's hard to tell whether a bottle is oak-soaked or oak-free until you pull the cork.

2002
Marlborough
Unoaked Chardonnay

The Buzz on . . . the ABC Movement

Over the past few years oak-inundated wine lovers have started a movement to overthrow the queen of whites and begun to buy "Anything But Chardonnay." For a while Sauvignon Blanc was next in line for the throne, but now Pinot Grigio, Riesling, Grüner Veltliner, and others have captured the imaginations of oak-free-wine seekers.

Shopping Guide

As a wine writer, I sample hundreds of wines every month, sifting through the beasts to find the beauties to write about and recommend. These winning wines made my shopping list because they are consistently enjoyable from year to year, have a high quality-to-price ratio, and have a high pour-me-more quotient—in other words, they taste really good.

In each chapter I've categorized my wine picks according to price and overall style profile, making it easy for you to expand your wine horizons. If you like a light-bodied, unoaked, crisp, minerally Chardonnay, try a dry Riesling or Sauvignon Blanc with the same style profile and price range. Picks are listed from least expensive to most and from lightest to fullest. Note: Use these price ranges as guidelines not gospel since prices vary wildly (often doubling), depending upon the store and state.

I've chosen wines from the regions highlighted in the label links, so, if you can't find the exact wine I've recommended, look for other wines by the same producer.

Key

PF=Leslie's Personal Favorite: Though all these wines I recommend highly, those marked with a PF icon are ones I think are extra special.

GW=Gift Wine: Due to the combination of attractive packaging (label and bottle) and delicious taste, I highlight bottles that make ideal gifts in various price categories.

PW=Party Wine: These are generally inexpensive and top choices for a crowd.

CW=Cellar Worthy: If you want to age wine for a period of time, look for bottles I've tagged as cellar worthy.

Stash-Your-Cash Wines $15 and Under

	Name of Wine	From	Style Profile	Price Range
GW	J. Moreau & Fils, Chablis	Chablis, France	Light-bodied, unoaked, crisp, minerally	$10–12
	Antonin Rodet, Bourgogne Blanc	Burgundy, France	Light-bodied, unoaked, crisp, minerally	$10–12
PW	Fetzer Vineyards, "Five Rivers Ranch," Chardonnay	Monterey County, California	Medium-bodied, light oak, crisp and juicy	$10–12
	Beringer Vineyards, "Founders' Estate," Chardonnay	California	Medium-bodied, light oak, crisp and juicy	$9–11
	Sterling Vineyards, "Vintner's Collection," Chardonnay	Central Coast, California	Medium-bodied, light oak, crisp and juicy	$12–14
	Edna Valley Vineyard, "Paragon," Chardonnay	Edna Valley, California	Medium-bodied, light oak, crisp and juicy	$12–14
	Firestone Vineyards, Chardonnay	Santa Barbara County, California	Medium-bodied, light oak, crisp and juicy	$12–14
PW	Lindemans, "Bin 65," Chardonnay	South Eastern Australia	Full-bodied, oaky, ripe	$8–10
	Meridian Vineyards, Chardonnay	Santa Barbara County, California	Full-bodied, oaky, crisp, ripe	$9–11
GW	Sebastiani Vineyards, Chardonnay	Sonoma County, California	Full-bodied, oaky, ripe	$12–14

Well-Known Winners $15–25

Name of Wine	From	Style Profile	Price Range
William Fèvre, Chablis, "Champs Royaux"	Chablis, France	Light-bodied, unoaked, crisp, minerally	$16–18

	Name of Wine	From	Style Profile	Price Range
	La Crema, Chardonnay	Russian River Valley, California	Medium-bodied, light oak, crisp and juicy	$16–18
GW	Louis Jadot, Pouilly-Fuissé	Burgundy, France	Medium-bodied, light oak, crisp and juicy	$18–20
PF	Sapphire Hill, Chardonnay	Russian River Valley, California	Medium-bodied, light oak, crisp and juicy	$20–22
	Morgan Winery, Chardonnay	Monterey, California	Medium-bodied, light oak, crisp and juicy	$20–22
	Rodney Strong, "Chalk Hill," Chardonnay	Chalk Hill, Sonoma County, California	Full-bodied, oaky, ripe	$15–17
	Kendall-Jackson, "Great Estates," Santa Barbara	Santa Barbara County, California	Full-bodied, oaky, ripe	$20–22
GW	Landmark, "Overlook," Chardonnay	Sonoma County, California	Full-bodied, oaky, ripe	$23–25

Luxury Sips

Worth-the-Splurge Wines $22–50+

	Name of Wine	From	Style Profile	Price Range
	Grgich Hills, Chardonnay	Napa Valley, California	Medium-bodied, light oak, crisp and juicy	$25–28
PF	Patz & Hall, "Napa Valley," Chardonnay	Napa Valley, California	Medium-bodied, light oak, crisp and juicy	$30–34
PF	Shafer Vineyards, "Red Shoulder Ranch"	Carneros, California	Medium-bodied, light oak, crisp and juicy	$33–37
	Domaine Laroche, Chablis "Les Vaillons," Premier Cru	Chablis, France	Medium-bodied, light oak, crisp and juicy	$38–42
CW	Louis Carillon, Puligny-Montrachet	Puligny-Montrachet, Burgundy, France	Medium-bodied, light oak, crisp and juicy	$38–42
	Woodward Canyon Winery, Chardonnay	Columbia Valley, Washington	Full-bodied, oaky, ripe	$28–32

	Name of Wine	From	Style Profile	Price Range
GW	Catena Alta, "Adrianna Vineyard," Chardonnay	Mendoza, Argentina	Full-bodied, oaky, ripe	$28–32
	Cakebread Vineyards, Chardonnay	Napa Valley, California	Full-bodied, oaky, ripe	$32–35
CW	Joseph Drouhin, Puligny-Montrachet	Puligny-Montrachet, Burgundy, France	Full-bodied, oaky, crisp, ripe	$38–42
	Paul Hobbs, Chardonnay	Sonoma Mountain, California	Full-bodied, oaky, ripe	$37–40
CW	Olivier Leflaive, Puligny-Montrachet, Premier Cru, "Les Folatières"	Puligny-Montrachet, Burgundy, France	Full-bodied, oaky, crisp, ripe	$40–45
GW	Far Niente, Chardonnay	Napa Valley, California	Full-bodied, oaky, ripe	$55–60

Surprise Sips

Unique Wines Worth Seeking Out

	Name of Wine	From	Style Profile	Price Range
PW	[yellow tail]	South Eastern Australia	Medium-bodied, light oak, crisp and juicy	$6–8
	Domaine Verget, Saint-Véran	Saint-Véran, Burgundy, France	Medium-bodied, unoaked, crisp, juicy	$13–15
PF	Kim Crawford, "Unoaked" Chardonnay	Marlborough, New Zealand	Medium-bodied, unoaked, crisp, juicy	$14–18
	McWilliam's Hanwood Estate, Chardonnay	South Eastern Australia	Medium-bodied, oaky, juicy	$10–12
	Valentin Bianchi, Chardonnay	San Rafael, Argentina	Medium-bodied, oaky, juicy	$13–15
CW	Kumeu River, Chardonnay	New Zealand	Medium-bodied, oaky, juicy	$20–22
	Montes, "Alpha," Chardonnay	Curico Valley, Chile	Full-bodied, oaky, ripe	$18–20
	Domaine Serene, "Côte Sud"	Willamette Valley, Oregon	Full-bodied, oaky, crisp, ripe	$30–34

	Name of Wine	From	Style Profile	Price Range
PF	Testarossa, "Sleepy Hollow Vineyard," Chardonnay	Santa Lucia Highlands, California	Full-bodied, oaky, crisp, ripe	$30–33
	Franciscan Oakville Estate, "Cuvée Sauvage," Chardonnay	Napa Valley, California	Full-bodied, oaky, crisp, ripe	$34–38

pairing

NOW THAT THE CHARDONNAY IS HOME AND READY TO be uncorked, what should you eat with it?

Just like your basic black pants, which *can* go with everything but work better with certain tops, some styles of Chardonnay enhance the flavors and textures of particular foods better than others.

Swirl that Chardonnay in your glass and take a sip. Consider the wine's style profile and ask yourself some questions:

Let's Talk Texture First: Light, medium, or full, rich or racy? If the Chardonnay is full-bodied, look for food with substance such as chicken, veal, or salmon in a creamy sauce. If the Chardonnay is more crisp and delicate, pair it with lighter dishes like simple lemon-laced scallops or trout.

Consider It a Complement: Are there buttery, citrus, or tropical fruit notes?

You can highlight the aromas and flavors found in the wine by pairing the wine with similar food flavors. Serve drawn butter with lobster and a buttery Chardonnay or a mango chutney with a juicy, tropical-scented Chardonnay.

Kissed by Oak: Are there noticeable levels of toasty oak character?

Oak is a wonderful wine-making tool, but a heavily oaked Chardonnay with spicy, toasty aromas and flavors can overwhelm many foods. Wine with apparent oak (spicy, toasty aromas) needs weightier foods such as pasta in a butter or cream sauce and shouldn't be served too cold since it often makes the oak character appear out of balance.

About Acid: Is the wine crisp or smooth?

Crisp Chardonnays pair nicely with tangy food such as fruit salsas, but they also offset the fattiness of cheeses and rich dishes. Softer, smoother Chardonnays complement fuller dishes, such as roast chicken or salmon.

The Buzz from... Peggy Fleming Jenkins, Olympic Ice Skater, Broadcaster, and Grape Grower

"While my entire life has been dedicated to ice and cold, when it comes to white wine, there is such a thing as too cold. If white wine is too heavily chilled, it can hide flavors and aromas. My husband, Greg, and I found this out when we started growing Chardonnay grapes in our small northern California vineyard. It's become a family project that has brought us a lot of enjoyment, and we've learned about the subtlety of temperature when it comes to wine. So, if you want to fully experience the range of taste in a white wine, don't call in the Zamboni. Think gently chilled."

Design-a-Dinner

Stock your shelves with these Chardonnay-friendly ingredients, and dinner becomes a simple matter of mixing and matching ingredients, like a perfect pairing of blouse and blazer and scarf or necklace. Start with the base, or bottoms, then add the tops, and, finally accessorize.

STOCK YOUR SHELVES

Bottoms: Pork, chicken, salmon, lobster, potatoes, sweet potatoes, couscous, brown rice

Tops: Corn, squash, pumpkin, red peppers, avocados, peaches, mangoes, cheeses (Brie, fontina, Asiago), fruit chutneys, white sauces

Accessories: Dijon mustard, caramelized onions, toasted almonds, hazelnuts, tarragon, sage, clove, nutmeg

GET SAUCY . . . WITH CHARDONNAY

Creamy Mustard Dressing: Use 1 tablespoon Dijon mustard to 2 tablespoons olive oil and blend together with a fork or small whisk until creamy. Add 1 tablespoon red wine vinegar or balsamic vinegar (more for a thinner, tangier dressing). Add chopped fresh tarragon and salt and pepper to taste. Spread on sandwiches, top salads, or drizzle over grilled meats.

Sweet Sage Butter: Unwrap a stick of room-temperature butter and put it on some wax paper. Mash the butter with a fork and mix in a spoonful of dried or chopped fresh sage, dash of freshly grated nutmeg, and a dash of brown sugar. Roll the butter into a log and wrap it up. Keep it in the freezer and melt slices on pasta, vegetables, and rice.

Easy Chicken Sandwich: Warm a loaf of crusty French bread in the oven. Slice the bread in half. Top the warm bread with Brie, sautéed chicken breasts, sliced avocado, and caramelized onion. Drizzle with Creamy Mustard Dressing (page 42) and cut the sandwich into portions.

Crispy Corn Salad: Something about the sweetness and texture of corn and Chardonnay makes it seem as though they belong together, so I serve chicken sandwiches with this simple corn salad. Brown the contents of a bag of frozen white corn in olive oil in a pan. Chill in the refrigerator until cool (about 20 minutes), then toss with Creamy Mustard Dressing (page 42). Add chopped tomatoes or halved cherry tomatoes.

Spicy Mango Salmon: Grill or broil salmon. Add some diced pineapple chunks to store-bought mango chutney and put a dollop on top of each piece of salmon. Serve with boiled Yukon Gold potatoes or red new potatoes tossed with Sweet Sage Butter (page 42).

Sweet Sage Ravioli: While fresh or frozen cheese ravioli are cooking according to the package instructions, melt several Sweet Sage Butter (page 42) slices in a pan and cook until lightly browned. Toss with the ravioli and top with grated Asiago or Parmesan cheese. Serve with an avocado salad drizzled with the Creamy Mustard Dressing (page 42).

Roast Chicken and Squash: There's nothing better on a Sunday afternoon than roast chicken and potatoes. Serve with acorn or butternut squash that has been halved, seeded, brushed with a little melted butter and brown sugar, and then baked until soft.

sharing

GIRLS' NIGHT OUT: A CHARDONNAY TASTING PARTY

I MET LYN WHEN OUR KIDS STARTED GOING TO THE same school. Like me, she is a busy mom with little spare time. Before she traded in her convertible for an SUV, she was just beginning to get into wine. When we met, she wanted to rekindle her budding interest but didn't know where to start.

I recommended she start her own wine-tasting group. Book clubs and Bunco nights have sprung up all over, so why not wine-tasting clubs? Here are some tips for starting your own.

1. Put together your group and pick a regular meeting date. My tasting club meets once a month.
2. Set a budget and pick a wine to focus on. Have everyone buy a bottle in a certain price range or chip in money and let the host buy all the bottles. Chardonnay is a great place to begin because there are so many options for themes.

   The Big Boys: Gather a selection of wines that say *California* on the label and compare with a few Bourgogne bottles and some from South Eastern Australia.

   Keep It Cool: Explore the cool-climate wine-growing regions like Chablis, California's Russian River and Carneros regions, New Zealand's Marlborough region, and Chile's Casablanca Valley.

S-and-N Night: California's dueling regions of Sonoma and Napa offer a good look at California Chardonnay. Pour the two next to each other and see if you like one better than the other (or can even tell the difference).

3. When people arrive, the host should bag the bottles or cover them with foil and number them. This is called *blind tasting*, and it helps you focus on the wine without any preconceived ideas of place, price, or producer.

4. Set out spit buckets, which can be anything from paper cups to plastic buckets, and glasses.

5. Make tasting sheets for each wine. Note the color, aromas, flavors, and overall impression of each unidentified bottle of wine. After the bag or foil is removed, record the name of the producer, the type of wine, the country and region it came from, the year it was made, the cost of a bottle, and the foods you think it would go well with.

6. Put out some nibbles and start smelling, swirling, spitting, and tasting.

How to Taste Wine

As a professional wine taster I'm often asked how I can possibly spit out all that delicious wine. My answer is that spitting allows me to get the impression of the wine without the alcohol, a necessity since I regularly taste fifty to a hundred wines a week. Spitting or swallowing is actually the last part of the tasting process, which begins when you pick up the glass.

See: Look at the color and clarity of a wine, preferably holding the glass over a piece of white paper or tablecloth. Whites should be clear, not cloudy, from pale straw color to gold, depending on the wine. Color will also tell you things about how the wine is made and its age. For example, a wine that has been in oak barrels (as many Chardonnays are) will be more gold in color than whites aged in steel tanks. An older white wine will look darker than a younger white wine.

Swirl: Do you know why we swirl? Technically to release the aromas and fruity esters of the wine, but all we're really doing is making the wine comfortable in the glass. It's like taking off your pantyhose after a long day at work—you're stretching out and getting comfortable, and wine needs to do the same thing after it's been cooped up in the bottle.

Smell: Swirling stirs up the wine and allows it to coat the sides of the glass so you can smell the wine better. Smelling a wine is the most important part of wine tasting because you can detect thousands of smells but only a few tastes. Take a good long sniff and ask yourself what you smell: fruits, veggies, flowers, butter, spices, herbs? Let your mind go wild. (Note: *aroma* is used to describe the qualities of most young wines, while *bouquet* refers to the combination of smells developed after bottle aging.)

Sip: Take a sip and swish it around in your mouth. This coats your mouth with the wine, much like swirling does in the glass, and allows you to assess the wine better. Again, ask yourself questions about the aromas and flavors, then think about the way the wine feels in your mouth:

○ Is it light-, medium-, or full-bodied? (Look at the alcohol content on the label for a clue. Higher-alcohol wines, around 13 to 14 percent or more, have a fuller body and heavier impression in your mouth than light- to medium-bodied wines, with alcohol levels of 8 to 12 percent. Sweeter wines also feel fuller in body.)

Did You Know?

It's ironic that we talk about the "taste" of wine and call it "wine tasting" when in actuality we taste only sweetness, sourness, saltiness, and bitterness. (Scientists are currently studying other potential tastes, and have tagged a fifth taste named *umami,* which refers to the savory essence.) With wine you can dismiss saltiness and focus on a wine's sweetness, which we taste on the tip of our tongue, the wine's sourness or acidity, which we notice on the sides of our tongue, and any bitterness, perceived in the back of our mouth. Referring to a wine's overall "taste" generally means a combination of what you smell, taste, and feel.

○ Do you taste sweetness or tartness?

○ Does the wine feel smooth or astringent?

○ Is there a pleasant, lingering aftertaste (called the *finish*)?

Most important, do you like the wine? If you can't figure it out, I'm sure you need another sip, then another, then another . . .

The Buzz on...Women Are Tops at Tasting

Since wine tasting is essentially wine *smelling*, women tend to be better wine tasters. Why? According to Carole Meredith, professor emerita in viticulture and enology at the University of California at Davis, "It has been demonstrated scientifically that women, particularly women of reproductive age, have a better sense of smell than men. Smell, of course, is the most important sense with regard to wine because most of what we call wine 'flavor' is its aroma. Women are better at identifying aromas and can detect them at a lower concentration than men."

Pinot Gris/Pinot Grigio
THE "DENIM" OF WHITE WINE

PINOT GRIS IS THE WINE WORLD'S ANSWER TO denim. Sipping a glass of easy-drinking, affordable Pinot Gris is like throwing on your favorite well-worn pair of jeans. Both are about kicking back and getting comfortable.

"Every person I pour Pinot Gris for loves it," says David Adelsheim of Oregon's Adelsheim Vineyard. "You don't need a lot of explanation, just a little note that says 'try me.'"

Pinot Gris/Pinot Grigio has moved into second place behind Chardonnay in white wine sales and shows no signs of slowing down. It has quickly become an essential wine wardrobe basic, just like those jeans.

THE GRAPE STORY
PINOT GRIS = PINOT GRIGIO

Pinot Gris and Pinot Grigio are one and the same grape variety. Most of us are familiar with Italian bottlings dubbed Pinot Grigio, but the grape has its roots in France.

Pinot Gris actually means "gray Pinot" in French (and *grigio* is "gray" in Italian) and is the result of an ancient mutation of the red grape variety, Pinot Noir. Interestingly, the grapes are more pinkish brown than gray, but *pinot maroon* doesn't sound as good as *Pinot Gris*, I guess.

Inherently, Pinot Gris has a nice kick of acidity, pear and citrus fruit flavors, and often a hint of spice. Like Chardonnay, Pinot Gris can produce wines in an array of styles from light- to full-bodied. Unlike the ubiquitous Chard, however, Pinot Gris is inherently a cool-climate grape and thrives only in select regions of the world.

The nice thing about Pinot Gris is that where it's grown and what it's called will often tell us a particular wine's style. If you like lighter-style wines, try Pinot Grigio from Italy and California, which anchor the crisp side of the style spectrum. Want a little more power? Wines called *Pinot Gris* from Oregon, California, and the Alsace region of France are typically fuller and more richly fruity.

Lingo Lesson

Core Words

Dry: Most bottlings of Pinot Gris and Pinot Grigio are considered dry, though wines labeled *Pinot Gris* often sport a whisper of sweetness. It's not that sugar is added to the wine as many people think, rather that a little of the sweet grape juice was left unfermented during the making of the wine. The wines won't taste sweet, but will be juicy and fruity.

Crisp or smooth: When grapes are grown in cool climates or harvested earlier, as they often are in northern Italy, the wine tastes crisp and vibrant. If the grapes are grown in slightly warmer climates such as Alsace or Oregon, the acidity is lower and the final wine generally tastes softer and smoother.

Light- and medium-bodied: Pinot Grigio tends to be lighter-bodied and Pinot Gris medium-bodied. In Alsace, however, the Pinot Gris can be so full and fleshy it almost needs a girdle to contain itself.

Extra Credit Words
Fruit aromas:

> Tree fruits—pear, Asian pear, peach, green apple
> Citrus fruits—lime, lemon, grapefruit

Bright and fresh: The citrus fruit aromas and flavors and the higher levels of acidity combine in a way to make the wine taste tangy and refreshing. This is especially true for Italian Pinot Grigio.

Nutty and spicy: Usually Pinot Gris (but even some Italian Pinot Grigios) can smell of almonds and sweet spices like cinnamon and ginger. It's not because the wines are aged in new oak barrels like Chardonnay, but because Pinot Gris is a darker-skinned grape and when grown in places with long, cool growing seasons this character shines through in the final wine.

LIGHT AND FRESH PINOT GRIGIO

Most wines labeled *Pinot Grigio* will be light-bodied and fall into the "seriously fun" category as opposed to the "serious" one. Fresh citrus fruit flavors and a cooling streak of acidity make Pinot Grigio an ideal wine for food.

Viva Italia

The vast majority of Pinot Grigio sold in the United States comes from northeastern Italy. This mountainous area stretches from the seaside metropolis of Venice west to the romantic city of Verona and then north and east up to the country's border with Austria and Slovenia. Within this cool area influenced by the towering Alps, Dolomite Mountains, and glacial lakes, there are three large growing regions referred to as the Tre Venezie, or three Venices.

Trentino–Alto Adige is broken into two distinct subregions—Alto Adige and Trentino—and has a split personality. Alto Adige is the northernmost area, bordering Austria, and is so influenced by German culture that signs are in both Italian and German. Trentino, located a little farther south, is firmly rooted in Italian culture.

The Veneto covers the southern flank of the Tre Venezie, which runs from Venice to Verona and up to the gorgeous glacially carved Lake Garda. Most of us have sipped a bottle of the Veneto's well-known exports, Valpolicella and Soave, but this region also produces a sea of Pinot Grigio.

Friuli–Venezia Giulia hugs the eastern border with Slovenia, and the hilly region of Friuli is home to some of the best Pinot Grigio in Italy. Vineyards are terraced into the hillsides and benefit from warm, sunny days and cool nights.

While you may notice these regions on wine labels, what you normally see on bottles of Italian Pinot Grigio will include the following:

Place: delle Venezie, Italy

Taste: Labeling the wine this way indicates the grapes that went into the wine are from growing areas located in the large Tre Venezie region. Beware of bland, lemon-water versions (these are often the least expensive) and pay a little more

money for a top producer's bottling, which should have bright acidity and refreshing citrus flavors.

The Buzz on... Italian Wine Laws

In 1963 the Italian government began the process of defining the uniqueness of Italian wine regions and created guidelines to regulate them. According to the rules, wines from a certain region should taste a particular way. To achieve this lofty goal, the government (and a consortium of wine producers) controls factors such as the types of grapes that can be planted, the size of crops, alcohol content, and aging time. Though they certainly don't guarantee the quality of every wine, the following letters on an Italian label can be used as a guideline when buying wine.

DOCG—Denominazione di Origine Controllata e Garantita

DOCG status is supposedly the best of the best in terms of wines (think of Barolo, Chianti Classico, and Brunello di Montalcino). It essentially means "controlled and guaranteed place of origin."

DOC—Denominazione di Origine Controllata

When you see *DOC* on a label, you know the grapes came from the place indicated on the label and the wine meets the standards set out for that region. Most bottles are of good to very good quality.

IGT—Indicazione Geografica Tipica

A fairly recent addition to the classification lineup, *IGT* on a label indicates "typical" wines of a certain region. Though subject to regulation, this designation gives winemakers more latitude to make interesting wines from a host of grapes grown in regions often larger than those tagged *DOC* or *DOCG*. The quality can be from simply decent to absolutely great, and prices range from inexpensive to outrageous. I'll talk more about great bottles when discussing an Italian wine phenomenon called *Super Tuscans*.

Place: Trentino or Alto Adige, Italy

Taste: When you see these words on the label, think zingy, laserlike focus, crystalline flavors, and acidity that almost snaps, crackles, and pops—a perfect reflection of a place that mesmerized me with its landscape dotted with snow-covered peaks and ice-blue lakes as I flew over the Dolomite Mountains in a small plane.

The Buzz from...Nadia Zenato, Fratelli Zenato, Verona, Italy

Are there really differences in bottles of Pinot Grigio from northern Italy? "Absolutely," says Nadia Zenato. "Pinot Grigio from the Veneto is very drinkable and lighter than that from Collio, which tends to be more structured, rich, and persistent. Pinot Grigio from Alto Adige is leaner and very aromatic with high acidity and longevity."

Place: Collio and Colli Orientali, Italy

Taste: These small appellations fall within the larger Friuli–Venezia Giulia region and are truly the hotbed of quality for Italian Pinot Grigio. The wines originating here can be intoxicating, with perfumed aromas and rich fruit flavors. Both nature and nurture play a

role in the quality. Hills that eventually become the Alps in the North are home to vineyards terraced into the hillsides (*colli* means "hills" in Italian). Sun beats down on the grapes during the day, producing concentrated flavors, then breezes sweep in from the nearby Adriatic Sea to cool things down at night. Several decades ago a handful of important producers began focusing on making great Italian whites in a country where red rules.

Tasting Tip: Look for wines from one of the region's most influential producers, Jermann. From stylish Pinot Grigio and Chardonnay to aromatic Traminer, Jermann's wines are worth seeking out. They range in price from $20 to $50.

Place: California

Taste: Wines carrying the California appellation are generally uncomplicated, light, and fresh. These wines (usually priced around $10) reflect the California sun and showcase less tanginess and more fruit than their Italian counterparts.

Except to see more affordable bottlings from the Golden State, too. As consumers clamor for Pinot Grigio, California brands such as Talus, Sutter Home, Robert Mondavi's Woodbridge, Gallo, and Kendall-Jackson can't plant vineyards fast enough to meet demand. Also, watch for versions from all over California labeled Pinot Gris. Typically falling into the $15–$20 category, they tend to be complex and richly fruity.

Place: Napa Valley, California

Taste: Think melon and juicy pears, peaches, and fresh fruit salad. It can be very warm in Napa, which mimics sun-drenched Tuscany more than cool northeastern Italy, but a number of vintners are crafting deliciously fruity, rich Pinot Grigio carrying the Napa appellation.

Look for these places on the label, too ...

Washington state

Germany

New Zealand

leslie's label links

Connecting taste to place makes wine buying easy

RIPE, LUSCIOUS PINOT GRIS

Sip an Italian Pinot Grigio next to a Pinot Gris from Alsace and you'll find it hard to believe they're the same grape variety. There is a simi-

larity in flavor, but the textural differences are striking. Imagine biting into an airy lemon chiffon pie then nibbling on a dense lemon pound cake.

Place: Oregon

Taste: Oregon Pinot Gris is the bridge between a bright, light style and the fullest wines from Alsace. Many of the state's vineyards are influenced by cooling Pacific ocean breezes, and that creates a  long, slow growing season. Grapes spend a lot of time hanging on the vines, which allows the final wines to maintain a vibrant kick of acidity while possessing ripe, rich fruit flavors. Members of the Pinot family (including Pinot Gris, Pinot Blanc, and, of course, Pinot Noir) love these climatic conditions and have adapted well to growing in Oregon.

Place: Willamette Valley, Oregon

Taste: When you see *Willamette* on a label, expect to taste concentrated fruit in a bottle. This fertile valley approximately a hundred miles long and sixty miles wide is the epicenter of Oregon's wine industry and is home to more than two-thirds of the state's nearly two hundred wineries. Due to the Willamette Valley's combination of rich soils and maritime-influenced climate, days are warm and evenings mild and cool. Grapes have a chance to ripen fully and slowly, producing vibrant, fruity Pinot Gris.

Place: Alsace, France

Taste: Jean Trimbach of Maison Trimbach in Alsace believes, "The natural link from Chardonnay to Alsace is Pinot Gris." I agree in the sense that, to get American wine lovers to try wines from Alsace, we must put them in the context of what most people know—Chardonnay. Though Pinot Gris from Alsace has a fuller body and often pearlike flavors associated with Chardonnay, you don't have to contend with oak. Alsatian Pinot Gris leaves you with the overwhelming impression of smelling flowers and drinking silk, a sensation showcased by the local cuisine, from sausages and ham to Muenster cheese and foie gras.

A MATTER OF STYLE

How do the winemaker's decisions affect the ultimate taste of a bottle of Pinot Gris? It depends on the desired style of the wine.

Bright and Fresh Versions

Many winemakers, particularly in Italy, choose to harvest their grapes early to maintain high acid levels and give the wine a tangy, crisp character. You know how if you pick your strawberries early they are green and taste tart? The same is true of grapes.

Pinot Grigio is usually fermented and aged in stainless-steel tanks as opposed to oak barrels, which preserves the brightness of the fruit. Though some wines undergo the secondary malolactic fermentation, which lowers the high levels of acidity and makes the wine seem creamier, they are still light and fresh.

Rich and Luscious Versions

Thanks to warm weather or more time on the vine, the fruit gets riper, and the flavors reflect that juicy, full quality. A giveaway is an alcohol level in the 13 percent range.

In Alsace, Pinot Gris is often fermented and aged in huge old wooden vats called *foudres.* These vats don't impart any wood character to the wine but highlight the richness associated with Pinot Gris from Alsace. Sometimes the texture and body of Pinot Gris is also enhanced by a dash of sugar left in the wine after fermentation, which gives the final product a succulently full and fruity quality.

Shopping Guide

The beauty of shopping for these wines is that they're so easy to find, especially with the sea of Italian Pinot Grigio flooding store shelves.

Most bottlings are affordable, while a few require spending serious money, but I've highlighted several worth the cash drop.

Stash-Your-Cash Wines $15 and Under

	Name of Wine	From	Style Profile	Price Range
PW	Ecco Domani, Pinot Grigio	delle Venezie, Italy	Light-bodied, unoaked, crisp, aromatic	$8–10
PW	Zenato, Pinot Grigio	delle Venezie, Italy	Light-bodied, unoaked, crisp, aromatic	$8–10
	Montevina Winery, Pinot Grigio	California	Light-bodied, unoaked, crisp, aromatic	$9–11
	Tiefenbrunner, Pinot Grigio	delle Venezie, Italy	Light-bodied, unoaked, crisp, aromatic	$10–12
GW	Franz Haas, "Kris" Pinot Grigio	delle Venezie, Italy	Light-bodied, unoaked, crisp, aromatic	$9–11
	Bollini, Pinot Grigio	Trentino, Italy	Light-bodied, unoaked, crisp, aromatic	$9–11
	Bolla, "Arcale," Pinot Grigio	Collio, Italy	Light-bodied, unoaked, crisp, aromatic	$9–12
	King Estate Winery, Pinot Gris	Oregon	Medium-bodied, unoaked, crisp, juicy	$13–15
PF	Adelsheim Vineyard, Pinot Gris	Oregon	Medium-bodied, unoaked, crisp, juicy	$13–15
	Trimbach, Pinot Gris, "Reserve"	Alsace, France	Medium-bodied, unoaked, crisp, juicy	$13–15
	Jean-Baptiste Adam, Tokay Pinot Gris	Alsace, France	Medium-bodied, unoaked, crisp, juicy	$13–15

Well-Known Winners $15–40

	Name of Wine	From	Style Profile	Price Range
GW	La Famiglia di Robert Mondavi, Pinot Grigio	California	Light-bodied, unoaked, crisp, aromatic	$15–18

	Name of Wine	From	Style Profile	Price Range
	Santa Margherita, Pinot Grigio	Alto Adige, Italy	Light-bodied, unoaked, crisp, aromatic	$18–22
	Long Vineyards, Pinot Grigio	Napa Valley, California	Medium-bodied, light oak, crisp and juicy	$14–16
GW	Luna Vineyards, Pinot Grigio	Napa Valley, California	Medium-bodied, light oak, crisp and juicy	$15–18
PW	Swanson Vineyards, Pinot Grigio	Napa Valley, California	Medium-bodied, light oak, crisp and juicy	$17–19
	Pighin, Pinot Grigio	Collio, Italy	Medium-bodied, unoaked, crisp, juicy	$15–18
GW	Sokol Blosser, Pinot Gris	Willamette Valley, Oregon	Medium-bodied, unoaked, crisp, juicy	$16–18
	WillaKenzie Estate, Pinot Gris	Willamette Valley, Oregon	Medium-bodied, unoaked, crisp, juicy	$17–19
	Domaine Schlumberger, "Les Princes Abbes," Pinot Gris	Alsace, France	Full-bodied, unoaked and aromatic	$15–18
PF	Jermann, Pinot Grigio	Venezia Giulia, Italy	Full-bodied, unoaked and aromatic	$20–24
CW	Domaine Weinbach, "Cuvée Sainte Catherine," Tokay Pinot Gris	Alsace, France	Full-bodied, unoaked and aromatic	$40–42

pairing

HERE'S AN EASY FOOD AND WINE PAIRING TIP: WHEN in doubt about which white wine to serve with food, choose Pinot Gris.

Think of its French and Italian heritage. In Alsace, Pinot Gris is served alongside pungent cheeses and rich cream sauces, chicken as well as game. In Italy it is the ideal companion to seafood pasta, antipasto, and northeastern Italian staples such as provolone and prosciutto.

What about its compatibility with spicy cuisine? Go for it. Pinot Gris from Alsace happens to be my favorite with anything curried.

You Sweet Thing: Is the wine dry or medium-dry?

With these wines it's often difficult to detect any sense of sweetness because they just taste fruity and full. If the wine does have a touch of residual sugar, it only enhances its ability to pair with full-flavored and spicy dishes.

Let's Talk Texture: Light or full, delicate or fleshy?

Pinot Grigios usually fall on the lighter side, so stick with the dishes that are less robust. Pinot Gris from Oregon and Alsace will be big and full and can stand up to full-flavored meats, cheeses, and, best of all, foie gras.

Consider It a Complement: Are there spicy, citrus, or ripe fruit notes?

Serve citrusy wines with all those things fresh from the garden—peas, salads, fresh veggies, pesto sauces, and fruits. Or echo the spiciness by pairing a rich Pinot Gris with curry sauces.

About Acid: Is the wine crisp or smooth?

Acidity is the component in wine that makes it so lively. Think of it as the vinous equivalent of a bra that imparts a perky appearance—in this case to both food and wine. Pinot Grigio's lemon/lime tartness can act like a knife slicing through creamy dishes, while its palate-cooling freshness tames piquant ones. When the wine is smoother, it complements rich dishes and creamy cheeses.

The Buzz from…Catherine Faller, Domaine Weinbach, Alsace

Catherine Faller, whose family owns Domaine Weinbach, one of Alsace's most highly regarded wineries, suggests the perfect pairing with their rich Pinot Gris is asparagus in a cream sauce. Sauté sliced shallots and morel mushrooms in butter, then pour in some Pinot Gris or Riesling and reduce. Add cream or milk and cook until thickened. Pour over steamed green or white asparagus.

Design-a-Dinner

STOCK YOUR SHELVES

Bottoms: Ham, salami, chicken, turkey, salmon/smoked salmon, tuna, white fish, scallops, risotto, pasta

Tops: Mushrooms, tomatoes, figs, mandarin oranges, green apples, cheeses (goat cheese, mozzarella, Muenster, Camembert, provolone), curry sauces, Alfredo sauces, tomato sauce, pesto

Accessories: Hazelnuts, macadamia nuts, pine nuts, basil, ginger, curry

GET SAUCY . . . WITH PINOT GRIS/PINOT GRIGIO

Retro Green Goddess Dressing: I loved Green Goddess dressing as a kid. My mom made it, and I remember the greenish hue and creamy sweetness on her Iceberg lettuce salad. Here's a revved-up version. In a blender or food processor, puree the flesh of 1 large ripe avocado with a small handful each of fresh dill, parsley, and basil or tarragon, plus a couple of tablespoons mayonnaise. Thin with a bit of olive oil and lemon juice or vinegar. Season with salt and pepper. Spread on sandwiches, dress salads, or use as a dip.

Creamy Goat Cheese Sauce: Fresh goat cheese is an ideal companion for Pinot Grigio. Heat 1 cup chicken broth in a pan, then whisk in a round of creamy fresh goat cheese (if the sauce is too thin add more cheese). Season with salt, pepper, and some coarsely chopped fresh basil and parsley leaves. Toss the sauce on everything from pasta and rice to turkey scaloppine and chicken breasts. This sauce works beautifully when paired with Sauvignon Blanc, as well.

MEAL ENSEMBLES

Figs and Goat Cheese: Cut fresh figs in half. Place face up on a cookie sheet and top each fig half with a dollop of goat cheese. Broil just until bubbly. Squeeze a dash of lemon juice on top and sprinkle with salt and cracked black pepper. Serve as finger food at room temperature.

Prosciutto-Wrapped Melon: Cut a ripe melon such as Crenshaw or honeydew into 2-inch slices and remove the rind. Wrap each slice with a piece of thinly sliced prosciutto. Skewer each with a toothpick to hold the ham in place.

Chunky Turkey Salad: Sauté 1 large turkey breast fillet (approximately 2 pounds) with a bit of cooking oil, salt, and pepper. Let cool and chop into 1/2-inch cubes. While the turkey is cooking, peel and then toast 1/2 cup hazelnuts and let cool. In a separate bowl, combine 1 tart green apple that has been cored and cubed, 1 small can drained mandarin oranges, and the cubed turkey. Chop the hazelnuts and add them to the bowl. Add some Retro Green Goddess Dressing (page 59) and toss gently to coat, then spoon the salad onto lettuce leaves and serve.

Tuna Curry Quiche: Prebake a store-bought or homemade pie crust on high heat for several minutes and let cool. Use a traditional quiche recipe, but whisk 2 teaspoons curry powder into the egg mixture and then add shredded Muenster or mozzarella cheese and one can of well-drained white tuna. Bake at 325°F until set and lightly brown on top. Pair with Pinot Gris from Alsace.

Goat Cheese Vegetable Pasta: Cook rigatoni, bowtie, or orecchiette pasta al dente according to the package instructions. Toss with chopped fresh tomatoes and basil then add Creamy Goat Cheese Sauce (page 59). Top with cracked black pepper.

sharing

MISSION POSSIBLE:
SHOPPING FOR WINE

IF YOU WANT TO NAVIGATE THE WINE AISLES WITH confidence, I suggest a shopping checklist.

Ask Yourself What the Wine Is For

To serve with dinner at home? Now that you know about Pinot Gris, give it a try tonight.

To take to a dinner party? Pinot Noir is one of my top picks because it goes with everything.

To give as a gift? I like to give Champagne and dessert wines as gifts.

To pour for a party you are hosting? Look for a magnum, which is a large bottle that holds the equivalent of two regular-size bottles.

For a special occasion? Dream big! Try an aged red Bordeaux from France or an Italian Barolo.

Determine What You Want to Spend

Less than $10?

$10–20?

$20–30?

More than $30?

Figure Out Where to Shop

Grocery store: For those living in states where wine is available at supermarkets, this is a convenient and popular option. Stores such as Safeway, Trader Joe's, Albertsons, Jewel, and Food Lion offer many top-notch bottlings and terrific values on everyday wines. Unfortunately, it is illegal to sell wine in grocery stores in many states.

Specialty wine stores: These stores vary from mega-operations like Sam's Wines & Spirits in Chicago and Beverages & more! in California to small mom-and-pop shops. My best advice is to find a retailer you trust and rely upon their expertise. The good ones will give you personalized attention and respect your cost parameters and interests.

Retail chains with specialty wine departments: National stores such as Costco and Cost Plus World Market have terrific wine departments. (Costco is, in fact, the largest single wine seller in the country and carries several hundred types of wine including top-notch Bordeaux bottlings.) The wines are selected specifically for quality, and because these chains are able to purchase in large quantities and take a lower margin than other stores, prices are often the best around.

Online: Because it's illegal to ship wine between numerous states, online sales have suffered. If you're lucky enough to live in a state where shipping is not an issue, you can find unique and great-value wines online. I've highlighted some of my favorite web sites in the Checkout Counter: Resources in the back of the book.

The Buzz on...Wine Clubs

Want to have wine delivered to your doorstep without the worry of shopping for it? Join a wine club. I have belonged to many over the years and love having wine hand-picked for me every month, then showing up at my house in time for dinner. Individual wineries often have their own clubs, while retailers and specialty clubs offer everything from "International-only" clubs to "Oregon Pinot Noir" or "Cabernet lovers" clubs, which makes it easy to find ones you like. Make sure to check the club's policy regarding shipping, returning wine, and discontinuing membership. Check out a few favorites in the Checkout Counter: Resources.

Now that you have a picture of how much you want to spend, where to spend it, and why, it's time to head to the store.

Who's on Top? Take In the Layout of the Store

Most wine stores are laid out according to grape variety, such as Chardonnay, Sauvignon Blanc, Merlot, and Cabernet Sauvignon. Others have wines broken down by regions of the world instead. I've also found many stores put the inexpensive wines on the lowest shelves, the middle shelves hold moderately priced wines, and the most expensive are on the top shelves.

If Shelves Could Talk . . . Oh, But They Do

You know those little signs stuck to the wine shelves? These are called *shelf talkers*, and they tout point or star ratings or quotes from wine publications to attract buyers. I find the most useful shelf talkers are those with tasting notes handwritten by staffers, which often include food-pairing hints.

Help Me, Please!

I don't know why people are nervous about asking for help in a wine store or when dining out. We have no problem asking a restaurant server what's good on the menu or talking to a salesclerk about whether or not an outfit looks good on us, so why not wine? Ask as many questions as you can.

Tricks for Extra Bargains

Wine stores often give case discounts, usually 10 to 15 percent, when you buy twelve bottles. Make sure you look for sales, which often appear around Christmastime, when people buy wine for the holidays. That's a good time to stock up.

The Buzz on...Women and Wine—the Experience

Women usually approach wine from an experiential standpoint, and their interest lies not in ratings but in the way a wine tastes and the situation where the wine will be enjoyed. "I believe women tend to be less concerned with big-name collectors' wines that they are told to buy by the media and more likely to pick a bottle just for its pure, hedonistic value," notes Amy Wesselman, winemaker and owner of Oregon's Westrey Wine Company.

Sauvignon Blanc/Sancerre
THE "CRISP WHITE SHIRT" WINE

You know the shirt, a crisp white cotton number that works as easily under a wool suit as it does with a pair of linen pants. It can be tied at the waist for a fresh, sassy look, or tucked in for a more timeless image. The classic top is a year-round winner.

If you could button up a bottle, your "white shirt" wine would surely be Sauvignon Blanc. As one of the world's most favored whites, it is both traditional and trendy. Sauvignon's fruity freshness, tinged with an edge of wild herbs, makes it simple to sip in the heat of summer and the middle of winter when some sunshine-in-a-bottle is a welcome relief.

THE GRAPE STORY

It seems appropriate that Sauvignon Blanc tastes a little untamed since it takes its name from the French word for "savage." Naturally high levels of acidity are responsible for Sauvignon's sassiness and delicious fruit flavors for its friendliness, but its personality is multifaceted.

With origins harking back to the Bordeaux region of France, Sauvignon Blanc (along with Cabernet Franc) is the parent of the famous red grape variety Cabernet Sauvignon. As with most family members who have things in common, these varieties can produce wines that share an herbaceous streak. Sauvignon Blanc, in particular, often sports aromas of cut grass and fresh herbs.

If you're thinking that doesn't sound very appealing, you're right. If the wine smells like a vegetable salad and not a fruit salad, it's out of balance. But, when those herbal notes are simply part of the package, they give Sauvignon Blanc an air of eclectic distinction.

The Buzz on…When Do They Put the Peaches in the Wine?

Once when I was waxing poetic about a bottle of wine that reminded me of peaches, someone asked if they actually put peaches in the wine. The answer is no, but there are scientific reasons we smell and taste what we do in wine. First, grapes are fruits and contain some of the same chemical compounds as other fruits and vegetables. As a result they share similar aromas and flavors. Each grape variety has a slightly different chemical makeup, so what we smell and taste in the glass is different for each wine, too. Sauvignon Blanc is an ideal illustration. The grape's fresh herbal character stems from a chemical compound called *methoxypyrazines*, which are found in grape varieties such as Sauvignon Blanc and Cabernet Sauvignon. Pyrazines also contribute to the flavors of foods such as bell peppers, asparagus, and peas.

THE NAME GAME

Sauvignon Blanc = Sancerre and Pouilly-Fumé

Sancerre and Pouilly-Fumé whites are made from Sauvignon Blanc grapes. Located in the Loire region of France, these wine-growing areas are home to some of the most distinctive Sauvignon Blancs in the world.

Sauvignon Blanc + Sémillon = white Bordeaux (appellations such as Graves, Pessac-Léognan, and Entre-Deux-Mers)

While Sancerre and Pouilly-Fumé are the best-known regions where Sauvignon Blanc is grown, they're not the grape's only claim to French fame. When you see a bottle of white Bordeaux, chances are it will have a healthy dose of Sauvignon Blanc.

YOU SAY SAUVIGNON, I SAY FUMÉ

Though France is certainly the home of zesty Sauvignon, many wine lovers are familiar with juicy versions from California, which are sometimes called *Fumé Blanc.*

In 1966 winemaking icon Robert Mondavi founded his namesake winery in Napa Valley. One of Mr. Mondavi's passions was to upgrade the image of domestic Sauvignon Blanc. As he says in his book *Harvests of Joy,* "I knew that in the Loire Valley they produced delightful white wines made from the Sauvignon Blanc grape, including Sancerre, Pouilly-Fumé, and Blanc Fumé. So I wondered why we couldn't find a way to reinvent Sauvignon Blanc and turn it into a success in America."

By taking advantage of California's sunshine to get ripe fruit flavors, then aging the wine in small oak barrels (something quite revolutionary at the time), and finally giving the wine a name he felt the American public could pronounce and embrace—Fumé Blanc—Robert Mondavi changed the face of Sauvignon Blanc forever.

While Mondavi kicked off awareness of Sauvignon Blanc in this country, French producers from Sancerre took the ball and ran. When Americans discovered the crisp whites in the early to mid-1980s, the wines became extremely popular. Nowadays, hot French Sauvignon Blancs include those from Sancerre but also from the Bordeaux appellation of Pessac-Léognan.

Not to be outdone, New Zealand became a player in the SB game by crafting what I call the "Andy Warhol" of Sauvignon Blancs. Just as Warhol's bold, stylish images of Campbell's soup cans turned the art world upside down, New Zealand Sauvignon Blanc transformed the wine scene. Consumers clamored to get their hands on the pungent wine that smelled like freshly cut grass and tasted like passion fruit.

The winery that caused the frenzy in 1985 was Cloudy Bay. As owner David Hohnen says, "I truly believe the right combination of varietal, soil, and microclimate can be magic. The best winemakers are really matchmakers."

Magical results in the bottle have to do with that marriage between grape variety and location, which is especially important to Sauvignon

Blanc. Cooler regions emphasize the grape's crisp, herbal character, while warmer climates bring out its fruity, succulent side.

Lingo Lesson

Core Words

Dry: Sauvignon Blanc–based wines are considered dry (with the exception of those made as sweet dessert wines). Sauvignon Blanc can often taste very dry in comparison to other white wines due to the combination of tangy acidity and lack of sweetness.

Crisp: Sauvignon Blanc has a lovely freshness and high-toned acidity that makes your mouth water. I think of good Sauvignon Blanc as almost crunchy, there is so much crispy acidity (imagine biting into a tangy green apple).

Light- and Medium-Bodied: Most versions are light- or medium-bodied whites, but when blended with Sémillon, they often feel full-bodied.

Extra Credit Words

Fruit aromas:

> Citrus fruits—lemon, lime, grapefruit
> Tropical fruits—pineapple, melon
> Exotic fruits—gooseberry, passion fruit

Herbal aromas: The inherent herbal character is usually described as grassy or like fresh herbs, or bell pepper, which becomes more pronounced when the grapes are grown in cooler regions. Think of the smell of freshly mown grass or basil just picked from the garden.

Flinty and minerally: Sauvignon Blanc–based wines from the French region of Pouilly-Fumé and Sancerre are often described this way. It's a difficult aroma to pinpoint, but I liken it to the smell of wet stones.

Smoky: Wines aged in oak barrels as some from Bordeaux or New World versions called Fumé Blanc often sport toasty, smoky aromas.

All About Structure

PART I

Now that you've gotten the hang of the Lingo Lessons and feel comfortable describing Chardonnay as smooth and full-bodied, Pinot Gris or Pinot Grigio as dry and medium-bodied, or Sauvignon Blanc as crisp and light-bodied, we're ready to look more closely at the structural components of wine associated with my core words.

Core Words = Structural Component

1. **Crisp, bright, smooth = acidity level**
2. **Dry, medium-dry, sweet = sweetness level**
   See page 91 for more.
3. **Light, medium, strong tannins = tannin level** (in red wines)
   See page 139 for more.
4. **Light-, medium-, and full-bodied = alcohol level**
   See page 240 for more.

Think of these four elements, which comprise the basic structure of a wine, as you would the important parts of a house. I consider acidity the foundation. The tannins and sweetness level are the frame and wood siding, and the alcohol level is the roof. They all need to support each other and integrate to create a wine's basic shape and style. Balance is the key.

You may be asking, why not fruit? Fruit aromas and flavors are important, but since very few people buy wine just because it's subjectively described as lemon versus pineapple or cherry versus plum, I've included the fruit character of a wine as an extra credit term. Other extra credit terms I have highlighted are qualities derived from growing and wine-making techniques.

Understanding what the core words mean is very helpful in determining the style of wine you like. We'll explore each one of these four structural components in the chapters most relevant to each, starting with acidity, which is particularly important to zesty Sauvignon Blanc.

Crisp, Bright, Smooth = Acidity Level

Just as the acidity in a squirt of lemon juice perks up food and drink, the acidity naturally present in grapes gives wine life and lift. Wine can be fresh, lively, crisp and bright or smooth, soft, creamy, depending on its levels of acidity. In general, wines from cooler regions have higher acidity and tangier fruit flavors while those from warmer growing regions have lower acidity and a riper fruit character.

How does wine develop acidity? Let's go back and visit our little friend, a grape named Brut, to find out.

Brut, like all his pals in the cluster, starts life as a tiny little grape with so much tart acidity you wouldn't be able to eat him. Only when Brut ripens by basking in the sunshine does he become something that would make a tasty wine. Brut gleefully suns himself during the day, which produces sugar. At the same time, he's using up acidity as energy and "sweating" it out. (Basically the two are inversely related, so as sugar rises, acidity drops.) If the nighttime temperature stays warm, Brut's acidity level continues to drop. However, if the temperature gets nice and cool at night, the vine shuts down and takes a rest and Brut's acidity is maintained. When this happens the resulting wine is crisp and bright. That's why I say cool nights act like a resealable plastic bag, preserving the juicy flavors developed during sunny days, but locking in vibrant acidity.

leslie's label links
Connecting taste to place makes wine buying easy

CRISP AND HERBAL
Climate is arguably the most important factor in the final taste of Sauvignon Blanc. These growing regions range from cool to downright cold and produce Sauvignon Blanc with herbal crispness that wakes up your palate like a quick dip in a cool lake wakes up your body.

Place: Sancerre, France

Taste: Herbs, minerals, citrus, and green apple notes combine to make Sancerre one of the purest expressions of Sauvignon Blanc in the world. This appellation in France's eastern Loire Valley is where Sauvignon Blanc reaches its heights. Literally. The town of Sancerre is built on a hill rising out of the surrounding flat landscape with a stone-walled village on top. Driving up to it reminds me of the moment Dorothy saw the city

MIS EN BOUTEILLE A LA PROPRIÉTÉ

Pascal Jolivet

SANCERRE
APPELLATION SANCERRE CONTRÔLÉE

12.5% ALC. BY VOL - PRODUCT OF FRANCE - 750 ML
VINIFIED AND BOTTLED AT THE PROPERTY
BY PASCAL JOLIVET
ROUTE DE CHAVIGNOL - 18300 SANCERRE FRANCE

of Oz emerging from the poppy fields. The vineyards are planted around the town on hillsides, which expose them to sun for maximum ripeness—a necessity in this cool-climate northern region. The soil is limestone and silex, or flint, which helps to give the wines their telltale mineral character.

Value Tip: Look for wines from the lesser-known appellation named Ménétou-Salon located next to Sancerre. These wines sport the same refreshing zip as bottles from their famous neighbor but for a fraction of the price.

Place: Pouilly-Fumé, France

Taste: From the hilltop town of Sancerre, you can look across the Loire River to the neighboring town of Pouilly-sur-Loire. It's in this flatter area with vineyards stretching over gently rolling hills that wines named Pouilly-Fumé are produced from the Sauvi-  gnon Blanc grape. The soil is rust colored and flinty. Picking up pieces as I walked through rolling vineyards helped me understand why these wines smell and taste the way they do—not necessarily of smoke and gunflint as many people say, but minerally and earthy. The rocks act like mini solar panels trapping the heat of the day, so it makes sense that the wines are often more opulent, full, and round than those from neighboring Sancerre.

Tasting Tip: Many wineries bottle both Sancerre and Pouilly-Fumé wines, so find producers you like—I recommend Pascal Jolivet or Henri Bourgeois—and sip their wines side by side to taste the differences.

Place: Entre-Deux-Mers, Bordeaux, France

Taste: This a good place to start to move from the steely Sauvignon Blancs of the Loire Valley to softer though still bright and citrusy whites. Traditionally, white wines labeled *Entre-Deux-Mers* will be a blend of Sauvignon Blanc, Sémillon, and the aromatic grape Muscadelle. *Entre-Deux-Mers* means "between two seas," and the region is cradled in the

fork of Bordeaux's Dordogne and Garonne waterways. With rolling, vineyard-covered hills, it is pastorally lush, with moisture hanging in the air, making the whole place smell faintly of fresh sea grass.

Place: Marlborough, New Zealand

Taste: New Zealand Sauvignon Blanc is addictive. It may be the juicy fruit flavors or the herbal overtones. It could be the vibrant tartness or the distinctive aromas of freshly cut grass . . . Whatever it is, once you start sipping a glass, it's hard to stop.

I've been a fan of these wines for so long that I went to see what makes them unique. New Zealand is made up of two islands: the North Island and the South Island. Flying a short twenty-minute route from the rain-shrouded town of Wellington on the North Island to Marlborough at the tip of the South Island, I understood why the wines taste the way they do. Emerging from the gray clouds to land in Marlborough, we were met by bright sun and pristine weather. Rimmed by steep mountains, Marlborough is protected from harsh ocean weather. Along with the combination of cool ocean breezes and long growing days, the climate allows the grapes to mature and gain fruit intensity while retaining high acidity levels and a pleasing touch of fresh herbs.

Value Tip: One of my consistent favorites from Marlborough is Brancott Vineyards Sauvignon Blanc, which can be found for around $10–12.

Place: Stellenbosch, South Africa

Taste: What I enjoy about the Sauvignon Blanc from South Africa is its distinctive bell pepper aromas and tropical fruit flavors, which are rounded out by a plump texture. South Africa has a rich wine tra-

dition, and the Stellenbosch region is one of the most naturally beautiful. Steep, swerving mountain ranges rim a large bay, and though it's warm in Stellenbosch, grapes are planted on hillsides, where it's cooler and the soil is better suited to growing high-quality grapes.

Place: Casablanca, Chile

Taste: On my first trip to Chile, my daughter asked if I was going to take my winter coat. I was visiting in Chile's summer season, so I was puzzled and said no. She said, "Mommy, you must; it's chilly in Chile." When I got down there, I was sorry I hadn't listened to her. The days are very hot, but with the influence of snowcapped mountains to the east and the nearby Pacific Ocean to the west of the Casablanca region, it cools quickly at
night. These ideal climatic conditions help to produce Sauvignon Blanc with crispness, exotic fruit flavors, and hints of sweet herbs.

Look for these places on the label, too . . .

Quincy, France

Reuilly, France

Alto Adige, Italy

Santa Barbara, California

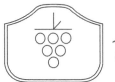

leslie's label links

Connecting taste to place makes wine buying easy

JUICY AND RIPE

If you like the fruitiness of Sauvignon Blanc but aren't enamored of the more herbal versions, then look for wines from the following regions.

Place: Graves, Bordeaux, France

Taste: In France, the Sauvignon Blanc seems to go from sleek to silk as we move from the eastern area of Sancerre to the western region of Bordeaux. Located on the Atlantic seaboard, Bordeaux has a moderate maritime climate. Graves is one of the subregions in Bordeaux, and the name describes why the wines are so special. Graves means "gravel," and the soil in this part of Bordeaux is full of vine-loving stones. The well-drained earth imparts a mineral-like quality to the wine, much like the limestone does in Chablis or silex/flint in Pouilly-Fumé, and keeps the vines dry and warm. Graves whites are also traditionally blended with lush Sémillon, which rounds out lean Sauvignon Blanc and gives the wines a fullness and ripe, rich quality.

Place: Pessac-Léognan, Bordeaux, France

Taste: This area is the jewel in the crown of Graves and is home to some of the world's top white wines. Named for the primo stretch of ultragravelly land surrounding the towns of Pessac and Léognan, the appellation is a fairly new addition to the Bordeaux lineup. It was actually delineated as a distinct appellation in  1987 through the efforts of a group of winegrowers, led by the owner of Château Couhins-Lurton, André Lurton, who wanted to protect the special place from the encroachment of Bordeaux's city sprawl. As with Graves whites, the blend often includes Sémillon and creates whites with intensity and richness.

Place: Sonoma County, California

Taste: One of every four bottles of Sauvignon Blanc sold carrying a price tag of $8 or more comes from Sonoma County. That's a lot of Sauvignon Blanc. Because the appellation has such a diversity of climates (there are ten sub-appellations within Sonoma County, from the  cool Russian River Valley and Carneros regions to the warmer spots like Sonoma Valley and Alexander Valley), wine-makers have quite a palette to paint a lush style of Sauvignon Blanc. Cooler regions give zest and zip, while warmer ones add ripe, smooth character to these wines.

Place: Dry Creek Valley, California

Taste: From this subappellation of Sonoma County come Sauvignon Blancs that are ripe and juicy yet vibrant. I think of them as fruit salad with a refreshing squirt of lemon. Dry Creek Valley is a narrow swath of land in the northern part of Sonoma County. The ocean

lies west of the valley over a range of coastal hills, and the region can get incredibly warm during the day but chill down at night, which produces fruity and rich Sauvignon Blanc.

Dry Creek holds a special place in my heart because my husband and I spent long weekends biking and sipping our way through the valley during our engagement. As we explored the winding country roads of Dry Creek, which is famous for hearty Zinfandel, we also discovered what a terrific spot it is for Sauvignon Blanc.

Place: Margaret River, Australia

Taste: If you want crisp but lush Sauvignon Blanc, look for wines from the Western Australian area of Margaret River. Situated in the far west corner of the country along the Indian Ocean, it's a windy spot with a climate more akin to Bordeaux than the hotter Barossa Valley. And as in France, producers often

blend Semillon with Sauvignon Blanc to achieve a rich yet vibrant character.

Place: Texas

Taste: Yes, Texas, ya'll. Not only can the Lone Star State boast of nearly fifty wineries, it's home to the nation's largest wine-growing region, called the Texas Hill Country. That's not all. According to the Texas Wine Research and Marketing Institute, the state ranks fifth in wine production behind California, New York, Washington, and Oregon. Since many of the grapes are planted at higher altitudes, where they can get ripe but also keep cool, the Sauvignon Blancs sport a juicy ripeness with just a hint of herbs and tropical fruit.

Look for these places on the label, too . . .
Hawkes Bay, New Zealand
Russian River Valley, California
Livermore Valley, California
Washington state

A MATTER OF STYLE

The old adage that wine is made on the vine applies particularly to Sauvignon Blanc. The winemaker's main goal is to capture that crisp, fresh-from-the-vine quality in the bottle. When they want a more lush style of Sauvignon Blanc, however, winemakers can get the fruit very ripe and fine-tune flavors using various techniques.

Many winemakers in the Bordeaux regions of Graves and Pessac-Léognan, for example, use oak barrels to ferment and age their whites, which lends a deeper color and spicy richness to the wine. Domestic producers—some who call their wines Fumé Blanc—do the same.

The wine's final taste can also be affected by adding another grape variety to the mix, usually Sémillon. This blend tends to round out the angular quality of the wine, with the Sémillon's richness and honey character taming the snap of the Sauvignon Blanc.

The Buzz on . . . Meritage means what?

Ever notice the word *Meritage* (rhymes with *heritage*) on a label of American white or red wine? It means that the wine is a blend of classic Bordeaux varieties grown on our very own shores. White Meritage wines are

> **ST. SUPÉRY**
> 2000
> **MERITAGE**
> **NAPA VALLEY WHITE WINE**
> ....
> PRODUCED AND BOTTLED BY ST. SUPÉRY VINEYARDS & WINERY
> RUTHERFORD CALIFORNIA 94573   13.5% ALCOHOL BY VOLUME

generally made from a blend of Sauvignon Blanc and Sémillon and reds from traditional Bordeaux grapes such as Cabernet Sauvignon, Merlot, Cabernet Franc, Malbec, and Petit Verdot. But not all Bordeaux-style wines can call themselves Meritage. They must belong to and abide by the regulations set out by the nonprofit Meritage Association.

Shopping Guide

Stash-Your-Cash Wines $15 and Under

	Name of Wine	From	Style Profile	Price Range
PW	Canyon Road, Sauvignon Blanc	California	Light-bodied, unoaked and crisp	$7–10
GW	Château Bonnet, Entre-Deux-Mers	Entre-Deux-Mers, France	Light-bodied, unoaked, crisp, herbal	$7–10
	Veramonte, Sauvignon Blanc	Casablanca Valley, Chile	Light-bodied, unoaked, crisp, herbal	$7–10
PF	Brancott Vineyards, Sauvignon Blanc	Marlborough, New Zealand	Medium-bodied, unoaked, crisp, juicy, herbal	$9–12
	Villa Maria, "Private Bin," Sauvignon Blanc	Marlborough, New Zealand	Medium-bodied, unoaked, crisp, juicy, herbal	$12–14
	Lawson's Dry Hills, Sauvignon Blanc	Marlborough, New Zealand	Medium-bodied, unoaked, crisp, juicy, herbal	$12–15
	Llano Estacado Winery, Sauvignon Blanc	Texas	Medium-bodied, unoaked, crisp, juicy, herbal	$12–14
	St. Supéry, Sauvignon Blanc	Napa Valley, California	Medium-bodied, unoaked, crisp, juicy	$13–15
	Château St. Jean, Fumé Blanc	Sonoma County, California	Medium-bodied, light oak, crisp, juicy	$9–12
GW	Château Coucheroy	Pessac-Léognan, Graves, France	Medium-bodied, light oak, crisp, juicy	$10–12

Well-Known Winners $15–25

	Name of Wine	From	Style Profile	Price Range
	Château de Sancerre	Sancerre, France	Light-bodied, unoaked, crisp, minerally	$15–18
PF	Pascal Jolivet, Sancerre	Sancerre, France	Light-bodied, unoaked, crisp, minerally	$18–20

	Name of Wine	From	Style Profile	Price Range
	Michel Redde, "La Moynerie," Pouilly-Fumé	Pouilly-Fumé, France	Medium-bodied, unoaked, crisp, juicy	$20–42
PW	Goldwater "Dogpoint" Sauvignon Blanc	Marlborough, New Zealand	Medium-bodied, unoaked, crisp, juicy, herbal	$16–18
	Wairau River, Sauvignon Blanc	Marlborough, New Zealand	Medium-bodied, unoaked, crisp, juicy, herbal	$16–18
GW	Dry Creek Vineyard, "Reserve," Fumé Blanc	Dry Creek Valley, California	Medium-bodied, light oak, crisp, juicy	$15–18
	Robert Mondavi Winery, Fumé Blanc	Napa Valley, California	Medium-bodied, light oak, crisp, juicy	$16–19
	Simi, Reserve, "Sendal"	Sonoma County, California	Full-bodied, oaky, crisp, ripe	$18–22

Luxury Sips

Worth-the-Splurge Wines $25–50+

	Name of Wine	From	Style Profile	Price Range
	de Ladoucette, Pouilly-Fumé	Pouilly-Fumé, France	Medium-bodied, unoaked, crisp, juicy	$25–28
CW	Château Carbonnieux, Sauvignon Blanc	Pessac-Léognan, Graves, France	Medium-bodied, oaky, juicy	$28–32
	Rochioli Vineyards, Sauvignon Blanc	Russian River Valley, California	Medium-bodied, light oak, crisp, juicy	$28–32
	Flora Springs "Soliloquy"	Napa Valley, California	Full-bodied, light oak, juicy	$25–28
GW	DeLille Cellars, "Chaleur Estate," Sauvignon Blanc	Columbia Valley, Washington	Full-bodied, oaky, crisp, ripe	$37–40
PF	Château Smith-Haut-Lafitte, Sauvignon Blanc	Pessac-Léognan, Graves, France	Medium-bodied, oaky, juicy	$40–44

Unique Wines Worth Seeking Out

	Name of Wine	From	Style Profile	Price Range
PF	Delaire, Sauvignon Blanc	Stellenbosch, South Africa	Medium-bodied, unoaked, crisp, juicy, herbal	$14–16
	Thelema, Sauvignon Blanc	Stellenbosch, South Africa	Medium-bodied, unoaked, crisp, juicy, herbal	$16–18
GW	Henri Bourgeois, Sancerre, "Les Baronnes"	Sancerre, France	Light-bodied, unoaked, crisp, minerally	$16–20
	Concha y Toro, "Terrunyo," Sauvignon Blanc	Casablanca Valley, Chile	Medium-bodied, unoaked, crisp, juicy, herbal	$18–22
GW	Errazuriz, Fumé Blanc	Casablanca Valley, Chile	Medium-bodied, light oak, crisp, juicy	$10–12
	Leeuwin Estate, "Siblings," Sauvignon Blanc/ Semillon	Margaret River, Australia	Medium-bodied, light oak, crisp, juicy	$16–20
PF	Seresin Estate, Sauvignon Blanc	Marlborough, New Zealand	Medium-bodied, light oak, crisp, juicy	$20–24
	Voss Vineyards, Sauvignon Blanc	Napa Valley, California	Medium-bodied, light oak, crisp, juicy	$20–24
GW	Origin-Napa, "Gamble Vineyard," Sauvignon Blanc	Napa Valley, California	Medium-bodied, light oak, crisp, juicy	$20–24

pairing

WHEN IT COMES TO PAIRING WITH FOOD, SAUVIGNON Blanc is one of the most versatile basics in any wine wardrobe. It has always been on the short list of popular alternative varieties to Chardonnay, in part because it goes so well with so many styles of food.

What are its ideal companions at the dinner table? Try everything from shellfish to salmon, goat cheese to Parmesan, and even creamy pasta dishes.

Let's Talk Texture First: Light, medium, or full?

Most of these wines are light- to medium-bodied, which makes them ideal with delicate fish and seafood. Full-bodied versions work with salmon, lobster, pork, and chicken.

Consider It a Complement: Are there pungent herbal or citrus aromas?

These are often pungent wines, so the intensity of the food should match the intensity of the wines. Consider the dominant qualities— acidity and bright fruit with herbal overtones—then think fresh-from-the garden snap peas or oysters with a squirt of lemon juice.

Kissed by Oak: Does the wine have any oak character?

Oaky versions can resemble Chardonnay and stand up well to full-bodied, richer dishes.

About Acid: Is the wine crisp?

Acid, acid, acid. I sound like a broken record, but that's what makes Sauvignon Blanc such a food-friendly wine. It can complement acidic foods like tomatoes and goat cheese yet foil the fattiness of cheese pizza (Sauvignon Blanc with veggie pizza is great!).

Design-a-Dinner

STOCK YOUR SHELVES

Bottoms: Veal, chicken, white meat pork, white-flesh fish, crab, scallops, shrimp, pasta, rice

Tops: Zucchini, asparagus, peas, green bell pepper, tomato, olives, citrus fruits, cheeses (goat cheese, feta, Parmesan), crème fraîche, teriyaki sauces, lime/lemon juice, salsa, pesto

Accessories: Basil, oregano, fennel, lemongrass, black pepper, garlic

Pesto: In a food processor or blender, puree 2 bunches basil leaves, a few mint sprigs, 1 peeled and sliced garlic clove, and a parsley sprig. Add a handful of pine nuts and grated Parmesan, then drizzle with olive oil and puree until smooth. Add more olive oil if the mixture is too thick.

Spicy Fruit Salsa: Dice 1 mango, 1 papaya, and ½ small pineapple and combine in a bowl. Seed and mince 1 jalapeño and another spicy pepper of your choice. Wash, dry, and finely chop 1 bunch basil and 1 bunch cilantro. Add the peppers, basil, lemon juice, and salt to the fruit and let sit for 20 minutes.

MEAL ENSEMBLES

Fresh-from-the-Garden Platter: Arrange a platter of olives, snap peas, steamed fresh beets, and steamed asparagus and serve with Retro Green Goddess Dressing (page 59) as a dipping sauce. Slice flour tortillas into wedges and toast until brown. Top with Spicy Fruit Salsa (page see above).

Chèvre Chaud Salad: Roll fresh goat cheese into golf-ball-size rounds. Whisk 1 egg and roll the rounds of cheese through it before coating in a mixture of bread crumbs and parsley. Chill on a plate in the refrigerator for 20 minutes or so, then brown in a shallow pan of cooking oil. Don't jostle them in the pan. Let them sit in one position and fry until golden brown, then turn them to the other side and do the same. Drain on paper towels for a minute or so before placing them on a bed of baby greens dressed in Creamy Mustard Dressing (page 42).

Fruity Fish Tacos: Rub boneless fillets of firm-fleshed fish such as orange roughy with seafood seasoning. Coat the fillets in bread crumbs and fry in vegetable or olive oil. Wrap tortillas in foil and warm in the oven, then fill each tortilla with flaked fried fish, Spicy Fruit Salsa (page see above), shredded lettuce, and sour cream.

Grilled Teriyaki Chicken and Asparagus: Marinate chicken breasts in teriyaki sauce and bake or grill them. Throw asparagus into a resealable plastic bag with olive oil, some fresh herbs of your choice, and salt and pepper. Shake around to distribute the seasonings and then cook on the grill or under the broiler until crispy. Using a vegetable peeler, make large shavings of Parmigiano-Reggiano and arrange the cheese over the asparagus spears.

Pesto Pasta Salad: Cook small-shaped pasta al dente. Drain and rinse thoroughly and let sit for a few minutes. Chop several tomatoes, ¼ cup olives, and 1 red bell pepper into small chunks and combine with the pasta. Add enough Pesto (page 80) to generously coat the vegetables and pasta. Crumble feta cheese over the salad, stir gently, and serve at room temperature or slightly chilled.

The Buzz from…Michaela Rodeno,
CEO, St. Supéry Winery, Napa Valley

As head of a major winery, Michaela is one of Napa Valley's most respected women in wine. St. Supéry also happens to make one of California's most lauded Sauvignon Blancs, which Michaela recommends pairing with seviche. Her version: Chop canned chiles, tomatoes, and cilantro, then add shredded fish or whole bay scallops and mix with lime juice. Let marinate until "cooked," about 8 hours. Serve it on lettuce leaves or in martini glasses for a festive twist.

---

sharing

GADGETS GALORE . . . WHAT DO YOU REALLY NEED? There are almost as many wine gadgets and accessories as there are types of wine. But which ones are hype and which ones help? Whether shopping for gifts or for use in your own home, these are basics worth buying.

THE BASICS
One nice set of glasses plus sparkling wine flutes
Cost: $5–8 per stem
Reason: A glass is a glass is a glass, right? Well, yes and no. Any glass with wine in it is technically a wineglass, but there are ways to enhance your enjoyment of wine through stemware.

Tips for Sips

Size matters: All you really need to buy is an affordable all-purpose set of wineglasses. I recommend ones with a generous-size bowl that holds around sixteen to twenty-two ounces. A big bowl leaves plenty of room for swirling, which gives the wine space to release its aromas. If you want separate glasses for red and white, buy stemware with a big bowl for reds and a set with a slightly smaller bowl for whites. Reds need more room to express themselves, while whites stay cooler in smaller glasses.

Shape it up: Avoid glasses that curve out at the top of the bowl. You want wineglasses that are shaped like a tulip, with a bowl that is narrower at the top and wider toward the bottom to focus the aromas and flavors of the wine. A decent-length stem is preferable to give you something to hold on to other than the bowl. The body heat from your hands warms up the wine if you hold it too long, which is why wine drinkers often hold their glasses by the stem or base.

Clear is better: If you can't see the color of the wine, you're missing one of its key pleasures.

Don't spend more than you can afford to replace: Wineglasses do break, and if you have only "the really good ones," you may be afraid to use them.

Long and lean: When it comes to sparkling wineglasses, look for the clear flutes, not the saucer-shaped glasses. This allows the bubbles to rise to the top and show-off the beauty of bubbly.

Waiter's Friend Corkscrew

Cost: $5

Reason: I used to hate this kind of corkscrew because I would inevitably need to put the bottle between my legs to get the cork all the way out (I admit I still have to do this sometimes). Actually, though, once you get the hang of it, it's easy. The nice thing about these corkscrews is that they come with a little knife so you can first remove the foil. Put the corkscrew in the center of the cork at an angle, then slowly straighten it up as you turn the corkscrew.

Lever-Style Cork Pullers

Cost: $20–100

Reason: There are many versions of a fancy corkscrew that use a lever mechanism to remove a cork in one motion. If you open as much wine as I do, or simply want to make opening a bottle a breeze, then you'll want to own one of these.

Tip: You still need to cut or remove the foil capsule before opening the bottle, or it will wear out the cork puller prematurely. These cork pullers also don't work well on synthetic corks.

The Buzz on...Screw Caps Take on the Wine World

I'm a huge fan of screw caps. Not only can you easily open the bottle without the use of a fancy gadget, but if you don't finish it, closing the wine is simple, and you can store an opened bottle on its side in the refrigerator. The best part about this simple closure, however, is that there is no chance the wine will be spoiled by something called *cork taint*. Cork taint causes a musty, moldy smell in wine that often reminds me of wet cardboard. Though the cork industry has been working to eliminate "corked" wines, some wineries estimate that up to 5 percent of all wines are affected.

Previously associated with inferior-quality wine, the screw top suffers an image problem as a closure for high quality wines, but the evidence of its advantage is overwhelming. I participated in one of the most enlightening experiences of my wine life in New Zealand, organized by members of New Zealand's Screwcap Wine Seal Initiative. I tasted more than thirty bottles side by side with the same wine bottled under screw cap and cork. What a difference! With screw caps whites tasted fresher and more vibrant, while reds seemed brighter and fruitier. Thanks to leaders in New Zealand such as Lawson's Dry Hills and Kumeu River, Australia's Clare Valley Riesling producers and California wine producers like Bonny Doon Vineyard, Calera, and Plump Jack Winery, the screw cap is slowly being accepted.

Foil Cutter

Costs: $5

Reason: The biggest pain about opening a bottle of wine is dealing with the foil capsule on the outside of the bottle. I always try first to yank the whole thing off (some of them are loose enough to do it). Or I reach for a foil cutter, which easily cuts the top foil section so a corkscrew can be inserted.

Bottle Collar

Cost: $3–5

Reason: I can't tell you how many stains I've had to remove du[e]
wine dripping down the side of the bottle. A bottle collar is a la[rge]
ring that fits over the neck of a bottle, easily preventing the proble[m]

IF YOU HAVE EXTRA CASH

Specialized Glasses

Cost: $6–100 per glass

Reason: The purpose of these glasses is that the shape of each one cor-
responds to a particular type of wine. Due to the shape, each glass
focuses the wine on a different place on your tongue, thereby highlighting its unique set of aromas and flavors.

Tips for Sips

Riedel: The Riedel brand has long been considered the crème de la crème
of fine wine crystal. The company currently makes more than a hundred types of wineglass in all shapes and sizes. Personally, I've found the
most dramatic change by drinking Pinot Noir from the Riedel Burgundy
glass and would recommend you start by buying these. If you have the
money and drink pricey wines, it's worth it to invest in various Riedel
glasses.

Spiegelau: There is a terrific brand of crystal from Germany called
Spiegelau (if you look at the base of the glass, you will find a small
S logo). It is used by many restaurants and hotels around the world
because it's top quality but also very sturdy. Spiegelau glasses are easy
to stock up on in numerous shapes and sizes because they are affordable. I've bought many for $6 per stem.

The Buzz on...Squeaky-Clean Glasses

Soap residue on a wineglass will ruin a perfectly good glass of wine. The
best way to protect against residue is simply to hand-wash the glass using hot
water, then letting it air-dry. If you want to use detergent or put wineglasses in
the dishwasher, make sure they are rinsed thoroughly.

Sparkling Wine Stopper

Cost: $3–5

Reason: If you find yourself with left-over sparkling wine or Champagne, this inexpensive rubber and metal stopper will keep the bottle fresh for days. It's shaped like a cork but with metal wings. Lift the wings and insert the rubber portion into the bottle. Put pressure on the top and close the wings. It secures itself on the lip of the bottle and keeps those glorious bubbles inside. Stand back when you remove it, though, since I've had several of them blast off like a rocket.

Wine Preserver Gas

Cost: $10 per bottle

Reason: A cork does just fine preserving wine for three to five days or more, especially if the wine is refrigerated. I keep a can of wine-preserving gas on hand, however, and give my open bottles a squirt before putting the cork back in. This lays down a layer of gas, which keeps the wine from coming into contact with air and causing spoilage.

Riesling/Gewurztraminer
THE "SPRING DRESSES" OF WHITES

EVERY APRIL, WHEN SUN PEEKS THROUGH THE RAIN clouds, I relish switching my wardrobe from heavy winter wear to breezy spring clothes.

Out go sweaters, boots, and wool pants, and into the closet go floral print blouses, sling-back pumps, and light-as-air linen dresses. Slipping into that perfect springtime dress just makes me feel rejuvenated and refreshed.

Wines do the same thing. After oak-laden whites and rich reds imbibed during cold weather, uncorking a Riesling or Gewurztraminer is like putting on that breezy spring clothing. With seductive scents of

---

The Buzz on...Sweetness in Wine

Sweetness is detected on the tip of the tongue and is a taste that most everyone appreciates. Most people start to perceive a wine as having sweetness at anywhere from 1–2 percent sugar. This doesn't refer to sugar added to the wine as many people think, but to the amount of residual sugar (*RS*) left in the finished wine at the end of alcoholic fermentation. Since sweetness is a subjective taste in terms of detection, a wine can be referred to in many terms ranging from dry to off-dry, slightly sweet to medium-sweet and semisweet, depending upon the person. I find it helpful to separate wines into three simple sweetness categories: **dry** (tastes dry); **medium-dry** (sports a pleasing touch of sweetness); or **sweet** (dessert wines that taste very sweet).

honeysuckle and orange blossom and delicate flavors of peach and spice, these aromatic whites are my wine wardrobe's breath of fresh air.

GIMME A LITTLE SUGAR

Not familiar with Riesling or Gewurztraminer? No problem. Most bottles are affordable, which makes exploring their joys a breeze. If you have heard of these whites but think of them as cloying sippers meant for inexperienced wine drinkers, think again. Many versions are dry, while sweeter styles can be fantastic.

Believe it or not, Riesling and Gewurztraminer aren't the only wines with a little sugar. A good portion of whites, including Chardonnay, and even reds like big-name California Cabernet Sauvignon and full-bodied Australian Shiraz contain residual sugar. Though the wines are still considered dry, this dash of sweetness is part of their appeal.

You may be wondering how wine can contain residual sugar and still taste dry. Sweetness in wine is all about perception and balance. For a white wine to taste fresh and not overly sweet, residual sugar needs to be balanced by acidity.

Imagine sugar and acidity as partners dancing the tango. Despite the appearance of gliding effortlessly across the dance floor, the couple must maintain a push/pull dynamic. This underlying muscular tension is what makes the dips, twists, and curves appear so seamless yet exciting.

The same is true of wine. When the interplay of acidity and sugar captures a sense of tautness or tension, a wine is in perfect balance. At that point the sweetness of a wine is perceived simply as rich, ripe fruit.

The Buzz on…Liebfraumilch

Who among us hasn't had a bottle of Blue Nun or Black Tower? These well-known German imports fall into a category known as Liebfraumilch, which accounts for the majority of wine exported from Germany. Though they've improved over the years, many versions still serve up pure sugar water, while others offer a fairly sweet, inexpensive quaff.

Tasting Tip: If you want to explore a delicious tongue-in-cheek version, check out Frog's Leap Winery of Napa Valley, which has bottled a Riesling/Chardonnay mix and named it—what else?—**Leapfrögmilch.**

As Johannes Selbach of Germany's Selbach-Oster Winery says, "When people ask me if our Riesling is a sweet wine, I tell them 'no,' it's a dry wine with fruit. You don't like your strawberries green, do you? They should be ripe and juicy."

When I serve Riesling or Gewurztraminer at a dinner party, my guests inevitably comment on how terrific the wine tastes. Maybe it's a matter of their overcoming the wines' outdated images or simply a matter of trying the wine. Whatever it is, these "spring dress" whites deserve to be brought out into the fresh air and allowed to shine.

THE GRAPE STORY

Both Gewurztraminer and Riesling are highly aromatic varieties, but have uniquely different personalities. The two share intensely floral, spicy, and fruity qualities and an uncanny ability to age, yet Gewurztraminer shows its appeal the minute it's poured. Riesling tends to be more reserved, revealing itself slowly in the glass.

Gewurztraminer: The Flower of the Vine

When you pour Gewurztraminer, a mélange of floral, fruity, and spice aromas jumps from the glass and begs you to take a sip. Once you do, the wine can range from crisp and fresh to soft and smooth, depending on its birthplace.

Though Gewurztraminer reaches its pinnacle of expression in the French region of Alsace, the name comes from the German word for "spiced"—*gewürz*. The *traminer* part harks to a village named Tramin in northern Italy, which is where the grape is thought to have originated.

Like Pinot Gris, the skin of Gewurztraminer grapes is more deeply colored than many other white grapes. Its pinkish/golden skin often imparts a more golden color and gives the wine oomph. The acidity is generally lower than in Riesling, which adds to the wine's voluptuous character.

One of the most memorable wines I've ever tasted was a Gewurztraminer from Alsace's Domaine Schlumberger. As I was hiking through steep hillside vineyards with Séverine Schlumberger, the fresh face of this classic Alsatian producer, I was mesmerized by the sweeping views of the countryside. We could look across the Rhine River past the border and see Germany's Black Forest. The vista was breathtaking.

As a reward for my strenuously physical day, Séverine graciously opened a special bottle in the Schlumberger cellars. It was a 1971 Domaine Schlumberger, Gewurztraminer, Cuvée Anne. I was blown away by the youthfulness of this wine. There was not a wrinkle or age spot, which is a huge feat for something more than thirty years old. Rich and honeyed, but with vibrancy and life, it made me feel like I was partaking of the fountain of youth.

As Jean Trimbach of another of Alsace's famous properties, Maison Trimbach, says, "Gewurztraminer is unique, ageworthy, affordable, and pairs with food. What else do you want from wine?"

The Incredible Lightness of Riesling

While Gewurztraminer is a crowd pleaser, Riesling can be a bit harder to understand. Some Rieslings are fruity and lightly sweet, while others are so steely and acidic they take years to soften and express themselves. For lovers of the elusive grape, though, there's nothing better. It is arguably the world's greatest white variety and produces wines of ethereal lightness and complexity.

Riesling can smell of minerals and fruit. In the mouth there's a sparkling snap of acidity and juicy freshness. But in its youth it can be angular, like a young supermodel's face. When the best wines age, however, they become fleshy and immensely interesting.

While delicious Rieslings can come from a variety of locations, the grape's origin is Germany. It is planted all over the country in cool to downright cold regions. Riesling gleefully takes the climatic abuse and keeps coming back for more, thriving in conditions that would make most other varieties run for the sun.

That's because Germany pushes the northernmost limit for growing grapes. To maximize their exposure to the sun and actually get the fruit ripe, winegrowers in places like the Mosel River Valley plant vineyards on slopes that would make skiers salivate. It works, though, because the grapes get ripe, gloriously so in many cases, and produce some of the world's most coveted white wines.

Lingo Lesson

Core Words

Dry, medium-dry: Bottlings from Alsace are described as dry, while those from California, New Zealand, Australia, and Germany have varying levels of sugar and can range from dry to medium-dry. (We'll discuss the delicious sweet versions in the "Dessert Wines" chapter.) A dry Gewurztraminer or Riesling will taste approximately like the dryness level of Viognier or Pinot Gris.

Crisp or smooth: Rieslings will feature vibrant, high acid levels, and Gewurztraminer, a naturally less acidic grape, will often be softer. When a wine has too much sugar and not enough acidity, it is referred to as *cloying*.

Light- to medium-bodied: Imagine the most delicate chiffon and that's Riesling. It's light and almost airy when you sip it. On the other hand, Gewurztraminers tend to be medium-bodied with the occasional full-bodied, fleshy version. Think of silk or even satin next to that chiffon and you get the picture.

Extra Credit Words

Fruit aromas:

> Citrus fruits—tangerine, pink grapefruit
> Stone/dried fruits—white peach, peach, apricot
> Tropical fruits—papaya, pineapple, litchi

Aromatic: Due to their pronounced floral, fruity, and spicy aromas, both Riesling and Gewurztraminer are considered aromatic grape varieties. Other naturally perfumed grapes include Sauvignon Blanc, Muscat and Viognier, while Chardonnay is not an aromatic variety.

Spicy: Used primarily for Gewurztraminer, which is reminiscent of clove, nutmeg, and white pepper.

Minerally: Riesling often has unique mineral quality aromas and flavors, especially in wines from the Mosel region of Germany. Think of the delicate aromas of wet stones after a rain.

All About Structure
PART II

In the last chapter I showed how the core words I use to describe wine relate to its structural components (see page 68). We began with acidity, which I consider a wine's foundation. The next step is to talk about the sweetness level, which is particularly relevant to Riesling and Gewurztraminer. Let's go back and visit our grape Brut and find out more.

Dry, Medium-Dry, Sweet = Sweetness Level

Sugar is Brut's reason for living. As leaves on the vine turn sunshine into sugar through photosynthesis, they send it through the vine to Brut and his fellow grapes in the cluster. Their jobs are to ripen from tart, pea-size fellows into sweet, juicy wonders. But the winemaker is also concerned with Brut's sugar content since sugar is what gets converted to alcohol during fermentation. For a wine to be dry, just about all that sugar must be eaten by the yeast. For a slightly sweeter wine, the winemaker needs to choose the right point during fermentation to kill the yeast to retain residual sugar. It's a skill to find the perfect point where sugar and acidity are in balance—too much of one, and the result is a sweet and cloying wine or one with mouth-puckering tartness. For sweet wines, Brut and his buddies are left to hang on the vine until their sugar levels are very high. During fermentation the yeast tends to peter out in a happy state of intoxication before converting all that delicious sugar to alcohol.

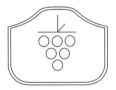 *leslie's label links*
Connecting taste to place makes wine buying easy

CRISP AND AROMATIC

Rieslings produced in these regions can range from dry to slightly sweet, and most are light-bodied with succulent fruit flavors and a breathtaking streak of acidity that draws you in hook, line, and sinker. Gewurztraminers lean more toward the medium-bodied side with softer acidity and ripe fruit.

Place: Mosel-Saar-Ruwer, Germany
Grape: Riesling
Sweetness: Kabinett and/or Trocken on the label = lighter, drier
   wines; Spätlese and/or Halbtrocken = fuller, medium-dry wines

Taste: I encourage you—no, plead with you—to try Rieslings from the Mosel-Saar-Ruwer region of Germany. Their bracing acidity, bright fruit flavors, and low alcohol levels make them unusually thirst quenching and easy to sip. Many Mosel Rieslings offer a mere 8 percent alcohol compared to warm-weather California Chardonnay, which can tip the scales at 14 percent. To discover why  they're so special, however, you need to understand a little bit about the place. Just think slope, sugar, and slate.

Following the snakelike curves of the Mosel River (the Saar and Ruwer rivers are tributaries), Riesling vines are planted on steep riverbanks. In many vineyards harvesters need harnesses to keep their footing while picking grapes. These skyscraperlike hillsides help expose the grapes to the maximum amount of sun during the long, cool growing season, allowing for intense flavor development without excessive alcohol. Carl von Schubert, producer of the highly regarded Maximin Grünhaus wines, calls his Riesling Kabinett a "no regret wine. You can drink, enjoy, relax, and not feel overwhelmed with oak and alcohol. You can even head back to work after wine at lunch."

Nowhere in the world is the dance between sugar and acidity done so masterfully as in top Mosel wines. Some are dry, while others sweet, yet the most skillful winemakers make finding the balance between the two seem effortless. These whites express something even more distinctive, however, and wine lovers call it *minerality*. In the Mosel it comes from vines reaching deep into the blue and red slate soils. When I sip a classic Mosel Riesling, it's like tasting the earth and the sun at the same time.

Place: New Zealand

Grapes: Riesling and Gewurztraminer

Sweetness: Dry to medium-dry

Taste: Rieslings from New Zealand sport a limy freshness with zesty acidity. Gewurztraminer, though often more fleshy, will still be crisp, floral, and fruity. From Hawkes Bay on the North Island, where the weather is warmer, to Marlborough on the

The Buzz on...German Wine Labels and Classifications

After years of tastings I can look at California wine labels and read them with ease. That's kindergarten stuff. Australian wines are grade-school territory, while learning about French and Italian labels seems more like high school. But German labels—ouch! Once you've mastered them, you'll feel like you've earned a graduate degree. German wines have an exceptionally detailed classification system, and it's all on the label to be deciphered. Here are a few clues to help you unlock the secrets:

Producer name: Look for the word *Weingut,* which means "winery" or "domaine."

Grape variety: In high-quality wines the grape variety, such as Riesling, is listed on the label.

Specific vineyard: If there is a specific vineyard where the grapes are grown, it will be mentioned on the label. The vineyard name will be preceded by the name of the village where the vineyard is located.

Clue: an *er* is added to the village name, so Riesling from the Goldtröpfchen vineyard in the village of Piesport becomes Riesling Piesporter Goldtröpfchen.

Style: Here's where it gets really tricky. Wines labeled *Qualitätswein mit Prädikat* (*QmP*) are of the highest quality level. They are divided into categories that correspond to ripeness levels at harvest:

Kabinett—These are the first grapes picked, and produce wines that are lighter and generally drier. Many delicious wines can be found for around $10–15.

Spätlese—Means "late-picked" and is made from grapes riper than the ones picked for Kabinett wines. These wines tend to be fuller, round, and medium-dry, but can be made in a dry style. Typically $15–20 will buy a top version.

Auslese—Very, very ripe grapes produce these opulent wines. They are usually fairly sweet, but can be made in a dry style. Expect to pay between $25–35.

Beerenauslese or BA and Trockenbeerenauslese or TBA—Pickers select individual berries of incredibly ripe grapes affected by *noble rot* (for more on noble rot, see page 98) to make these honeyed, concentrated wines. They are rare, very expensive (from $50 to hundreds of dollars), and gloriously sweet.

Sweetness: If you want a very dry wine, look for the word *Trocken* on the label, which means "dry." You might also find drier wines with the newly coined terms *Classic* and *Selection* on the label. For a slightly sweeter wine, look for the word *Halbtrocken* on the label, which means "half-dry."

South Island, where the climate is more like Germany, these aromatic varieties show great promise.

Place: Washington state

Grapes: Riesling and Gewurztraminer

Sweetness: Dry to medium-dry

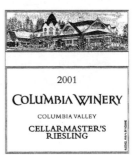

Taste: Riesling is one of the original grape varieties planted in Washington and is the second most planted white grape variety in the state after Chardonnay, while Gewurztraminer is gaining ground. It's downright cold at night in many parts of eastern Washington where the grapes are grown, and this allows these varieties to showcase their floral qualities coupled with grapefruity flavors and a refreshing ping of acidity.

Place: The Finger Lakes, New York State

Grape: Riesling

Sweetness: Dry to medium-dry

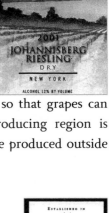

Taste: This bucolic wine country is one of the top spots for domestic Riesling, producing crisp, peachy versions most often with a touch of sweetness. The region is named for the glacially formed lakes that dot the landscape like fingers on a hand, which help moderate the temperature so that grapes can actually grow this far north. This huge wine-producing region is responsible for nearly half of all the domestic wine produced outside of California.

Place: California

Grape: Riesling and Gewurztraminer

Sweetness: Dry to medium-dry

Taste: Most bottles labeled simply with the California appellation will be medium-dry and have a softer acidity than their cool-climate counterparts. When you see the California appellation, expect an affordable quaffing wine.

Value Tip: Numerous affordable dry versions of these wines are coming out of specific appellations in California. I recommend Napa's classic Riesling producers Smith-Madrone and Trefethen Vineyards and Gewurztraminer from Sonoma's Gundlach-Bundschu Winery.

Look for these places on the label, too . . .

Alto Adige, Italy

Willamette Valley, Oregon

leslie's label links

Connecting taste to place makes wine buying easy

RIPE AND AROMATIC

Whether sipping a Gewurztraminer or a Riesling from one of these regions, expect a wallop of spicy, fruity aromas and a smooth, mouth-filling texture. When you discover these fruit bombs with flesh on their bones, you'll be a convert to these spring dress whites.

Place: Alsace, France

Grapes: Riesling and Gewurztraminer

Sweetness: Dry

Taste: Gewurztraminer from Alsace is the best in the world, period. It's forward, flirtatious, fleshy, explosively aromatic, and downright fun to drink. More

rounded with softer acidity than its German neighbors, Alsatian Riesling exudes vibrant aromas of peaches and cream.

Not only are these Rieslings and Gewurztraminers dry and delicious, but the labels are simple to understand: they indicate the grape variety and that they come from Alsace. Some will highlight the vineyard or mention the words *Grand Cru*, which means they're produced with grapes from Alsace's best vineyards. The label will even tell you about sweetness. All Alsatian whites are basically dry unless you see these words on the label: *Vendange Tardive* or *Sélection de Grains Nobles*, which indicate sweet wines.

Alsace is arguably the most beautiful wine region in the world. The Route des Vins winds through the foothills of the Vosges Mountains, between the cities of Colmar and Strasbourg, and driving it is like stepping back in time. Half-timbered houses and cobblestone streets adorn fairy-tale villages such as Riquewihr and Ribeauvillé. Vineyards blanket the rolling hills, and there is a sense of history that transcends winemaking. "Our family has been making wine in Alsace for a few years—well, since 1626," jokes the lighthearted Hubert Trimbach of Maison Trimbach. "It was the same year that the Dutch settlers bought Manhattan Island for $26."

Alsace lies in the northern portion of France (only Champagne is farther north), and you'd think it would be too cold to produce such opulent wines. But the Vosges Mountains, the French counterpart of the German Black Forest, shelter Alsace, keeping it warm and dry.

Place: Eden Valley, Australia

Grape: Riesling

Sweetness: Dry

Taste: I call Rieslings from Eden Valley my secret-weapon wines. Medium-bodied, bordering on full, they sport a  nutty, creamy, citrus character that reminds me of key lime pie. People are often surprised when I introduce them to Australian Riesling. "It's too hot there. Don't they just make reds?" Sure, the famous wine of the neighboring Barossa Valley is powerhouse Shiraz, but high above the warm valley floor is a little slice of vinous heaven. It's called the Eden Valley. When the area was settled by German immigrants in the mid-1800s, they brought with them foods and, of course, Riesling vines.

Eden Valley is more like a high plateau than a valley. Driving around with Jane Ferrari of Eden Valley's well-known winery Yalumba—a dynamo winemaker whose personality fits her name—I was mesmerized not only by the beauty of the vineyards chock-full of sixty- to one-hundred-year-old vines, but also by the coolness.

Moments before, as we tooled up the road, we had had the windows open, but once we hit the higher altitude of Eden Valley you could feel the temperature drop. Riesling thrives in those conditions, developing ripeness and complexity while keeping its refreshing kick of acidity.

Place: Clare Valley, Australia

Grape: Riesling

Sweetness: Dry

Taste: About an hour north of the Eden Valley lies the Clare Valley, another fan-

tastic spot for Riesling. The Clare isn't just one valley but a series of valleys with vines planted high on the hillsides. It can be hot, but there is a telltale breeze that whips through the Clare, cooling it down at night, which produces Rieslings with a limelike freshness.

Place: Anderson Valley, California

Grape: Gewurztraminer

Sweetness: Dry to medium-dry

Taste: In my estimation, this is the best place in the United States to grow Gewurztraminer. "Everyone talks cool climate. Hey, even Napa doesn't admit to

being a warm climate. But Anderson Valley goes beyond that to a cold climate! That's what puts the stamp on our wines," says wine-maker Milla Handley of Anderson Valley's Handley Cellars. Cold is right. There can be more than fifty degrees' difference between day-time and nighttime temperatures, and this helps to produce Alsatian-style Gewurztraminer that is both spicy and vibrant but rich.

Place: Pfalz, Germany

Grape: Riesling

Sweetness: Kabinett and/or Trocken = lighter, drier wines; Spätlese and/or Halbtrocken = fuller, medium-dry wines

Taste: Other than the Mosel, wines from the Pfalz are a great place to start when exploring

German wines. While Mosel Rieslings are taut and fine, Rieslings from the Pfalz are fleshy and friendly. This southern region borders France, and, like Alsace, is protected by a mountain range (in this case the Haardt Mountains), so the climate is warmer and drier than at other spots in Germany, resulting in riper grapes and wines with higher alcohol levels and a fuller body.

Look for these places on the label, too . . .
Hawkes Bay, New Zealand
Nahe, Germany

A MATTER OF STYLE

If use of oak barrels makes a big difference in the final taste and style profile of Chardonnay, then sweetness (or lack thereof) is the crucial factor with Riesling and Gewurztraminer. These wines fall into the "oak be damned" category, and what you smell and taste in the glass is all about fruit, not wood.

In addition to a higher level of residual sugar, one of the methods a winemaker may employ to gain richness, sweetness, and complexity in the final wine is to use grapes that have been affected by an ugly but beneficial mold named *Botrytis cinerea.*

When conditions are right, the mold, which is also called *noble rot,* covers the grapes, making them appear furry and shriveled. The grape clusters look horrible, but as the roots of the mold bore into the grape and suck out the moisture, it concentrates the sugars and flavors. Many dessert wines, including Sauternes, owe their existence to noble rot, but dry to medium-dry Gewurztraminer and Riesling gain a rich, honeyed note when a few grapes with noble rot are crushed alongside unaffected bunches of grapes.

Shopping Guide

Stash-Your-Cash Wines $15 and Under

	Name of Wine	From	Style Profile	Price Range
	Rudolf Müeller, Riesling, Kabinett	Mosel-Saar-Ruwer, Germany	Light-bodied, unoaked and crisp	$7–9
PW	Bonny Doon, "Pacific Rim," Riesling	California	Light-bodied, unoaked and crisp	$8–10
PF	Selbach-Oster, Riesling, QbA	Mosel-Saar-Ruwer, Germany	Light-bodied, unoaked and crisp	$10–13
	Dr. Konstantin Frank, Dry Riesling	Finger Lakes, New York	Light-bodied, unoaked and crisp	$12–14
PW	Château Ste. Michelle, Johannisberg Riesling	Columbia Valley, Washington	Light-bodied, unoaked, crisp, aromatic, medium-dry	$6–10
	Weingut Erich Bender, Riesling, Kabinett, Halbtrocken	Pfalz, Germany	Medium-bodied, aromatic, medium-dry	$10–14
	Allan Scott, Riesling	Marlborough, New Zealand	Light-bodied, unoaked, crisp, medium-dry	$13–15
	Husch Vineyards, Gewurztraminer	Anderson Valley, California	Medium-bodied, unoaked, crisp, juicy	$10–12
GW	Thomas Fogarty, Gewurztraminer	Monterey, California	Medium-bodied, unoaked, crisp, juicy	$12–14
GW	Handley Cellars, Gewurztraminer	Anderson Valley, California	Medium-bodied, unoaked, crisp, juicy	$12–14
	Navarro Vineyards, "Estate Bottled," Dry Gewurztraminer	Anderson Valley, California	Medium-bodied, unoaked, crisp, juicy	$13–15

Well-Known Winners $15–40

Name of Wine	From	Style Profile	Price Range
Edmeades, Gewurztraminer	Anderson Valley, California	Medium-bodied, unoaked, crisp, juicy	$15–16

	Name of Wine	From	Style Profile	Price Range
	J.J. Prum, "Wehlener Sonnenuhr," Riesling, Kabinett	Mosel-Saar-Ruwer, Germany	Light-bodied, unoaked and crisp	$18–22
PF	von Schubert, Maximin Grünhaus, "Herrenberg," Riesling, Kabinett	Mosel-Saar-Ruwer, Germany	Light-bodied, unoaked, crisp, minerally	$18–22
GW	Wolf Blass, "Gold Label," Riesling	Eden and Clare Valleys, South Australia	Medium-bodied, unoaked, crisp, minerally	$15–16
	Smith-Madrone, Riesling	Napa Valley, California	Medium-bodied, unoaked, crisp, minerally	$15–17
	Grosset, "Polish Hill," Riesling	Clare Valley, South Australia	Medium-bodied, unoaked, crisp, minerally	$26–30
GW	Dr. H. Thanish, "Bernkasteler Lay," Riesling, Auslese	Mosel-Saar-Ruwer, Germany	Medium-bodied, aromatic, medium-dry	$17–20
	Müller-Catoir, "Haardter Herzog," Riesling, Spätlese	Pfalz, Germany	Medium-bodied, aromatic, medium-dry	$26–32
PF	Fritz Haag, "Brauneberger Juffer-Sonnenuhr" Riesling, Spätlese	Mosel-Saar-Ruwer, Germany	Medium-bodied, aromatic, medium-dry	$33–35
PF	Domaines Schlumberger, "Fleur," Gewurztraminer	Alsace, France	Full-bodied, unoaked and aromatic	$20–22
CW	Trimbach, "Cuvée Frédéric Émile," Riesling	Alsace, France	Full-bodied, unoaked and aromatic	$36–40

Unique Wines Worth Seeking Out

	Name of Wine	From	Style Profile	Price Range
PW	Columbia Winery, "Cellarmaster's Riesling"	Columbia Valley, Washington	Medium-bodied, aromatic, medium-dry	$8–10

	Name of Wine	From	Style Profile	Price Range
PW	Jacob's Creek, Eden Valley, Riesling	Eden Valley, Australia	Medium-bodied, unoaked, crisp, minerally	$13–15
	Jim Barry, "The Lodge Hill," Riesling	Clare Valley, Australia	Medium-bodied, unoaked, crisp, minerally	$13–15
	Annie's Lane, Riesling	Clare Valley, Australia	Medium-bodied, unoaked, crisp, minerally	$14–16
PW	Isabel Estate, Dry Riesling	Marlborough, New Zealand	Medium-bodied, unoaked, crisp, minerally	$18–20
GW	Dr. Loosen/Château Ste. Michelle, "Eroica," Riesling	Columbia Valley, Washington	Medium-bodied, unoaked, crisp, minerally	$20–22
PF	Craggy Range, "Rapaura Road Vineyard," Riesling	Marlborough, New Zealand	Medium-bodied, aromatic, medium-dry	$20–24

pairing

CONSIDER THE HOMELAND OF THESE TWO WINES WHEN you think about the food. From pungent Muenster cheese to sausage and sauerkraut choucroûte, foie gras, and the onion and cream flatbread known as *tarte flambée*, the cuisine of Alsace is gorgeously rich. And German cuisine is no less powerful, so you need wine that stands up to the food's intensity while cutting through it to refresh your palate. Riesling and Gewurztraminer are up to the challenge.

These wines also have a flair for all things international and can take on spicy fare from Mexican burritos to Chinese kung pao chicken and Indian curry dishes. With their lack of oak and loads of fruit, acidity, sweetness, and spice, Riesling and Gewurztraminer can put out the fire of just about any dish thrown their way.

The Sweet Side: Does the wine taste sweet or dry?

You will notice sweetness on the tip of your tongue. When a wine is too sweet, it will make food taste dull, but when there is a balanced level of sweetness, it rounds out a wine. Medium-dry Rieslings pair particularly well with spicy foods.

Let's Talk Texture: Light- or medium-bodied?

Most Rieslings will be light-bodied, especially those from the Mosel region of Germany, so think about dishes with a similar texture. Gewurztraminer will usually be medium-bodied. And those Alsatians—well, watch out; they can take on foods with weight and power, from sausages to ham and cream-based sauces.

Consider It a Complement: Are there sweet fruit and spicy notes?

The slight level of sweetness in many of these wines augments the sweetness in things like fruit sauces or mango chutney. Their inherent spiciness also complements the spice in many dishes. For example, Gewurztraminer goes great with Thai noodles or curry.

About Acid: Is the wine crisp or smooth?

Food loves acidity, and Riesling has it in spades to partner with tangy foods or offset rich ones. Gewurztraminer has a lower, softer character from lower acidity so it can counterbalance heavier cuisine.

Design-a-Dinner

STOCK YOUR SHELVES

Bottoms: Ham, pork, sausages, tuna, salmon/smoked salmon, scallops, rice noodles, jasmine rice

Tops: Red bell peppers, sweet potatoes, apricots, peaches, cheeses (Muenster, Camembert, goat cheese, Monterey Jack), teriyaki sauce, spicy peanut sauce, mango chutney, mustard sauces

Accessories: Sesame seeds, caramelized onions, curry seasonings, coriander/cilantro, ginger

GET SAUCY . . . WITH RIESLING AND GEWURZTRAMINER

Quick Stir-Fry Sauce: Mince several garlic cloves into a bowl. Cover with sesame oil or vegetable oil. Mince a 2-inch piece of ginger (no need to peel) and add to the bowl. Keep this mixture tightly covered in the refrigerator for up to 4 days and use a spoonful or two whenever you make a stir-fry.

Red Pepper Honey Mustard: Roast a whole red bell pepper under the broiler. Let it cool, then rub off the burned skin with a paper towel. Chop the pepper into small pieces. Mix about $1/2$ cup Dijon mustard with 1 tablespoon honey and stir in the pepper pieces. If you want it spicier, add a sprinkle of hot pepper flakes. Spread on sandwiches, sausages, or burgers.

MEAL ENSEMBLES

Sausage Sandwich and Sweet Potato Fries: This is a favorite at my house, especially when made with chicken apple sausage. Cook the sausages and slice in half lengthwise. Cut warm, crusty bread into sandwich-size pieces, then layer with the Red Pepper Honey Mustard (see above), sausage, and caramelized onions. To make Sweet Potato Fries, peel several sweet potatoes and cut into thick wedges. Sprinkle with a dash of olive oil, sea salt, and cracked pepper. Bake until lightly browned in a 375°F oven, about 30 minutes. These are delicious with Chardonnay, too.

Peanut-Pork Skewers: Cube mango and pineapple and pork and lace onto skewers with fresh basil leaves. Grill or broil and serve over sticky jasmine rice or brown rice. Top with store-bought peanut sauce.

Fish and Flash-Fried Beans: In a heavy skillet, heat a small amount of Quick Stir-Fry Sauce (see above). Once hot, add green beans and fry for about 5 minutes, until tender. Season the beans with soy sauce or hoisin sauce. You can also sprinkle them with black or white sesame seeds for added texture and flavor. Serve with grilled or broiled tuna and rice noodles.

Wild White Pizza: This is a quick take on the traditional *tarte flambée* from Alsace. Instead of the sort-of flatbread used in Alsace, slather a flour tortilla with fromage blanc (if you can't find this creamy cheese, use a mixture of half ricotta and half mascarpone). Then top with caramelized onions, cooked crumbled bacon or ham pieces, and shredded Muenster or Monterey Jack cheese. Bake until bubbly in a 400°F oven, 8 to 10 minutes.

> The Buzz from...Wendy Stuckey,
> Winemaker, Wolf Blass Winery, Australia
>
> As one of Australia's top Riesling winemakers, Wendy loves the combination of sushi and racy Riesling. "My husband and I love to drink it while rolling our own sushi and then, of course, while eating it."

sharing

THE PERFECT BRUNCH WINE

RAE ANN, ONE OF MY DEAREST FRIENDS FROM HIGH school, recently called me from Chicago with a wine dilemma: she wanted to host an impressive dinner for her work colleagues but was on a budget. How could she find wines that were affordable but would appeal to a diverse group of people that ranged from wine newbies to wine know-it-alls?

I suggested that she forget dinner and make the party a Sunday brunch instead. I've started hosting weekend brunches as an alternative to lavish dinner soirees because of kids, conflicts with schedules, and cost. More casual than evening gatherings, brunch makes it possible to whip food together quickly and gives you a chance to showcase some really delicious, unique wines that will impress for less.

WINE IDEAS

Whites

Riesling—Fruity and refreshing with a low alcohol level, Riesling is the ideal brunch wine.

Gewurztraminer—Another winner because it can take on typical brunch fare like eggs and salmon with ease.

Chenin Blanc—Light, medium-dry, and juicy, Chenin pairs well with fruit salads and spicy sausages.

Crémant de Loire—No brunch would be complete without some fizz, so here's an idea: instead of Champagne, drink Crémant de Loire. It's a sparkling wine made in the Loire region of France that's inexpensive, bright, and bubbly.

Tip: Freeze orange juice in ice cube trays and plop one cube in each flute of bubbly for a twist on the traditional Mimosa.

Reds

Rosé—Think of this as Kool-Aid for adults because it's so fruity and fresh.

Beaujolais—Drinking Beaujolais is like popping a freshly picked grape into your mouth. Juicy berry and a kick of spice make this an easy quaffing wine.

The Buzz on... Removing Wine Stains

What's the best way to remove red or white wine stains from fabric or carpet after a party? According to a study conducted by the University of California at Davis, the best way is with a mixture of equal parts hydrogen peroxide and Dawn liquid soap.

Margaret Lehmann is one of those lovely people you meet once and remember for life. Her husband, Peter Lehmann, is an icon in the Australian wine industry. When traveling through Australia, I made a point of visiting their winery, not only because the wines are world famous but also because I'm enamored of their colorful labels depicting images of the Queen of Clubs. Meeting Margaret early one morning, she introduced me to the joys of breakfast wine. After a nibble of the local German specialty called *streusel kuchen,* which is a moist coffeecake topped with streusel, she poured me a much-needed coffee. The best part of the morning, however, was sipping Lehmann's late-harvest, Botrytis Semillon. Now there's a lady who knows how to brunch.

Chinon—Chinon from France's Loire Valley is an ideal companion at the brunch buffet due to its bright acidity and refreshing cherry flavors.

FOOD IDEAS

These suggestions all go with the wines just mentioned and require little time to prepare:

- Platter of smoked salmon with bagels and cream cheese
- Spicy sausages served with a selection of interesting mustards and chutneys
- Breadsticks: Serve standing up in a sparkling wine flute filled with sesame seeds (used to hold them in place). They can be served to dip in a mustard and chutney selection.
- Sweet and savory breakfast crêpes: My mother makes these for Sunday brunch, and they're a family favorite. She whips up crêpes and puts two on everyone's plate. One is filled with sautéed mushrooms, broccoli, and melted cheese, and the other contains sliced strawberries with a dollop of crème fraîche.
- Quiche

○ Coffeecake

○ Fruit salads

Viognier, Chenin Blanc, and Sémillon
THE "FEMMES FATALES" OF WHITES

T HE MAINSTAY WHITES NOW ADORN YOUR WINE WARDROBE, BUT WHAT about all those other interesting bottlings from Albariño to Arneis, Garganega to Grüner Veltliner, Tocai to Trebbiano and Verdelho to Verdicchio? I could write another book just on the wonderful world of exotic whites but will limit myself to three favorites that are likely to appear on store shelves.

buying

Viognier

THE NAME GAME

Viognier = Condrieu

When you see the French growing region Condrieu on a label, it means the white wine was made from the Viognier grape. Condrieu is a small appellation in the northern Rhône Valley, and its white wines are famous floral, spicy, and rare. Château-Grillet is the name of a winery but also the name of France's smallest appellation (it contains only one winery), which is tucked away on a hill in the heart of Condrieu.

THE GRAPE STORY

Viognier is a vixen, a husky-throated, curvaceous, and ever-so-seductive Kathleen Turner of a wine. Aromatic and full-bodied, it smells like a floral Gewurztraminer and tastes like a creamy Chardonnay.

I remember sipping my first Viognier many years ago in a wine-tasting class. Picking up the glass, I immediately realized I didn't need to swirl it because the aromas were so pronounced they practically knocked me off my chair. Orange blossom, freesia, clove, honey, and apricot intertwined in a vinous potpourri. When I took a sip, the wine melted in my mouth, coating it with warmth and rich fruit. I blurted out, "This is amazing!" The teacher's lips curled in a sly smile, and he simply said, "Château-Grillet."

After swallowing (didn't want to spit this one out), it dawned on me that I had read about this wine and knew it was rare and expensive. At that moment, I understood why.

Unfortunately, not all Viognier is great, because it's a temperamental grape to grow. Less-than-successful versions lack the enchanting floral aromas and simply wallop you with high alcohol. But when Viognier is successful, oh la la . . .

In the past decade much has been written about its virtues, and wineries have scrambled to plant what they tout as the next Chardonnay. At one point just a few years ago, Viognier was definitely the

Lingo Lesson: Viognier

Core Words

Dry: Most versions are dry, although dessert-style wines are also produced in Condrieu. Due to their high alcohol levels and deep fruitiness, though, these wines can often seem sweeter.

Medium- to full-bodied: High alcohol is a trademark of Viognier (many versions top 14 percent), and it generally has a full, mouth-filling texture.

Smooth: Typically a lower-acid grape, Viognier is soft and silky in the mouth.

Extra Credit Words

Fruit aromas: peach, apricot, and melon
Spicy aromas: allspice, white pepper, and clove
Floral aromas: orange blossom, honeysuckle, and jasmine
Opulent: All the elements combine to make Viognier seem curvaceous, voluptuous, and opulent.

"It-girl" wine. Everyone who was sick of Chardonnay smugly sipped it while slapping themselves on the back for their innovation.

However, Viognier has never been able to reach critical mass, since prices are often high and the amount produced is comparatively low. So, Viognier remains a treat to indulge your senses when you're in the mood for seduction in a glass.

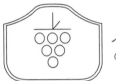

leslie's label links
Connecting taste to place makes wine buying easy

Place: Condrieu, France

Taste: Aromas of honeysuckle and jasmine combine with peachy, spicy flavors in the opulent wines of Condrieu. These whites are distinct (and usually expensive), coming from a region whose wine  roots can be traced back to Roman times. Grapes are planted on extremely steep hillsides in this northern Rhône Valley appellation. Sandwiched between two famous red wine appellations, Côte Rôtie and Saint-Joseph, Condrieu is like the cream in the middle of an Oreo cookie.

After falling in love with these rare wines, I made a trip to explore the source of my Viognier obsession. I could hardly contain my excitement when I arrived in the small town of Condrieu. Unfortunately, it was a national holiday, and everything was closed. So, instead of visiting wineries, I decided to "go native" and join the townspeople at the local May Day festival. When the aroma of garlic butter wafted my way, I knew I was in the right spot. Passing a cheese cart that sold dozens of different local varieties, I made my way to the source of the savory smell—a stand hawking fresh escargots and glasses of Condrieu. That's my kind of holiday.

Place: Virginia

Taste: Not too many places in this country can claim a wine history that goes back hundreds of years, but Virginians at Jamestown were making wine in 1609. It must have been pretty good, because Thomas Jefferson, America's original oenophile, felt Virginia could produce wines of the caliber he had tasted in France.

It's taken some time, but Virginia's wine industry is soaring and currently boasts more than eighty wineries. The warm conditions favor aromatic yet powerful Viognier. Look for leaders such as Horton Cellars and Chrysalis Vineyards.

Place: Sonoma and Santa Barbara counties, California

Taste: Everyone in California seems to be dabbling in a bit of Viognier these days. Though it's not a common varietal, it is on the rise in the Golden State. I recom-

mend looking for wines from Sonoma and Santa Barbara counties, since both seem to have an affinity for the grape. The versions emerging from these spots are lush, ripe, and voluptuous.

Look for these places on the label, too . . .

South Australia

Yakima Valley, Washington

Lodi, California

Shopping Guide

Viognier-Based Wines Sure to Impress

	Name of Wine	From	Style Profile	Price Range
PW	Pepperwood Grove, Viognier	California	Medium-bodied, unoaked, juicy	$7–10
	Clay Station, Viognier	Lodi, California	Medium-bodied, light oak, crisp and juicy	$15–16
PF	Yalumba, "Y Series," Viognier	South Australia	Full-bodied, light oak and aromatic	$9–11
GW	Fess Parker, Viognier	Santa Barbara County, California	Full-bodied, light oak and aromatic	$18–20
GW	Horton Cellars, Viognier	Virginia	Full-bodied, light oak and aromatic	$16–18
	Arrowood Vineyards, "Arrowood Estate," Viognier	Sonoma Valley, California	Full-bodied, light oak and aromatic	$28–30
PF	McCrea Cellars, Viognier	Yakima Valley, Washington	Full-bodied, light oak and aromatic	$28–30
	Calera, "Mt. Harlan," Viognier	Mt. Harlan, California	Full-bodied, light oak and aromatic	$32–34
	Domaine Georges Vernay, "Coteau de Vernon," Condrieu	Condrieu, France	Full-bodied, light oak and aromatic	$70–75
CW	M. Chapoutier, Condrieu	Condrieu, France	Full-bodied, light oak and aromatic	$70–75

pairing

VIOGNIER IS NOT A SHY WINE. THOUGH THERE ARE delicate aromas, its texture is one of viscous richness. The use of oak is rarely apparent, and lower levels of acidity lend a soft smoothness to the wine. I recommend highlighting the exotically aromatic, supple qualities of Viognier with like-minded fare from curries and Asian-influenced dishes to full-flavored cheese and creamy sauces.

Design-a-Dinner

Roast Chicken and Squash (page 43)
Tuna Curry Quiche (page 60)
Sausage Sandwich and Sweet Potato Fries (page 103)

The Buzz from…Susan Neel, McCrea Cellars, Washington State

McCrea is one of this country's Syrah and Viognier specialists. Co-owner Susan Neel pairs Viognier with crab, shrimp, and lobster, but her favorite match is with spicy Asian soups. "All those exotic, tropical flavors blend so well on the palate and are transporting," she notes. "One of my customers even describes our Viognier as his vacation in a glass!"

Buying: Chenin Blanc

THE GRAPE STORY

If Viognier is Kathleen Turner, then Chenin Blanc is Audrey Hepburn. For every curve and voluptuous quality in a glass of top Viognier, there is a sleek, slender, and enchanting character in great Chenin Blanc.

I purposely said "great" because the key with Chenin Blanc is quality. It is a versatile grape variety that can produce both ugly duckling wines and graceful swans. Though there are some delicious New World versions, the grape is too often planted in hot areas, where it grows like a weed and makes lackluster wines. When grown with care in classic areas of France's cool-climate Loire Valley, however, Chenin Blanc turns into that regal swan.

Naturally high in acidity, young Loire Chenin Blancs can be downright mouth puckering. Though they'll actually taste dry, some versions will include residual sugar to flesh out the penetrating tartness of the wine. But, when top Chenin Blanc ages (some last for decades), its acidity softens and the wine develops complexity, character, and elegance. Audrey Hepburn was even more fabulous in her later years, wasn't she?

THE NAME GAME

Chenin Blanc = whites of Vouvray and Savennières, Loire Valley, France

When you see *Vouvray* on the label, you know the wine was made from Chenin Blanc in the Vouvray appellation of France's Loire Valley region. Savennières is a neighboring appellation, and the high-quality dry whites are made from Chenin Blanc as well.

The Buzz from... Kim Stare Wallace, Owner of
Dry Creek Vineyards, Sonoma County, California

Dry Creek Vineyards is California's best producer of Chenin Blanc. According to Kim, "One of my favorite Chenin Blanc recipes is unbelievably simple and fun. It's called 'Chenin Shooters.' Just take a shot glass, put one oyster in it (Kumamotos are good), and fill with Dry Creek Chenin Blanc, then down the hatch."

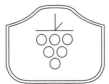

leslie's label links

Connecting taste to place makes wine buying easy

Place: Vouvray, France

Sweetness: Vouvray Sec = dry, Vouvray Demi-Sec = medium-dry, Vouvray Moelleux = medium-sweet, Doux = sweet (these categories are often indicated on the label)

CHATEAU DE VALMER
VOUVRAY
APPELLATION VOUVRAY CONTRÔLÉE

MIS EN BOUTEILLE AU CHATEAU
A CHANÇAY (I&L) PAR
Langlois-Château
Nég. 21. à ST-HILAIRE, ST-FLORENT (M&L) FRANCE
PRODUCE OF FRANCE

SOLE AGENTS *Dreyfus, Ashby & Co* NEW YORK N.Y.
750 ML WHITE TABLE WINE Alcohol 11% by vol.

Taste: It was the thousand-year-old caves that I'll remember most about Vouvray. Tunneled into the river valley's vertical chalk cliffs, these former quarries were the source of material used for building some of the famed châteaux that run the length of the middle Loire. Walking through a labyrinth of hand-carved tunnels at Marc Brédif winery, I pulled my jacket closed and felt a sense of damp coolness. I think of it every time I drink crisp Vouvray.

The Loire River begins in the heart of France and traverses nearly half the country. It winds around Sancerre and Pouilly-Fumé, carves a path through Vouvray and Savennières, and finally makes its way—several hundred miles later—to the Atlantic Ocean. Because Vouvray is inland, it does not benefit from the ocean's moderating effects. This part of the middle Loire gets warm days but often bitterly cold nights. The continental climate coupled with limestone soil produces Chenin Blancs with the potential to be downright biting. But the French are ingenious and have had centuries of winemaking to deal with Mother Nature's whims.

The best producers keep yields low so the grape's flavors are more concentrated. Some wines have residual sugar to soften the snap of acidity. Others make bone-dry, acidic Chenin Blancs, then age them into delicious submission. In really cold vintages, producers ramp up the production of their sparkling Vouvray (which, by the way, is fizz worth finding). Whatever shape Vouvray takes, it's apt to tingle your taste buds.

Place: Stellenbosch, South Africa

Sweetness: Generally medium-dry

Taste: Chenin Blanc, or *steen* as it's called in South  Africa, is the country's workhorse white. Like Chardonnay in California, Chenin Blanc is prolific in South Africa. Due to the warm climate, vines can be high yielding and churn out tasteless wine, but when grown with care, the resulting whites can be scrumptious. Usually inexpensive, they are fruity and refreshing, making them ideal for summertime sipping.

Place: Clarksburg, California

Sweetness: Dry to medium-dry

Taste: Chenin Blanc is grown widely in parts of 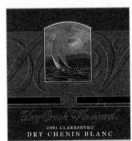 California. But because the grapes don't command as high a price as Chardonnay or other white varieties, most high-rent, grape-growing districts have just about given up on it. This is one place, however, where Chenin Blanc is actually embraced. Located just south of the state capital of Sacramento, the hot region is positively influenced by the Sacramento River, so its warm days are tempered by cool nights. Clarksburg Chenin Blanc expresses a ripe yet zippy nectarine character. I usually hunt down these bottlings when heading out on a picnic. Uncork them with sandwiches, hot dogs, and fresh fruit salads.

Look for these places on the label, too . . .

Savennières, Loire Valley, France

Montlouis, Loire Valley, France

Columbia Valley, Washington

For a wine to be kosher, it has nothing to do with the grape varieties, sweetness level, or type of wine, but rather how the wine is made. Kosher wines must follow a set of guidelines including maintaining separate equipment dedicated to the production of kosher wines, using kosher products such as yeast for fermentation, and allowing only Sabbath-observing Jews to handle the grapes from the beginning of the winemaking process to the end. If the crushed grape juice used to make the wine is flash pasteurized for a few seconds, the wine is Mevushal. This means non-Jewish people can deal with the wine (for example, a waiter serving it in a restaurant) and the wine remains kosher. One of my top picks is California's Baron Herzog Winery whose kosher Chenin Blanc is delicious any time of the year.

Shopping Guide

Recommended Sips

Chenin Blanc–Based Wines Sure to Impress

	Name of Wine	From	Style Profile	Price Range
PF	Baron Herzog, Chenin Blanc	Clarksburg, California	Light-bodied, unoaked, crisp, aromatic, medium-dry	$6–8
PW	Monmousseau, Vouvray	Vouvray, France	Light-bodied, unoaked, crisp, aromatic, medium-dry	$6–9
	Simonsig, Chenin Blanc	South Africa	Light-bodied, unoaked, crisp, aromatic, medium-dry	$8–10
PW	Pine Ridge Winery, Chenin Blanc/ Viognier	California	Light-bodied, unoaked, crisp, aromatic, medium-dry	$9–11
GW	Mulderbosch, Chenin Blanc	Stellenbosch, South Africa	Light-bodied, unoaked, crisp, aromatic, medium-dry	$10–13
	Marc Brédif, Vouvray	Vouvray, France	Light-bodied, unoaked, crisp, aromatic, medium-dry	$12–14
GW	Dry Creek Vineyards, Dry Chenin Blanc	Clarksburg, California	Medium-bodied, unoaked, crisp, juicy	$7–9

	Name of Wine	From	Style Profile	Price Range
	Chappellet, Dry Chenin Blanc	Napa Valley, California	Medium-bodied, unoaked, crisp, juicy	$9–12
CW	Domaine du Closel, "Le Clos du Papillon"	Savennières, France	Full-bodied, unoaked and aromatic, minerally	$17–20
CW	Coulée de Serrant	Savennières, France	Full-bodied, unoaked and aromatic, minerally	$70–75

The Buzz from ... Evelyne de Pontbriand, Domaine du Closel, Savennières, France

Evelyne and her mother are the winemakers and owners of the highly regarded Domaine du Closel in the Loire Valley appellation of Savennières. Her top choices for food pairings with the family's luscious Chenin Blanc–based wines include fish poached in wine topped with a beurre blanc sauce and grilled lobster with artichoke hearts filled with a little bit of caviar and sour cream. Delicious!

pairing

CHENIN BLANC WORKS SO WELL WITH A VARIETY OF foods that it's a shame more people don't enjoy its charms and its affordable price tag. With a character similar to Riesling, Chenin Blanc's acidity and often slight sweetness are ideal with spicy fare, shellfish, and fresh-from-the-garden salads, herbs, and fruit. The texture of the wine matches with delicate dishes, and since oak would pummel the wine's prettiness, it's not much of an issue.

Design-a-Dinner

Fish and Flash-Fried Beans (page 103)
Chunky Turkey Salad (page 60)
Prosciutto-Wrapped Melon (page 60)
Pesto Pasta Salad (page 81)

buying

Sémillon

THE NAME GAME

Sémillon = Graves, Pessac-Léognan, sweet wines of Sauternes

Whites from the Bordeaux regions of Graves and Pessac-Léognan or Entre-Deux-Mers are usually made with a healthy dose of Sémillon (along with Sauvignon Blanc and, occasionally, Muscadelle). Sémillon is also the primary grape in the sweet wines of Sauternes.

THE GRAPE STORY

Completing the trio of femmes fatale whites is Sémillon. Think of it as being like the timeless Susan Sarandon—fresh and vibrant in youth, complex and interesting with age.

Though highly regarded on its own, especially in Australia's Hunter Valley, Sémillon is the traditional companion of Sauvignon Blanc in the whites of France's Bordeaux region. But Sauvignon Blanc isn't the only partner for this master blender. Sémillon is known to step out with Chardonnay to form the Australian partnership called *Sem/Chard*.

Due to its easygoing personality, Sémillon might be the grape variety closest in character to Chardonnay. It can round out Sauvignon Blanc's tartness with its soft, plush character while imparting a sense of fullness when paired with fruity Chardonnay. If uncorked and enjoyed while young, Sémillon's floral, citrus qualities are refreshing, but when allowed to age it moves into opulent territory, gaining a nutty and creamy complexity.

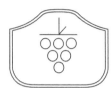

leslie's label links

Connecting taste to place makes wine buying easy

Place: Hunter Valley, New South Wales, Australia

Taste: Sipping an aged Hunter Valley Semillon is an unforgettable experience (note the lack of an accent when the Semillon is Australian).

MOUNT PLEASANT

Single Vineyard

LOVEDALE

1997

Semillon

Deep golden in color, this dry, complex wine smells and tastes like a baked pear drizzled with cream and sprinkled with spiced, toasted nuts. When I was enjoying a dinner in Sydney, Australia, with Phillip Ryan, the wine-

---

Lingo Lesson: Semillon

Core Words

Dry: Most versions are dry, but packed with juicy fruit character. (See the "Dessert Wines" chapter for details on the sweet wines of Sauternes.)

Medium- to full-bodied: Often high-alcohol and fuller-bodied, these wines can resemble Chardonnay in texture.

Crisp or smooth: When young these wines often possess a zippy, crisp character, but as the wine ages it takes on a roundness and smoothness.

Extra Credit Words

Fruit aromas: fig, apricot, melon, pear, and citrus

Nutty and spicy: Sometimes oak is used when making Semillon, imparting a spicy, nutty character to the wine. The nutty quality also develops when the wine is aged, even if no oak barrels were used.

Lanolin, beeswax, honey: When these wines age, they often acquire a waxy, honeyed character reminiscent of beeswax. This term is used especially to describe aged wines of Australia's Hunter Valley.

maker of McWilliams Mount Pleasant Estate, I had a chance to taste an older version of its famous Semillon named "Lovedale." With my eyes closed, I swore I was drinking classic white Burgundy (spicy, nutty, full . . . telltale oak aging, I smugly said to myself). Not only was it not Burgundy, but an oak barrel hadn't been anywhere near this wine. As Phil explained, "With young Semillon the flavors and aromas lean toward lemon, grapefruit, and even grassy; however, with bottle maturation the wines mature into the toasty, nutty, honeyed characters that are unique to the Hunter Valley. These wines have the potential to mature for decades, and this unique flavor transformation takes place without the use of any oak! Remarkable."

Value Tip: Semillons from other areas of Australia, including the Barossa Valley, are also worth seeking out. Young versions seem to have a delicious split personality, offering light, zesty citrus fruit flavors followed up with a surprisingly weighty texture. Many delicious versions cost a cool $5–9.

Place: Graves, Bordeaux, France

Taste: This is the other half of the easy-drinking wines of Graves and Entre-Deux-Mers, and often part of the great whites of Pessac-Léognan. Taste a Sauvignon Blanc from New Zealand next to a white wine from Graves, and you'll taste Sémillon. It adds softness and weight to the wine and gives it a deeper character.

Place: Columbia Valley, Washington

Taste: Sémillon from Washington state is like a cross between dry Riesling and Chardonnay. It showcases citrus fruit and exotic fig and peachy flavors, but with a crisp acidity and a round texture. It is the third most planted white grape variety in Washington after Chardonnay and Riesling and is a staple in the upscale Bordeaux-

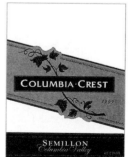

style blends emerging from leaders such as DeLille Cellars. As their winemaker Chris Upchurch notes, "I have always said that the real proof that Washington state is a Bordeauxesque region is the success of Sémillon in the vineyards. Cabernet does well everywhere, but Sémillon doesn't. Some of our soils are like Graves as well. It is these conditions that give us the concentrated dried fruits, minerals, and spice along with natural acidity that Sémillon can show."

Look for these places on the label, too . . .

New Zealand

Napa Valley, California (mostly in Meritage or Bordeaux-style wines)

Shopping Guide

Recommended Sips

These Sémillon-Based Wines Are Sure to Impress

	Name of Wine	From	Style Profile	Price Range
	Peter Lehmann, Semillon	Barossa Valley, Australia	Medium-bodied, unoaked, crisp, juicy	$11–13
PW	Rosemount, Semillon/ Chardonnay	South Eastern Australia	Medium-bodied, light oak, crisp and juicy	$6–9
PW	Columbia Crest Winery, Sémillon/ Chardonnay	Columbia Valley, Washington	Medium-bodied, light oak, crisp and juicy	$7–9
	Hogue Cellars, Sémillon	Columbia Valley, Washington	Medium-bodied, light oak, crisp and juicy	$8–10
PF	Angove's, Semillon/ Chardonnay	South Australia	Medium-bodied, light oak, crisp and juicy	$9–12
	Villa Bel-Air Blanc, Graves	Graves, France	Medium-bodied, light oak, crisp and juicy	$16–18
CW	Mt. Pleasant, "Lovedale," Semillon	Hunter Valley, New South Wales, Australia	Full-bodied, unoaked and aromatic	$15–20
	Signorello, "Seta," Sémillon/ Sauvignon Blanc	Napa Valley, California	Full-bodied, oaky, crisp, ripe	$22–25
	Clos Du Val, "Ariadne," Sémillon/Sauvignon Blanc	Napa Valley, California	Full-bodied, oaky, crisp, ripe	$26–30

pairing

DEPENDING ON WHETHER THEY CONTAIN ANOTHER grape variety such as Sauvignon Blanc or Chardonnay, Sémillon and Sémillon-based blends run the style gamut. Crisp, oak-free whites like Entre-Deux-Mers are ideal with shellfish and goat cheese. Blends from California, Washington, and France or aged Hunter Valley Semillons from Australia are usually full-bodied, opulent wines that shine when paired with creamy polenta, nutty couscous, and smoked salmon.

Design-a-Dinner

Easy Chicken Sandwich (page 43) and Crispy Corn Salad (page 43)
Spicy Mango Salmon (page 43)
Figs and Goat Cheese (page 59)

sharing

WILD WHITES
"AROMATHERAPY" PARTY

WHY NOT HOST A WILD WHITES PARTY? ROUND up bottles of the following affordable wines and prepare to sniff and sip your way through the evening. You will most likely need only one bottle of each wine since you can easily get ten or more healthy-size pours for tasting purposes.

Line up empty clear glasses and fill them with ingredients such as spices, cut flowers, sliced fruit, and condiments. Have guests swirl, smell, and taste the wines (see page 45 on how to taste wine) and then compare and contrast them with the scents of the ingredients in the glasses. It's fun and helps hone your wine-tasting skills.

Spicy and Rich

Gewurztraminer

Sémillon

Viognier

Pinot Gris (Alsace and Oregon)

Tip: Set out glasses with ginger, cinnamon, honey, toasted almonds, fresh flower petals, vanilla (beans or extract), sliced pears and apples, sliced melons.

Fruity and Bright

Riesling

Pinot Grigio (Italy and California)

Sauvignon Blanc

Chenin Blanc

Tip: Set out glasses with sliced peaches, lemons and limes, basil, sliced bell peppers, pebbles with a little water covering them for mineral aromas

AISLE

Red Wine

Cabernet Sauvignon/Bordeaux
THE "CLASSIC SUIT" RED

buying

IN MOST WOMEN'S CLOSETS, YOU WILL FIND AT LEAST one black dress, one pair of black pants, and one all-purpose suit, which can transition from the workday to dinner with ease. It doesn't matter what the ensemble costs, the basic suit is indispensable.

I feel the same way about classic Cabernet Sauvignon, which is a wine wardrobe essential. From coveted cult wines to quaffable every-day sippers, flexible Cabernet remains one of the most popular red wines on the market because it offers distinctive drinking in a wide range of prices and styles.

THE NAME GAME

Cabernet Sauvignon = red Bordeaux wines from places such as the Médoc and Graves regions

When you see the French growing region *Bordeaux* on a bottle of red wine, you know the wine was made from a blend of five main grape varieties: Cabernet Sauvignon, Merlot, Cabernet Franc, Petit Verdot, and Malbec. Some wines are dominated by Cabernet Sauvignon and others by Merlot, depending on where they're grown in the Bordeaux region. Those that are based primarily on Cabernet Sauvignon come from the vineyards on Bordeaux's Left Bank.

What distinguishes Cabernet Sauvignon from other grapes is its ability to maintain a varietal identity regardless of where it's grown. From France to California, Washington to Chile, you know what you're getting when you buy Cabernet—a deeply fruity, often noticeably tannic wine with a touch of earthiness.

The distinctive earthy, herbal character of Cabernet Sauvignon has much to do with its lineage since it is the offspring of the noble red grape Cabernet Franc and white grape Sauvignon Blanc. Adding to its good genes, Cabernet Sauvignon has developed its own strengths. Most noteworthy is its ability to make fruity wines that drink well when young but also age for decades.

The thick-skinned, blueberry-colored grape requires a fairly warm climate to ripen fully and thrives in well-drained soils that keep its roots dry. Because its needs are in sync with conditions in many top wine regions of the world, Cab globe-trots with ease.

This flexibility, coupled with the grape variety's knack for producing high-quality wine, puts Cabernet Sauvignon in a class by itself.

The Leader Among Reds

Cabernet Sauvignon has a rich history worthy of the noblest of the noble grapes. It has been one of the leaders in France's Bordeaux region for centuries. Called *claret* by the British, red Bordeaux has been the benchmark for the world's Cabernet Sauvignon–based wines. I've tasted hundred-year-old bottles of Bordeaux that were astonishing in their complexity and drinkability!

Cabernet's rise to the top in California began more than a century ago under the stewardship of the historic Inglenook winery. In the 1940s and 1950s, award-winning Cabernet from Napa Valley's Beaulieu Vineyards and Charles Krug sparked a revival after years of decline. And in 1976 Cabernet Sauvignon's status as California's great grape was solidified when a Napa Valley Cabernet bested top wines from Bordeaux in the landmark Paris Tasting (see page 129).

Across the globe the story is the same. Producing high-quality Cabernet Sauvignon is like a badge of honor for wine-growing regions.

It's easy to understand why Cabernet is a classic . . . just like that timeless suit.

Lingo Lesson

Core Words

Dry: Cabernet Sauvignon is considered dry wine. It often tastes more dry than Shiraz or Pinot Noir, for example, but not as dry as Sangiovese-based wines from Italy.

Bright: Cabernet Sauvignon grapes are naturally higher in acidity than Merlot grapes so the resulting wine often has a more vibrant character (think of green plums versus ripe, juicy ones), especially when the grapes are grown in cooler areas such as Bordeaux.

Medium- or full-bodied: Styles of Cabernet Sauvignon range from elegant to powerful, depending upon where the grapes are grown. Warmer regions equal riper grapes, higher alcohol (13.5–14 percent or more) and fuller body. Cooler regions equal less sugar in the grapes and slightly lower alcohol levels (12–13 percent). In the glass, that translates to the difference between satin and velvet, or brushed cotton and winter wool.

Medium to strong tannins: These are thick-skinned grapes, which means the wines are inherently more tannic than most all other reds. If you don't like the sometimes drying, astringent feel from tannins (see pages 138–140 for details on tannins), Cabernet Sauvignon may not be your top pick in reds. Try Merlot or Pinot Noir.

Extra Credit Words
Fruit aromas:

> Red fruits—cherry, raspberry
> Black fruits—black cherry, blueberry, blackberry, boysenberry, plum, black currant, and cassis

Oaky, toasty, cedar: Cabernet aged in oak barrels often has a roasted coffee, chocolate, and toasty character and, when older, a cedar and tobacco note.

Mint, herbal, olive: When grown in cooler climates or if it doesn't get fully ripe, Cabernet can have an earthy character reminiscent of eucalyptus and black olives. Aged Cabernet often smells of dried herbs.

Complex: There is a concentration to many Cabernets that delivers layer after layer of interesting aromas and flavors. Every time you take a sip another aroma, flavor, or feel emerges. Top Cabernet Sauvignons develop more complexity with age.

Balanced: This means that none of the components—acid, fruit, tannin, alcohol, or acidity—dominates the wine. If a wine is not in balance when it is bottled, it rarely gains balance over time.

BORDEAUX 101: TIPS FOR UNDERSTANDING AND BUYING BORDEAUX

Drinking Bordeaux is easy, but when the place produces nearly a billion bottles of wine per year and has fifty-seven individual appellations, how do you begin to make sense of it? The lightbulb went on in my head years ago when I realized the first step toward understanding Bordeaux was simply to hold my hands up and say "Left and Right."

Adjacent to the Atlantic Ocean, Bordeaux is essentially split by rivers into two regions popularly known as the *Left Bank* and *Right Bank*. Climate and soils dictate which grape varieties thrive on which side of the waterways. Cabernet Sauvignon is the Lord of the Left Bank because of the gravelly soils and temperate weather, while in the Right Bank's slightly cooler climate and clay soils Merlot reigns supreme.

Left Bank: The Wines are Cabernet Sauvignon–dominant, and the area includes the following main regions:

> Médoc—Most wines labeled simply *Médoc* or *Haut-Médoc* (which is part of the larger Médoc appellation) will be affordable, easy-

drinking reds, often only costing $10–15. Within the Haut-Médoc, look for wines from individual appellations, such as these favorites of mine:

○ Saint-Estèphe

○ Pauillac

○ Saint-Julien

○ Margaux

Graves is a smaller wine-growing area located on the outskirts of the city of Bordeaux and is famous for its Cabernet Sauvignon–dominant reds (as well as world-class whites). The high-quality appellation of Pessac-Léognan falls within the larger Graves region.

Right Bank: If you're a Merlot lover, search for wines from Right Bank spots such as these (see the next chapter for more information):

Saint-Émilion

Pomerol

Côtes de Castillon

The Cru Crew

In addition to geographical delineation, many individual wineries are classified according to quality. It's important to remember that in Bordeaux the producers are ranked, not the vineyard land. Fortunately, this can be a big help when buying red Bordeaux because it's often easier to remember a producer's name than various vineyards.

Classified Growths of 1855

In 1855 the Bordeaux trade "classified" sixty red wine producers in the Médoc region (and one famous Graves property, Château Haut-Brion) by quality level. They were organized into five categories from first growths, or premier crus, to fifth growths. My top selections to try include:

First Growths: Usually more than $100 per bottle but worth it

○ Château Mouton-Rothschild

○ Château Margaux

○ Château Haut-Brion

Value Tip: Look for these famous producers' "second label" wines, which are usually made from younger vines and sell for a fraction of the price of the regular versions:

- Pavillon Rouge du Château Margaux
- Le Petit Mouton from Mouton-Rothschild
- Bahans Haut-Brion from Haut-Brion

These favorites are relative bargains, ranging from $20 to $50 per bottle:

Second Growths
- Château Gruaud-Larose
- Château Pichon-Longueville-Baron

Third Growths
- Château Cantenac-Brown
- Château Calon-Ségur

Fourth Growths
- Château Beychevelle
- Château Duhart-Milon-Rothschild

Fifth Growths
- Château Lynch-Bages
- Château Cantemerle
- Château Clerc Milon

Tip: Cru Bourgeois—The Real Value Wines!

Wines labeled *Cru Bourgeois* are often the best values of all Bordeaux. This is a group of high-quality producers in the Médoc that weren't included in the 1855 classification but make delicious, affordable wines. These fall into the $10-to-$30 range. My top picks include:

- Château les Ormes-de-Pez
- Château Greysac
- Château Gloria
- Château Haut-Beauséjour
- Château Phélan-Ségur

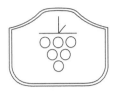

leslie's label links

Connecting taste to place makes wine buying easy

ELEGANT AND EARTHY

These cooler-climate regions push the limit on getting grapes ripe, so the Cabernet Sauvignon–based wines tend to have an elegant, vibrant quality with touches of earthiness. We'll start our journey on Bordeaux's Left Bank.

Place: Pauillac, France

Taste: On a golf club, the sweet spot is the perfect area on the club head where you're sure to hit a winning shot. That's Pauillac—the sweet spot of the Médoc. This area is home to three of the five first growths, top second growths, and numerous other classified properties, including my favorite fifth growth, Château Lynch-Bages. Wines from the commune, or village, of Pauillac are intense and concentrated with layers of cassis fruit, a touch of mineral and herbal aromas, and usually strong tannins.

Place: Saint-Estèphe, France

Taste: Although the village of Saint-Estèphe is only a ten-minute car ride from Pauillac, the wines of the two places differ significantly. The soil in Saint-Estèphe favors Merlot, so these wines tend to have more up-front fruitiness surrounding the structure provided by Cabernet Sauvignon. They're big and muscular with a fleshy texture and ripe, rich fruit. I think of them as equivalent to a big bear hug. That image comes from my past since my first Bordeaux "embrace" was from a wine of Saint-Estèphe. While looking for bargains at my local wine shop years ago, I was introduced to wine from Château les Ormes-de-Pez. It was affordable, seductively smooth, and deeply fruity. Suddenly I understood why everyone waxed poetic about Bordeaux.

Place: Pessac-Léognan, Graves, France

GRAND CRU CLASSÉ DE GRAVES

CHATEAU HAUT-BAILLY

PESSAC-LÉOGNAN
APPELLATION PESSAC-LÉOGNAN CONTRÔLÉE
2000
S.C.A. DU CHATEAU HAUT-BAILLY - PROPRIÉTAIRE A LÉOGNAN - GIRONDE
12,5% vol.   MIS EN BOUTEILLE AU CHATEAU   750 ml

Taste: The reds of Pessac-Léognan are something special—ultraelegant and often less full than those from Pauillac or Saint-Estèphe, but with delicate aromas of sweet earth and pipe tobacco. The wines are an expression of the place, certainly since the gravelly soil in this appellation is typical of the larger Graves region. Cabernet Sauvignon loves this well-drained land and flourishes in the warmth of the stony vineyards.

The Buzz on...That Louse!

In the mid- to late 1800s, Bordeaux and eventually most European vineyards were devastated by a louse named *phylloxera*. This tiny aphidlike insect eats grapevines, slowly killing them. To save the wine business, European vines were essentially cut-and-pasted (called *grafting*) onto rootstocks from phylloxera-resistant native American vines. California and other domestic vineyards fared no better than those in Europe. By the early 1900s this little bug had crippled the world's wine industry, which took decades to recover. However, vineyards in remote Chile and parts of Australia escaped the onslaught of the disease and today boast some of the only prephylloxera Cabernet Sauvignon vine material in the world.

Place: Coonawarra, Australia

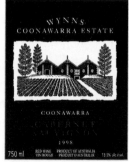

WYNNS
COONAWARRA ESTATE

COONAWARRA

1998

750 ml   RED WINE   PRODUCT OF AUSTRALIA   13.5% alc./vol.
          VIN ROUGE   PRODUIT D'AUSTRALIE

Taste: Coonawarra is a unique growing region in South Australia that is often called "the Médoc of Australia." The vineyards in Coonawarra are planted on land as flat as a Kansas farm, but the Cabs develop intensity due to the distinctive red, or *terra rossa*, soil and the cool, continental climate. Taste one and you won't forget it—elegant and vibrant with a touch of eucalyptus aromas and toasted earthiness.

Look for these places on the label, too . . .

Margaux, Bordeaux, France

Saint-Julien, Bordeaux, France

Margaret River, Australia

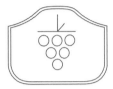

leslie's label links

Connecting taste to place makes wine buying easy

JUICY AND RICH

If you want a glassful of juicy fruit packed with power, search out Cabs produced in these regions. Some of them are full-bodied powerhouses with tannins to match, while others are medium-bodied, soft, and fresh.

Place: Chile

Taste: For affordable Cabernet you'd be hard pressed to find anything better than those from Chile. Most versions are fruity and light on the tannins, capturing Cabernet's softer side. How can the wines be good and be so inexpensive? The conditions are nearly perfect for growing high-quality grapes, and land is less expensive than in many other wine-producing countries. Most important, labor is cheap. No wonder so many international companies are investing in Chile and so many Americans are snapping up Chilean Cabernet Sauvignons.

Place: Aconcagua Valley, Chile

Taste: If you find you like Chilean Cabernet Sauvignon, I encourage you to seek out versions from the Aconcagua Valley. I predict it will be the Napa Valley of Chile and produce some of the world's best Cabernets. The ones I have sampled share an intensity of fruit, a touch of herbalness, and sweet, supple tannins. To better understand why they taste this way, we need to look at where the vines grow. As I traveled by small plane to reach the historic Viña Errazuriz winery, the dramatic Mount Aconcagua rose in the distance and craggy peaks practically touched the plane. Vines are planted on these hillsides, and because the Aconcagua Valley is the northernmost growing region in Chile, it benefits from tremendous heat and plunging nighttime temperatures. Cabernet Sauvignon grapes develop concentration and complexity and produce elegantly powerful wines.

The Buzz on...Super Chileans' Quest for the Best

Don't think that Chile is a place for value wines alone. Not satisfied with a reputation for producing only inexpensive bottles, Chilean wineries are raising the quality bar in their quest for recognition as a world-class wine-producing nation. Over the past decade impressive wines have begun to emerge, and these expensive "Super Chileans" are appearing alongside top Bordeaux, California Cabernets, and Super Tuscans from Italy. My picks include Almaviva, Seña, and "Don Melchor" Cabernet Sauvignon from Concha y Toro. (Prices range from $80 to $60 to $40, respectively.)

Place: California

Taste: Cabernet Sauvignon is one of those rare grape varieties that can produce affordable wine with character. It's the most widely planted red grape in the state, and good bottles labeled  with simply a *California* appellation generally sport juicy berry fruit quality, smooth but noticeable tannins, and sometimes an herbal tinge.

Place: Alexander Valley, California

Taste: If you want lush, ultrasmooth Cabernet, look for versions from Sonoma County's Alexander Valley. They're all about texture and deep, black fruit flavors with unique aromas of black olive.

Alexander Valley is located in the northern reaches of Sonoma County, and its expansive rolling hills look like someone shook out a carpet of vines, then laid them down gently. Flanked by the Russian River Valley, whose cooling fog provides relief from the heat, Alexander Valley has become home to so many top Cabernet Sauvignons—from Clos du Bois to Geyser Peak and Jordan—that it's a wonder the region isn't overrun with tourists. Yet it remains relatively unspoiled and pastoral.

Value Tip: One of the best-value Cabs on the market today comes from Gallo of Sonoma, whose affordable bottling (around $10) is produced with a healthy dose of Alexander Valley grapes.

The Buzz from…Gina Gallo, Winemaker, Gallo of Sonoma, California

Growing up in a historic wine family, Gina Gallo's most cherished memories include sharing family time around the dinner table. "Bringing food and wine and, most important, people together is the most rewarding part of making wine," says this third-generation winemaker. Gina recommends simplicity when it comes to pairing food with Cabernet. "Grill fresh vegetables, like bell pepper and asparagus, brushed with olive oil, pepper, and a little garlic, alongside a nice piece of meat, and that's all you need."

Place: Napa Valley, California

Taste: How can you not love juicy, luscious intensely fruity Napa Valley Cabernet Sauvignon? Cabernet is what put this wine region on the wine world map, and it remains the staple of Napa Valley. Certainly all different styles emerge from the valley, from the elegant versions from the cooler southern reaches 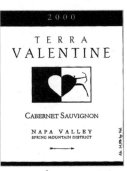 of the valley to the powerhouses from vines grown on the mountains rimming the valley floors, yielding something for everyone.

Place: Stags Leap District, California

Taste: The southeastern corner of the Napa Valley is the Pauillac of this California region: it's the sweet spot. The Stags Leap District is not a big place and has a slightly cooler micro-climate than places farther north, such as Rutherford and Calistoga. This lends elegance and focused fruit flavors to the wines. With names such as Silverado, Pine Ridge, Stag's Leap Wine Cellars, Clos du Val, and Chimney Rock, it's tough to find a more classic circle of Napa Valley Cabernet producers.

The Buzz on ... The Maestro of Napa Valley

André Tchelistcheff has been called "The Maestro" and the "Father of California Winemaking." He was identified most closely with the historic Beaulieu Vineyard (BV) where, in 1938, the Russian-born, French-trained winemaker began making legendary Napa Valley Cabernet Sauvignon, which became one of the world's most coveted wines—the BV "Georges de Latour" Private Reserve. Not only was Tchelistcheff the first to introduce modern winemaking techniques such as using French oak (and later American oak) barrels; he also mentored several generations of winemakers. Though he passed away in 1994, chances are you've drunk a Cabernet Sauvignon that was influenced by The Maestro's touch.

Look for these places on the label, too . . .

Oakville, California

Rutherford, California

Livermore, California

Barossa Valley, Australia

Priorat, Spain

A MATTER OF STYLE

When it comes to the final style profile of any Cabernet Sauvignon, we have to talk about the winemaking *T* word—tannin. As winemaker Chris Hatcher of Wolf Blass Winery in Australia emphasizes, "The tannin structure is the most important component of balance in any red wine, particularly in Cabernet."

Harsh or out-of-balance tannins make the final wine taste overly astringent and drying. Too few tannins and Cabernet loses its structure.

To understand its role, we have to start at the very beginning of the winemaking process.

Crush Me, Squeeze Me, Let Me Steep

Just about all grape varieties, whether red or white, have flesh that is clear. To make red wine, grapes are crushed and the dark skins stay in contact with the juice and start to turn it from light pink to deep purple. The longer the skins stay in contact with the juice, the more deeply colored the wine.

But color isn't the only thing that gets soaked up by the juice. The skins and seeds of grapes also contain tannins. The longer the grape skins stay in contact with the juice, the more tannic the final wine. Think of it as tea—another substance with noticeable tannins. If tea steeps for a long time, it will be darker and more mouth puckering. Also, the thicker the grape skins, the more tannic the wine. Pinot Noir and Merlot are both thinner-skinned grapes, and the wine they produce is generally less tannic than Cabernet Sauvignon, for example.

All About Structure
PART III

What exactly are tannins, and how do they affect the final style profile of the wine? Let's go back to our friend Brut to find out more.

Light, Medium, or Strong Tannins = Tannin Level

Brut, our little grape, has an astringent component in his skin, seeds, and stems called *tannin*. This chemical compound helps keep birds at bay until the fruit is fully mature. When the tannins have formed a protective brownish coating around the seeds and Brut's flesh is sweet and ripe, he is ready to fulfill his destiny in life—for birds to nosh away, spread his seeds, and propagate more vines. At that point Brut is what we call *physiologically ripe*. Winemakers judge whether the red grapes are ready to be harvested in part when the skins are no longer astringent and the seeds are the right shade of brown.

In finished wine, tannins play a different role, adding structure and acting as a preservative. Tannins in young red wines can be very apparent, but over time the tiny tannins bind together, get bigger, and fall to the bottom of the bottle as sediment. That's why wine appears softer and less tannic as it ages.

How do you detect the level of tannins in a red wine? We don't taste tannin but feel it. Light tannins are barely noticeable, medium tannins give a hint of drying feel in the mouth but are balanced by sweet fruit, and strong tannins create an obvious mouth-puckering sensation on the inside of your cheeks.

Shopping Guide

These winning wines made my shopping list because they are consistently enjoyable from year to year, have a high quality-to-price ratio, and have a high pour-me-more quotient—in other words, they taste really good.

In each chapter I've categorized my wine picks according to price and overall style profile, making it easy for you to expand your wine horizons. If you enjoy full-bodied Cabernet Sauvignon, branch out and try Syrah or Shiraz with a similar style profile. Do you prefer more elegantly styled Cabs? Seek out comparable Merlot bottlings or other Cabernet-based wines produced in places you have yet to explore. Picks are listed from least expensive to most and from lightest to fullest. Note: Use these price ranges as guidelines not gospel since prices vary wildly (often doubling), depending upon the store and state.

Key

PF=Leslie's Personal Favorite: Though I recommend all these wines highly, those marked with a PF are ones I think are extra special.

GW=Gift Wine: Due to the combination of attractive packaging (label and bottle) and delicious taste, I highlight bottles that make ideal gifts in various price categories.

PW=Party Wine: These are generally inexpensive and top choices for a crowd.

CW=Cellar Worthy: If you want to age wine for a period of time, look for bottles I've tagged as cellar worthy.

Stash-Your-Cash Wines $15 and Under

	Name of Wine	From	Style Profile	Price Range
PW	Gallo of Sonoma, Cabernet Sauvignon	California	Medium-bodied, supple tannins, smooth and fruity	$10–12
PW	Carmen, "Reserve," Cabernet Sauvignon	Valle Central, Chile	Medium-bodied, supple tannins, smooth and fruity	$10–12
PW	Laurel Glen Vineyard, "Terra Rosa," Cabernet Sauvignon	Valle Central, Chile	Medium-bodied, supple tannins, smooth and fruity	$10–12
GW	Cousiño Macul, "Antiguas Riservas," Cabernet Sauvignon	Maipo Valley, Chile	Medium-bodied, supple tannins, smooth and fruity	$12–14
	Wente Vineyards, "Vineyard Selection," Cabernet Sauvignon	Livermore Valley, California	Medium-bodied, light tannins, bright and earthy	$10–13
	Trinchero Family Selection, Cabernet Sauvignon	California	Medium-bodied, light tannins, bright and earthy	$11–14
	Echelon, Cabernet Sauvignon	California	Medium-bodied, supple tannins, smooth and fruity	$11–14
	Clos du Bois, Cabernet Sauvignon	Sonoma County, California	Medium-bodied, light tannins, bright and earthy	$11–14
PF	Château Greysac	Médoc, France	Medium-bodied, light tannins, bright and earthy	$14–15

Well-Known Winners $15–30

Name of Wine	From	Style Profile	Price Range
Rosemount Estate, "Show Reserve," Cabernet Sauvignon	Coonawarra, Australia	Medium-bodied, supple tannins, bright and earthy	$20–25

	Name of Wine	From	Style Profile	Price Range
CW	Château Cantemerle	Haut-Médoc, France	Medium-bodied, supple tannins, bright and earthy	$25–30
	Penley Estate, "Phoenix," Cabernet Sauvignon	Coonawarra, Australia	Medium-bodied, supple tannins, bright and earthy	$30–33
GW	Hess Estate, Cabernet Sauvignon	Napa Valley, California	Medium-bodied, supple tannins, smooth and fruity	$20–22
	Château Souverain, "Winemaker's Reserve," Cabernet Sauvignon	Alexander Valley, California	Medium-bodied, supple tannins, smooth and fruity	$26–30
PF	Château Phélan-Ségur	Saint-Estèphe, Bordeaux, France	Medium-bodied, strong tannins, bright and earthy	$26–30
	Casa Lapostolle, "Cuvée Alexandre," Cabernet Sauvignon	Rapel Valley, Chile	Full-bodied, supple tannins, smooth and ripe	$18–22
CW	Beaulieu Vineyard, "Rutherford," Cabernet Sauvignon	Rutherford, Napa Valley, California	Full-bodied, supple tannins, smooth and ripe	$18–22
	Conn Creek Vineyards, Cabernet Sauvignon	Napa Valley	Full-bodied, supple tannins, smooth and ripe	$24–26
GW	Rodney Strong, "Alexander's Crown," Cabernet Sauvignon	Alexander Valley, California	Full-bodied, strong tannins, smooth and ripe	$25–29

Luxury Sips

Worth-the-Splurge Wines $25–50+

	Name of Wine	From	Style Profile	Price Range
PF	Château Haut-Bailly	Pessac-Léognan, Graves, France	Medium-bodied, supple tannins, smooth and fruity	$35–42
	Wynns Coonawarra Estate, "John Riddoch," Cabernet Sauvignon	Coonawarra, Australia	Medium-bodied, strong tannins, bright and earthy	$42–48

	Name of Wine	From	Style Profile	Price Range
CW	Château Lynch-Bages	Pauillac, France	Medium-bodied, strong tannins, bright and earthy	$50–55
GW	Chimney Rock, Cabernet Sauvignon	Stags Leap District, Napa Valley, California	Full-bodied, supple tannins, smooth and ripe	$45–50
	Errazuriz, "Don Maximiano," Cabernet Sauvignon	Aconcagua Valley, Chile	Full-bodied, supple tannins, smooth and ripe	$50–55
	Paradigm, Cabernet Sauvignon	Oakville, Napa Valley, California	Full-bodied, supple tannins, smooth and ripe	$48–55
PF	Long Meadow Ranch, Cabernet Sauvignon	Napa Valley, California	Full-bodied, supple tannins, smooth and ripe	$58–62
GW	Staglin Family Vineyard, Cabernet Sauvignon	Rutherford, Napa Valley, California	Full-bodied, supple tannins, smooth and ripe	$72–80
PF	Stag's Leap Wine Cellars, "Fay"	Stags Leap District, Napa Valley, California	Full-bodied, supple tannins, smooth and ripe	$70–80
CW	Von Strasser, Cabernet Sauvignon	Diamond Mountain, Napa Valley, California	Full-bodied, strong tannins, smooth and ripe	$50–55

The Buzz on … Vintages

In this book I don't highlight vintages because if you find a good producer from a place you like, chances are each year it will make quality wine. One year might be more powerful while another elegant. One vintage might be worth cellaring while another is ready to drink right away. I say enjoy the differences of each vintage since that's what makes wine exciting. If you want to remember some notable vintages in Bordeaux and California Cabernet Sauvignon to impress your friends and neighbors, here they are:

Legendary red Bordeaux vintages: 1945, 1961, 1982, 1989, 1990, 1995, 2000

Great California Cabernet Sauvignon vintages: 1994, 1997, 1999, 2001

Classic Bordeaux-Style Blends

	Name of Wine	From	Style Profile	Price Range
PF	Quintessa, Meritage	Rutherford, Napa Valley, California	Full-bodied, supple tannins, smooth and ripe	$90–100
CW	Niebaum-Coppola, "Rubicon"	Rutherford, Napa Valley, California	Full-bodied, strong tannins, smooth and ripe	$90–100
CW	Joseph Phelps, "Insignia"	Napa Valley, California	Full-bodied, strong tannins, smooth and ripe	$100–120

The Buzz on…Cult Cabernet Makeovers

What exactly is a "cult" wine? Basically they are handcrafted, high-quality wines in very limited supply. Most are bought by collectors and the rich and famous, but you don't need to be a celebrity to drink like one. I've highlighted lower-priced alternatives to the impossible-to-find Napa cult Cabs. My make-over wines cost $35–50 versus the $150–500+ cults.

Instead of Screaming Eagle, try Paradigm Winery.
Instead of Harlan Estate, try Atalon Winery.
Instead of Bryant Family, try Staglin Family Vineyard.
Instead of Colgin, try Salvestrin Estate Vineyards.
Instead of Dalla Valle, try Long Meadow Ranch.

---

pairing

IT MAY BE A CLICHÉ, BUT ONE OF MY FAVORITE wine and food pairings in the world is a terrific bottle of Cabernet Sauvignon and a medium-rare grilled steak. In fact, most types of meat go well with Cabernet, but so do duck, vegetables, and a host of cheeses.

Though Cabernet is often the first choice for many diners, it does pose a challenge to some foods as big, tannic versions can overpower what's on the dinner table. Let's grab a glass, take a sip, and ask some questions about the wine.

Let's Talk Texture First: Medium or full, elegant or powerful?

Fuller wines need bigger dishes such as steak or lamb, but more elegantly styled wines have a wider range of options from chicken to duck, pasta to cheese.

Consider It a Complement: Do you smell earthy aromas or fresh herbs in the wine?

Lamb with mint underscores the minty character of some Cabs, while mushrooms or lentils complement an earthy Cabernet.

It's Tannin Time: Do you notice light, medium, or strong tannins?

Cabernet can be the most tannic red you will taste, especially among young wines. To tame them, go for protein, which softens tannins. Think cheese or a big steak.

Design-a-Dinner

STOCK YOUR SHELVES

Bottoms: Beef, lamb, chicken/dark meat, duck, turkey/dark meat, potatoes, brown rice

Tops: Bell peppers, eggplant, spinach, green beans, lentils, cheeses (provolone, blue/Gorgonzola, Parmesan, Gouda, strong Cheddar), meat sauces, brown gravy, red wine sauce

Accessories: Mustard, walnuts, black pepper, rosemary

GET SAUCY . . . WITH CABERNET SAUVIGNON

Tomato–Blue Cheese Butter: Soften 1 stick of butter and in a small mixing bowl use a fork to mix it well with several tablespoons of blue cheese, a bit of minced fresh chives, and a tablespoon of finely chopped sun-dried tomatoes. Spoon the mixture onto a piece of waxed paper or plastic wrap and roll into a cylinder shape. Chill or freeze and slice off a piece to melt on meat, stir into pasta, or top rice.

Gorgonzola Walnut Sauce: Toast 1/2 cup shelled walnuts and let cool before chopping them into small pieces. In a saucepan, sauté 1/2 onion, diced, in olive oil until translucent and beginning to brown. Add 1/2 cup each cream or half-and-half, chicken broth, and crumbled Gorgonzola cheese. Simmer until slightly thickened. Remove from the heat when the cheese is melted and toss in 1/2 cup shredded fresh spinach leaves, the chopped nuts, and loads of cracked black pepper. Serve on pasta or pour over meat.

MEAL ENSEMBLES

Roasted Leg of Lamb with Fresh Mint Sauce: Rub the outside of a leg of lamb with a mixture of honey, Dijon mustard, sea salt, cracked black pepper, and chopped fresh mint and rosemary. Grill or roast until cooked. For the Mint Sauce, mix chopped fresh mint with a little olive oil, salt, and lemon juice. Stir it into couscous or rice and serve with the thinly sliced lamb.

Grilled Steak Extravaganza: Grill filet mignon or New York strip steaks. When you remove them from the grill, top with a thin slice of Tomato–Blue Cheese Butter (page 146). Serve with Potato Gratin and Creamed Spinach.

Potato Gratin: Peel 3 or 4 russet potatoes and slice them a little more than ¼ inch thick. Layer in a buttered casserole dish and dab each layer with slices of butter and salt. Pour milk or cream into the pan until it just covers the potatoes and bake in a 375°F oven until the potatoes are tender and the top is crispy, approximately 30 minutes.

Creamed Spinach: Tear the contents of 1 bag prewashed spinach into small pieces and sauté in a few spoonfuls of melted butter. Cook over medium heat until the leaves are wilted, then season with salt, pepper, and a squeeze of lemon juice. Add several spoonfuls of sour cream or crème fraîche and stir together. For a smoother texture, puree with a hand blender.

Gorgonzola Nut Pasta: Cook toothsome pasta until al dente and then toss with Gorgonzola Walnut Sauce (page 146). Top with fresh parsley and shredded Parmesan. This dish also pairs beautifully with Merlot.

sharing

SUSAN AND HER HUSBAND, BOB, ARE REAL WINE lovers. They would like to plan their vacations around visiting wine regions and called me for a few pointers on planning their wine journeys.

This is one of my favorite topics, because traveling to wine regions is, in my opinion, the best way to learn about wine.

Not only is it fun, but you get a chance to meet winemakers, walk the vineyards, and eat wonderful local dishes. Each time you uncork a bottle from a place you've visited, you re-experience the joy of the trip.

These days you're never too far from wine country. Wine is produced in every state, so whether you live in Virginia, New York, Nebraska, Michigan, or Texas, you should be able to find your "local" wine country.

The Buzz on... Tasting Room Tips

- Don't be afraid to spit! Just try not to splash the person next to you.
- Expect to pay a fee in most tasting rooms (though you often get to keep the glass).
- Call ahead if you have kids, because some spots are kid friendly and others aren't.
- Many smaller wineries require an appointment, so be sure to check before dropping by.
- Avoid the crowds by visiting on a weekday.
- Assign a designated driver or hire a limo to take you around and split the cost among the group.

If you want to go global, here are some of my recommendations near and far. (Check out the Checkout Counter: Resources at the back of the book for contact information and winery associations.)

Where? *Napa Valley, California*

Why? This is *the* most famous wine region in the United States and draws more than five million visitors per year. I recommend avoiding the summer rush and visiting either during harvest in October or in the spring, when the whole valley is a sea of brilliant mustard blooms.

Must-see spots:
- the historic caves at Beringer Vineyards
- lunch at Tra Vigne or Mustards Grill
- a stop by the Oakville Grocery for picnic supplies

More? Contact the Napa Valley Visitors Bureau

Where? *Sonoma Valley, California*

Why? While Napa may be the most popular in terms of tourism, Sonoma Valley is truly delightful. A little more laid back than the Napa Valley, it's still easy to drive up and down the main drag of Highway 12 to visit wineries.

Must-see spots:
- Sonoma Plaza (great playground for kids)
- the vineyard tram tour at Benziger Family Winery
- lunch at the Girl and the Fig or Basque Boulangerie
- a stop by the Sonoma Cheese Factory

More? Contact the Sonoma Valley Visitors Bureau

Where? *Walla Walla, Washington*

Why? An up-and-coming wine region that's a step back in time with a charming downtown area and wineries so close together that it's a touring paradise.

The Buzz on...Spas and Sips

Wine country isn't just for wine anymore. Spas are popping up all over the world to pamper wine lovers. Give these a try if you really want to escape and relax:

The Silverado Country Club & Resort is as classic as Napa Valley's top Cabernets. Golf, tennis, wine, food—you name it, they've got it. Popular treatments include a grape-seed body polish, followed by a jasmine-ginger-green clay mask and massage.

Les Sources de Caudalie, Bordeaux, France is a four-star luxury hotel on the grounds of Château Smith-Haut-Lafitte, near the city of Bordeaux, and is home to the world's first vinotherapy treatments. You can enjoy a soak in a red-wine-barrel bath before heading off to lunch at the spa's bistro or taking culinary classes with Michelin-star chef Franck Salein.

The Willows Lodge, Woodinville, Washington, is a top spot for visiting some of Washington's best wineries. Book a room and a massage at the Willows Lodge and Spa, eat at the world-famous Herb Garden restaurant, and walk to nearby mega-wineries Château Ste. Michelle and Columbia Winery, then pop over to the upscale DeLille Cellars.

If you want to visit Bordeaux but don't know where to start, turn to Jean-Michel Cazes and his vivacious sister, Sylvie Cazes-Regimbeau, for help. The proprietors of Château Lynch-Bages have launched a venture dubbed *Bordeaux Saveurs*. You can set up specialized vineyard tours and take wine-tasting courses in downtown Bordeaux and cooking classes at the classic Le Chapon Fin restaurant. Stay at the Cazes-owned hotel, Cordeillan-Bages, located next to Château Lynch-Bages in Pauillac. It's the perfect way to learn about Bordeaux and have a great vacation.

Must-see spots:

- the glamorous Northstar and Pepper Bridge wineries
- a stay at historic Marcus Whitman Hotel
- dinner at Whitehouse-Crawford restaurant

More? Contact the Washington Wine Commission

Where? *Burgundy, France*

Why? If you're a Pinot Noir or Chardonnay fan, you must go at least once in your life to visit Burgundy. Only a few hours by train from downtown Paris, it's an easy place to navigate because it's small. Stay in the beautiful city of Beaune and branch out from there.

Must-see spots:

- the Hotel Dieu in Beaune
- the downtown food markets in Beaune
- the famed Château du Clos de Vougeot

More? Contact the Burgundy Tourism Bureau

Where? *Tuscany, Italy*

Why? Why not! Tuscany is an amazing place, and all the wonderful books written about it are true. Spending time in Florence is a must. Then, when you're ready for wine country, find an *agriturismo* (farmhouse bed and breakfast) near the small town of Greve in Chianti.

Must-see spots:

- the ancient Castello di Nippozano in Chianti Rufina, which is owned by the Frescobaldi family

◦ lunch at Il Cibreo restaurant in Florence

　　◦ the hillside town of Montelcino, with fabulous pottery shopping

More? Contact the Italian Government Tourist Board

Where? *Barossa Valley, South Australia*

Why? Not only are the Aussies a fun lot, but the Barossa is a terrific place to visit for the wine and the German-influenced local cuisine. Base yourself in the city of Adelaide, which is less than an hour's drive to the Barossa.

Must-see spots:

　　◦ Jacob's Creek Visitor Centre (or cellar door, as the Aussies say)

　　◦ Maggie Beer's Farm Shop for local delicacies

　　◦ Historic Yalumba Winery in nearby Eden Valley

More? Contact the South Australian Tourism Commission

Where? *Martinborough, New Zealand*

Why? Not as well known as spots such as Marlborough or even the tourist destination of Hawkes Bay, the tiny town of Martinborough (population around a thousand) is a bucolic spot worth visiting.

Must-see spots:

　　◦ Murdoch James Winery for a picnic lunch

　　◦ Palliser Estates for Pinot Noir

　　◦ a stay at the Martinborough Hotel

More? Contact the Wellington Tourism Bureau

The Buzz on … Women and Wine: Hey, Big Spenders!

Many attribute the sale of low-priced wine to women, but guess what? Women account for 60 percent of high-end wine buyers in this country, according to Christian Miller, director of research at Motto, Kryla & Fisher LLP, a wine industry research firm. MKF defines high-end buyers as people who fit at least two out of the following three criteria: purchase wine costing more than $15 occasionally to frequently, have more than twelve bottles on hand in their home, and would buy a wine costing over $15 for a casual meal at home.

Merlot/Bordeaux
"WRAP ME IN CASHMERE" RED

CASHMERE IS THE ULTIMATE IN LUXURIOUS TEXTURE. Whether it's a twin set, shawl, or cashmere-lined leather gloves, this sensuous material embraces us with its softness and warmth. We buy it when we feel the urge to splurge.

When Merlot is good, it's nothing short of vinous cashmere. Supple and plush, it simply feels good to drink. Layer on the juicy fruit flavors typical of Merlot, and you have a wine that's hard to resist.

In the past decade Merlot became the darling of wine drinkers because of these obvious charms. Not only is it easy to pronounce, but Merlot's easy-drinking style has made it simple for white wine lovers to slip into savoring reds.

THE NAME GAME

Merlot = red Bordeaux wines, including those labeled *Pomerol* and *Saint-Émilion*

Merlot is the dominant grape variety in the wines of Bordeaux's Right Bank, which includes the famous appellations of Pomerol and Saint-Émilion. Cabernet Franc is another important grape in the blends of Right Bank wines, followed by Cabernet Sauvignon.

THE GRAPE STORY

Merlot's rise to the top is similar to the story of the Broadway dancer who went onstage as a chorus girl and ended up a star.

In Bordeaux, where it partners with Cabernet Sauvignon and Cabernet Franc, Merlot has been an admired variety for centuries, but it was by no means the only attraction. As in all of Europe, place took precedence over grape, and France produced not great "Merlot," but great "Bordeaux."

It wasn't until California's Louis M. Martini Winery produced the first wine labeled *Merlot* more than thirty years ago that the grape variety slowly started its ascent to the top of the singles charts. Napa Valley's Sterling Vineyards did the same, and soon wineries from California to Washington and Italy were bottling the grape as a single varietal. Merlot was a star-in-training, and savvy consumers looking for a smooth, friendly red naturally gravitated to it.

Merlot madness really hit in the early 1990s, however, after CBS's "60 Minutes" reported that a team of esteemed scientists discovered the French had an overall lower incidence of heart disease despite their high-fat diet. The scientists partially attributed it to regular consumption of red wine. As winemaker Mike Martini of Louis M. Martini winery notes, "The French paradox kicked in, and people could slide across from whites into reds with an easy-drinking Merlot."

This was Merlot's breakthrough role, but then the pressure of stardom struck. Merlot became a huge moneymaker, and everyone wanted a piece of the action. Grapes were planted like wildfire, and store shelves were overflowing with the bounty.

The problem was that Merlot started to lose its distinction. It had built a following because of its characteristic fruity softness, but as Merlot vines multiplied, so did lackluster wines. In more recent years critics started declaring Merlot passé, and its star seemed to be tarnishing. No way. Though there are still many uninspiring Merlots, the wine remains extremely popular. No longer starstruck, many producers are recapturing what makes Merlot special—a mouthful of fruit and softness.

A Price for Quality

So, how do you navigate the wine aisles and wine lists to discover bottles you enjoy?

First, look for a place. Merlot can be majestic or monotonous depending on many factors, including where it's grown. Though not an overly fussy grape variety, early-ripening Merlot really shines when planted in cooler climates where clay-based soils dominate. Second, wines can be made in various styles, from the Cabernetlike blends with fullness and noticeable tannins to soft juicy quaffers, so it's important to find a producer whose style you like.

Third, expect to pay for it. There are delicious, affordable versions, and I've highlighted some of my favorites in "Bargain Sips" (page 161),

---

Lingo Lesson

Core Words

Dry: Though Merlot often has a "sweet fruit" character (think of biting into a ripe, juicy plum), it is categorized as dry wine. If you like this dry, but not drying, taste in red wine, seek out Australian Shiraz, too.

Smooth: A lower-acid grape than most other reds, Merlot produces wines that have an inviting smoothness.

Medium-bodied: Style range from light to full, especially when blended with a healthy dose of Cabernet Sauvignon, but most wines will fall into the medium-bodied category.

Light to medium tannins: Merlot is a thinner-skinned grape than Cabernet Sauvignon, for example, and is inherently less tannic. If you don't like back-talkin' tannins, Merlot is your wine.

Extra Credit Words

Fruit aromas:

> Red fruits—raspberry, cherry
> Black fruits—black cherry, blackberry, plum

Chocolate and spice: Cinnamon, sweet spices, and hints of chocolate are often apparent when the wine has been aged in toasty oak barrels.

Herbal aromas: Although it's not as herbal as Cabernet Franc or even Cabernet Sauvignon, there is often a touch of herbal aromas in Merlot from cooler-climate regions.

Velvety, plush: Lighter tannins, juicy fruit notes, and smooth acidity combine to give the best Merlots a velvety, plush feeling in the mouth.

but to really capture the lush smoothness of top Merlot you have to be willing to lay out some cash. If you've ever bought thinner, less expensive one-ply cashmere versus the finest, most plush two-ply, you know how different it feels.

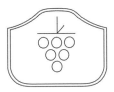

leslie's label links
Connecting taste to place makes wine buying easy

STYLISH AND SMOOTH

These areas offer Merlot the right set of conditions, from soil to climate, to produce wines of elegance and smooth texture. Some are more vibrant and light, others fleshy, concentrated, and full, but all highlight some facet of Merlot's friendly personality.

Place: Bordeaux, France

Taste: Wines that simply carry the general *Bordeaux* appellation are likely to be primarily Merlot since it is the most widely planted red grape in Bordeaux. In the hands of a good producer, these light-bodied reds offer bright cherry fruit and a touch of tannins and herbs at a price tag that won't break the bank.

Look for brands from Bordeaux's famous names, such as Château Mouton-Rothschild's Mouton-Cadet, Château Lynch-Bages' Michel Lynch brand, and Marquis de Chasse from Château Chasse Spleen. All sell for around $10 or less.

Place: Saint-Émilion, France

Taste: If there is a prettier spot than the medieval hillside village of Saint-Émilion, I haven't seen it, and if there is a prettier wine than Saint-Émilion, I haven't tasted it. With clay/limestone soils and a combination of warm days and cold nights, this area is planted in mostly Merlot, the reigning queen of the Right Bank, with its lady-in-waiting, Cabernet Franc, playing a supporting role. Floral, elegant, and sumptuously smooth, the reds of Saint-Émilion are the ideal place to begin and end a journey of discovery with Bordeaux. Labels that simply say *Saint-Émilion* offer enjoyable drinking for as little at $10, while those tagged *grand cru* are elegant, velvety, and hover in the $50–100 luxury category.

Value Tip: Search for affordable reds from the nearby Côtes de Castillon, which are also made from Merlot and Cabernet Franc. They offer everyday drinking in the $8–12 range.

Place: Pomerol, France

Taste: If Saint-Émilion's wines are pretty, Pomerols are out-of-this-world plush. What makes these wines so deeply fruity and velvety rich? As in neighboring Saint-Émilion, soils and climate unite to produce the best expression of Merlot in the world. Interestingly, it's one of Bordeaux's smallest appellations, but its  reputation is huge. Two of the world's most expensive wines that can cost more than $1,000 per newly released bottle, the legendary Château Petrus and the cult wine Château Le Pin, are produced in Pomerol. They epitomize the intersection of classic quality and innovative energy that is sweeping Pomerol and Saint-Émilion.

Value Tip: Try wines from nearby appellations named Lalande-de-Pomerol and Fronsac. My favorite value bottling is from Château Fontenil, the Fronsac property of famed wine consultant Michel Rolland and his wife, Dany. It will set you back a mere $20!

Place: Long Island, New York

Taste: New York's Long Island and Bordeaux share similarities from maritime-influenced climate to flat, gravelly soils, and both are centers of Merlot production. Although the first vines in the North Fork of Long Island weren't planted until 1973, by pioneering vintner Louisa Hargrave, Merlot has gained a

real foothold in the vineyards that line this sliver of land. Not quite as plush and lush as Pomerol, Long Island Merlots remind me of the elegance of Saint-Émilions.

Place: Carneros, California

Taste: The cool-climate Carneros region straddles both Napa and Sonoma valleys as they meet near San Pablo Bay. The undulating hills are swathed in Chardon-nay and Pinot Noir vineyards—Carneros's claim to fame for both still and sparkling

wine production. But guess what? Merlot is coming on strong. Versions from Carneros are intense and supple, deeply rich, and yet manage to maintain a sense of vibrancy. Why does Merlot thrive in this area? As winemaker Michael Havens of Napa's Havens Wine Cellars says, "The reasons Carneros is thought to be superior for Pinot Noir and Chardon-nay are the same reasons it's great for Merlot. The limiting soils keep vigor down, and the longer, cooler growing season allows for true ripeness."

Look for these places on the label, too . . .

Veneto, Italy

Fronsac, Bordeaux

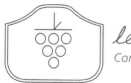

leslie's label links

Connecting taste to place makes wine buying easy

FRUITY AND RICH

Merlot from the following places is both rich and supple, but with an intensity of fruit that comes from basking in the sunshine. Some can be superlush and others more vibrant, but for intensity of rich, ripe fruit flavors, look for these regions on the label.

Place: Columbia Valley, Washington

Taste: Do you know a couple who has the marriage that everyone envies? They never fight, complete each other's sentences, and produce delightful children. That's the relationship between Merlot and the state of Washington—a marriage made in heaven. As the number-one red grape in this northwestern state, Merlot has found its ideal companion in the soils and climate of Washington's Columbia Valley. From these vines comes sumptuously textured wine with bright cherry and red berry fruit that marries French elegance and New World fruitiness.

Grapes aren't grown in soggy Seattle; they come from the arid eastern side of the Cascade mountain range. With rain a constant presence in western Washington, it's hard to believe that the Columbia Valley—where 98 percent of the wine grapes are planted—is so dry vineyards need irrigation to survive. But what the region lacks in rainfall, it more than makes up for in climate. The Columbia Valley's long sunny days (usually two more hours per day than California) and cool nights gives grapes time to slowly gain complexity and ripeness while not losing acidity.

Place: Walla Walla Valley, Washington

Taste: Walla Walla may be the home of famous sweet onions, but the sweetest thing to emerge from this part of Washington's larger Columbia Valley is Merlot. Intense, voluptuous, and velvety, it's as Pomerollike as you can get outside of France. Leaders such as Leonetti Cellar and Woodward Canyon started the ball rolling in the late 1970s and early 1980s. Today Merlot is a mainstay, and upcoming stars include Northstar, Spring Valley Vineyard, and Pepper Bridge Winery.

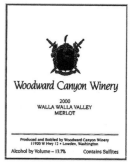

Place: Hawkes Bay, New Zealand

Taste: Just when I thought most of the amazing places for Merlot in the world had been discovered, I began tasting the bottles coming from an area in New Zealand's North Island called Hawkes Bay. Often blended with Cabernet Sauvignon, the wines share spicy aromas and vibrant fruit flavors wrapped in smoothness. The wines are so lush because Hawkes Bay enjoys a moderate climate that is one of the warmest and driest in all of New Zealand. Merlot has just enough of what it needs to get nice and ripe while keeping a zippy character.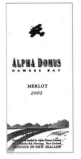

Tasting Tip: You may see wine from Hawkes Bay with a special seal on the label. There is a new growing area called the Gimblett Gravels, which is a small swath of land created by an old riverbed. It has a unique gravelly soil and specialized climate similar to Bordeaux, and it may prove to be the hottest spot for Merlot, Cabernet Sauvignon, and Syrah.

Place: Napa Valley, California

Taste: These wines range from elegant to full, vibrant to ripe, and spicy to chocolaty. Though there are grapes grown in cooler areas such as Carneros, Napa is a warm place overall, and most bottles capture the ripe, fruit-forward 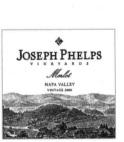 qualities of Merlot. It's impossible for me to talk about Napa Merlot without mentioning what is one of my benchmark wines—the Beringer Howell Mountain, "Bancroft Ranch" Merlot. If you want to experience the full potential of Merlot, get a bottle of this inky elixir and age it for a few years. (This is definitely a special occasion wine as a bottle costs about $60.)

Look for these places on the label, too . . .

Maipo Valley, Chile

Languedoc, France

Sonoma, California

A MATTER OF STYLE

When it comes to the winemaker's influence on Merlot, many techniques can affect the wine's final taste and style profile. Two worth exploring are what comes at the beginning of the process and what goes on at the end.

From Ground to Glass: Soil

We've been talking about soil this and soil that, but what does it really mean? Why are some soil types better for certain kinds of grapes?

Well-drained, gravelly soils are warm since the water percolates through the large particles and drains away. It's like putting rocks or pottery shards at the bottom of your potted plants to keep the roots well drained. Certain grapes, like Cabernet Sauvignon, need warm, dry soils to produce intense fruit.

On the other hand, Merlot likes cooler soils and thrives in places where clay is predominant. This thicker type of soil releases moisture to the grapes slowly over time and keeps the roots at a cooler temperature.

Clay soils are important to the final taste of a Merlot because its telltale smoothness is related directly to how long the grapes stay ripening on the vine. In cooler soils the grapes can develop properly and take their time to acquire ripe, supple tannins and smooth, soft acids. When Merlot is planted in the wrong types of soil, it lacks the all-important lushness that makes the wines unique.

From Ground to Glass: Blending

Merlot may be a star grape, but it loves being in an ensemble cast. Its strengths are texture and juicy fruit; its weakness is its lack of structure. Combining it with Cabernet Sauvignon, which provides the skeleton for Merlot's fleshiness, can produce a wine that's better than the sum of its parts. When Cabernet Franc is thrown into the mix, as it is in Saint-Émilion and Pomerol, its floral, mineral aromas and touch of herbal character help to fill in any holes that Merlot may have.

Bordeaux isn't the only place where it's important to blend. The final taste of many New World versions, from California to Washington and Chile, depends on Merlot's affinity for its Bordeaux partners.

Wines with a heavy proportion of Cabernet Sauvignon, for example, will be much fuller and tannic than straight Merlot.

The Buzz on ... Bordeaux-Style Blends

You'll often hear about reds described as "Bordeaux-style blends," which simply means they're made outside Bordeaux but with the same grape varieties, such as Cabernet Sauvignon, Merlot, and Cabernet Franc. You might also hear about a luxury class of wines dubbed Meritage (see page 75).

Shopping Guide

Bargain Sips

Stash-Your-Cash Merlot $15 and Under

	Name of Wine	From	Style Profile	Price Range
PW	Forestville, Merlot	California	Light-bodied, light tannins, bright and earthy	$5–8
GW	Marquis de Chasse, Merlot	Bordeaux, France	Light-bodied, light tannins, bright and earthy	$8–10
PW	Fetzer, "Eagle Peak," Merlot	California	Medium-bodied, light tannins, bright and fruity	$7–8
	Hogue, Merlot	Columbia Valley, Washington	Medium-bodied, light tannins, bright and fruity	$8–10
	Buena Vista, Merlot	California	Medium-bodied, light tannins, bright and fruity	$7–10
	Louis M. Martini, Merlot	California	Medium-bodied, light tannins, bright and fruity	$9–11
PW	Blackstone, Merlot	California	Medium-bodied, supple tannins, smooth and fruity	$8–10

	Name of Wine	From	Style Profile	Price Range
PF	Sterling Vineyards, "Vintner's Collection," Merlot	Central Coast, California	Medium-bodied, supple tannins, smooth and fruity	$12–15
	Alpha Domus, Merlot	Hawkes Bay, New Zealand	Medium-bodied, supple tannins, smooth and fruity	$13–15

Classic Sips

Well-Known Winners $15–30

	Name of Wine	From	Style Profile	Price Range
	Château Clos l'Eglise	Côtes de Castillon, Bordeaux, France	Medium-bodied, light tannins, bright and fruity	$15–18
PF	Kim Crawford, Merlot	East Coast, New Zealand	Medium-bodied, light tannins, bright and fruity	$18–20
GW	Wölffer Estate, "Reserve," Merlot	The Hamptons, Long Island, New York	Medium-bodied, light tannins, bright and fruity	$28–32
	Château La Chenade	Lalande-de-Pomerol, France	Medium-bodied, supple tannins, smooth and fruity	$15–18
	Markham Vineyards, Merlot	Napa Valley, California	Medium-bodied, supple tannins, smooth and fruity	$18–22
	Havens Wine Cellars, Merlot	Carneros, Napa Valley, California	Medium-bodied, supple tannins, smooth and fruity	$22–26
GW	Robert Sinskey, "los Carneros," Merlot	Carneros, Napa Valley, California	Medium-bodied, supple tannins, smooth and fruity	$23–28
	Baron Philippe de Rothschild, Pomerol	Pomerol, Bordeaux, France	Medium-bodied, supple tannins, bright and earthy	$25–30
GW	Silverado Vineyards, Merlot	Napa Valley, California	Full-bodied, supple tannins, smooth and ripe	$22–25
PF	Swanson Vineyards, Merlot	Napa Valley, California	Full-bodied, supple tannins, smooth and ripe	$23–28

Name of Wine	From	Style Profile	Price Range
Château Ste. Michelle, "Canoe Ridge," Merlot	Columbia Valley, Washington	Full-bodied, supple tannins, smooth and ripe	$23–28

Luxury Sips

Worth-the-Splurge Wines $30–50+

	Name of Wine	From	Style Profile	Price Range
	Château la Croix du Casse	Pomerol, France	Medium-bodied, supple tannins, bright and earthy	$35–40
CW	Château Clos Fourtet	Saint-Émilion, Bordeaux, France	Full-bodied, supple tannins, smooth and ripe	$35–40
PW	Andrew Will, "Seven Hills Vineyard," Merlot	Walla Walla, Washington	Full-bodied, supple tannins, smooth and ripe	$48–52
	Château Gazin	Pomerol, Bordeaux, France	Full-bodied, supple tannins, smooth and ripe	$60–65
CW	Château Angélus	Saint-Émilion, Bordeaux, France	Full-bodied, supple tannins, smooth and ripe	$80–100
CW	Pepper Bridge Winery, Merlot	Walla Walla, Washington	Full-bodied, strong tannins, smooth and ripe	$44–48
GW	Duckhorn Vineyards, Merlot	Napa Valley, California	Full-bodied, strong tannins, smooth and ripe	$45–50
	Northstar Winery, Merlot	Columbia Valley, Washington	Full-bodied, strong tannins, smooth and ripe	$52–56

pairing

MERLOT CAN COME IN A VARIETY OF STYLES AND GOES as easily with macaroni and cheese as it does with meat loaf. Believe it or not, though, Merlot is my top pick when pairing dry reds with chocolate.

From Valrhona to Scharffen Berger, Guittard to

Richart, Hershey's to Ghirardelli, chocolate is a girl's best friend. When a Merlot has soft tannins, loads of deep berry fruit, and a velvety texture, it's the ideal complement. As winemaker Kim Nicholls of Napa Valley's Markham Vineyards says, "Red wine pairs fabulously with chocolate! Luckily, I am a fan of dark chocolate, which is really the best match since it is less sweet and competitive with the wine."

Let's Talk Texture First: Is it medium or full? Velvety and rich or light and fresh?

Lighter Merlots work well with lighter, less complex fare like a simple chicken sandwich or cup of tomato soup, whereas fuller and more complex wines (often those blended with Cabernet Sauvignon) can handle richer foods such as a pot roast or duck.

Consider It a Complement: Are there herbal notes or an intense, fruity character?

Wines that have a hint of herbal aromas go well with earthy foods containing lentils, herbs, and mushrooms, while ultrarich wines with a touch of cocoa powder aroma are the top pick for chocolate lovers.

About Acid: Is the wine smooth or bright?

Merlot is generally a lower acid wine than most other reds, which is part of its appeal as a sipping wine. But some versions, especially from Bordeaux, Washington state, and Long Island, have brighter levels of acidity and are my picks when it comes to echoing tangy, tomato-based sauces. These wines are ideal when used as a foil for creamy white and cheese sauces, too. Watch out mac and cheese!

It's Tannin Time: Are there light, medium, or strong tannins?

Most Merlots will fall on the light-to-medium side of the tannin scale, which makes them a good choice for sipping as a cocktail. For those wines with a grainy texture from strong tannins, reach for the steak since proteins help to make tannins feel smoother.

Design-a-Dinner

STOCK YOUR SHELVES

Bottoms: Chicken, pork, duck, beef, steak, veal, lentils, potatoes

Tops: Mushrooms, eggplant, bell peppers, blueberries, prunes, plums, cheeses (Cheddar, Swiss, Gorgonzola), white sauces, cheese sauces, tomato sauces

Accessories: Dijon mustard, caramelized onions, tarragon, fennel, chocolate

GET SAUCY . . . WITH MERLOT

Zesty Blueberry Sauce: Blueberries serve a dual purpose in this sauce since they underscore the fruitiness of Merlot and give the sauce a touch of sweetness. Sauté ½ diced onion and 1 minced garlic clove in olive oil until the onion is translucent. Add equal amounts of ketchup and Merlot, approximately 1 cup each, and 1 or 2 tablespoons balsamic vinegar to the pan. Put in a handful of fresh or frozen blueberries and cook until the blueberries start to burst. Remove from the heat and puree with a hand-held blender. Use on ribs, chicken, or meat loaf.

Gorgonzola Walnut Sauce on page 146 is another ideal sauce to serve with Merlot.

MEAL ENSEMBLES

Blueberry Chicken: Place skinned chicken thighs in a casserole dish and generously spread with Zesty Blueberry Sauce (see above). Bake uncovered in a 350°F oven for 30–35 minutes. Garnish with fresh parsley and serve over rice and seasoned lentils. Simple and delicious.

Onion Tart: Roughly chop 2 large white or red onions and sauté in olive oil over medium heat until lightly browned, soft, and sweet. Let

1 box frozen puff pastry dough, which typically contains 2 sheets of dough, thaw and place 1 sheet on a greased cookie sheet. Spoon the caramelized onions (approximately 1 cup) on the dough and spread them out, leaving a 1-inch margin around the edges. Next, sprinkle grated sharp Cheddar cheese on the caramelized onions. Place the other piece of pastry dough on the first and pinch the edges together firmly. Make several incisions on the top of the tart using a sharp knife and bake at 375°F for 30–40 minutes, until golden brown. Cut into small squares and serve with soup or as an appetizer.

Gorgonzola Steak: Grill or broil flank steak or London broil and slice into thick strips. Top with Gorgonzola Walnut Sauce (page 146) and serve with boiled Yukon Gold potatoes tossed with butter and tarragon.

Eggplant and Mushroom Sandwich: Sauté several portobello mushrooms in olive oil and slice into wide strips. Cut 1 large eggplant into rounds about 3/4 inch thick and sprinkle salt on each round. Fry each piece in a generous amount of olive oil for 5 to 6 minutes, until brown on both sides and soft in the middle. Place them on paper towels to drain. Toast crusty bread cut in half lengthwise and spread with Dijon mustard. Layer on the cooked vegetables and fresh spinach leaves. Cut into portions and serve warm.

sharing

STASHING AND SERVING WINE

Two of the most common questions I hear have to do with storing and serving wine. Most women aren't concerned with building the perfect cellar for aging collectible wines but are looking for tips for stashing wine on hand. Here are some simple guidelines:

○ Inexpensive racking is fine as long as it is sturdy.
○ Store the bottles on their sides to keep the corks moist so they won't dry out.

○ Maintain the wine at a constant temperature—not too hot, not too cold.

○ Keep bottles in a dark place since light can damage wine. Good spots include a closet, under the bed, the garage, and under the stairs.

The Buzz from ... David Andrew, Global Wine Director, Costco

Costco is a top spot to stock up on good-value wine from all over the world, so it makes sense that David's advice for a home stash is simply to be adventurous. "Variety is the spice of life! Have some Sancerre, Chablis, maybe a New Zealand Sauvignon Blanc stored somewhere cool. Then load up on Washington Merlot and Chilean Cabernet Sauvignon. There's nothing more fun than having three or four different bottles on the table to share with friends."

The Buzz on ... How Many Glasses in That Bottle?

Wine bottles come in many different sizes, from big boys like a Balthazar (the equivalent of sixteen regular bottles) or an Imperial (eight bottles) to small splits (think one glass). Besides a standard wine bottle, my favorites are the half bottle, which is the ideal size for a two-person dinner, and the party-size magnum.

Half bottle (.375 ml) equals two big glasses or three smaller ones
Standard-size bottle (.750 ml) serves five to six glasses
Magnum (1.5 l) equals two bottles and serves ten to twelve glasses

---

Another common question has to do with serving wine at the right temperature. We tend to serve whites too cold and reds too warm, but how do you know the "proper" temperature? In reality no one whips a thermometer out of her pocket to sample the wine before uncorking (and be on geek alert for anyone who does). But it does help to serve each wine in an appropriate temperature range. Keep these points in mind:

○ The lighter the body and color of the wine, the cooler the serving temperature, meaning light-bodied whites should be cool and deep purple wines the warmest.

- Oak tastes even stronger when a wine is cold, so be careful not to overchill oaky whites like Chardonnay.
- Sweetness tastes more pronounced when a wine is too warm.
- Alcohol appears more powerful when warm, so don't serve high-alcohol wines like Zinfandel too warm.

Try These Temperature Ranges

Serve: Cold to the touch (40–50°F).
How: Usually an hour or two in a standard-temperature refrigerator or 20–25 minutes in a half-water, half-ice bath.
- Lighter sparkling wine
- Most white dessert wines
- Riesling
- Chenin Blanc
- Pinot Grigio
- Sauvignon Blanc (lighter styles such as Sancerre)
- Lighter Chardonnay (such as Chablis)
- Blush wine/medium-dry Rosé

Serve: Cool to touch (50–60°F)
How: Half an hour to an hour in the refrigerator or 15–20 minutes in an ice bath.
- Full-bodied Champagne
- Chardonnay
- White Bordeaux
- Sémillon
- Viognier
- Dry Rosé

Serve: Slightly cool to the touch (around 55–65°F)
How: 5–15 minutes in the refrigerator if not stored in a cool area
- Beaujolais
- Dolcetto
- Lighter-bodied Pinot Noir
- Lighter-bodied Chianti

Serve: Slightly lower than room temperature (60–68°F)

How: When the *room-temperature* verbiage became popular many years ago, rooms were a lot colder than they are now. If stored somewhere fairly warm, it doesn't hurt to put even your biggest, boldest reds in the refrigerator for several minutes. This prevents them from heating up too quickly in the glass.

- Most Chianti Classico and other Sangiovese-based wines
- Fuller-bodied Pinot Noir
- Merlot
- Cabernet Sauvignon
- Zinfandel
- Syrah
- Port

The Buzz from…Signe Zoller, Winemaker
Meridian Vineyards, California

When Signe Zoller's children were grown, she went back to school to become a winemaker and currently crafts wine for California's Meridian Vineyards. A study completed by her company showed that women were not treated as well as men in restaurant wine situations. As a result Signe penned a brochure entitled *7 Things Every Gal Should Know About Ordering Wine*. The free pamphlet has proven so popular that a second has followed: *7 Things Every Woman Should Know About Serving Wine*. As Signe notes, "Women are now competing in what has been a man's world. I'm hoping to help show the way by empowering them with information."

Syrah/Shiraz
THE "RED-HOT" RED

IF CHARDONNAY IS THE "BASIC BLACK" OF YOUR WINE wardrobe, then Syrah is the must-have red accessory. Just as a garnet handbag, crimson scarf, or scarlet lips make an outfit sizzle, Syrah adds a dash of sex appeal to any meal.

Peppery, smoky, and powerful, Syrah is exotic but approachable. Like wearing that splash of red, sipping Syrah is wildly fun. It was one of the wines that captured my heart early on, and I'm so enamored with the grape I even make my own Syrah.

How can you discover its allure? Easy. Store shelves are full of versions from Australia (where it's called Shiraz), France, California, Washington, and even Chile. With styles ranging from plush to elegant and price tags from designer to discount, there's a bottle with your name on it.

That's why Syrah is currently the fastest-growing wine type in the country. And, though it's nowhere near knocking Cabernet Sauvignon or Merlot from their perches, Syrah is red-hot.

THE NAME GAME
Syrah = Shiraz

Syrah = northern Rhône Valley reds

Shiraz **is simply another name for the Syrah grape. Why the difference? Shiraz could have been named for the wine center of** ancient Persia, a city named Shiraz, but no one knows for sure. It is very common to call grape varieties by different names, though, such as Grenache versus Garnacha and Mataro or Mourvèdre.

Syrah is also the grape variety responsible for producing the great red wines of France's northern Rhône Valley. Red-wine labels with place names such as *Côte Rôtie, Hermitage, Crozes-Hermitage, St.-Joseph,* and *Cornas* all signify wine made from Syrah.

THE GRAPE STORY

Just how did Syrah get to be so popular? It's the grape equivalent of that seventies pop culture image: the smiley face sticker. No matter where you plant it, it's happy.

Unlike fussy Pinot Noir or particular Pinot Gris, laid-back Syrah has the wonderful ability to adapt to various growing conditions. It likes cool climates but shines in warmer ones. It excels when planted on hillsides yet does well in flat vineyards. It can produce tannic, rustic reds but just as easily make smooth, quaffable wines. Who wouldn't want to plant this versatile grape?

Hi-Ho, Syrah, Away . . .

Despite all the current buzz surrounding Syrah, it is an ancient variety dating to Roman times. In its homeland of France, Syrah grape vines hug the steep hillsides of the northern Rhône Valley, producing legendary wines that rank among the world's best.

Over time, the variety has adapted happily to life in spots around the globe. For example, Syrah has been planted in California for more than a century. Its prominence in the Golden State has risen only since the mid-1980s, when a number of renegade winemakers—dubbed the Rhône Rangers—began crafting Rhône-style wines.

Syrah gained popularity among a clique of wine drinkers and was threatening full-fledged name recognition when the Australians came ashore. By 1989, Rosemount Estate's Diamond Label Shiraz was leading the way, and Americans quickly took to the fruity, spicy red.

In little more than a decade, the Aussie tsunami has flooded our shores with consistently good, affordable Shiraz. Now, with impressive versions emerging from hot spots such as Washington state and

Chile, the great grape race is heating up. Touch up your scarlet lipstick, grab a glass, and come with me on a worldwide ride. Hi-ho, Syrah . . . away!

Lingo Lesson

Core Words

Dry: Syrah is considered a dry wine, but many Australian Shiraz and other New World versions are made with residual sugar. The wine will not taste overly sweet but will have an appealing, succulent quality. If you like this style of wine, try Zinfandel, too.

Bright to smooth: In cooler climates of France and Washington State, for example, Syrah exhibits a vibrant quality from higher levels of acidity. In warmer regions of Australia and California, the fruit's ripeness lowers the acidity and imparts an embracing softness.

Medium- to full-bodied: These are some of the highest alcohol reds around (only trailing Zinfandel by a hair). Most tip the scales at 13.5–14+ percent, which puts them squarely in the "big boy" wine category.

Medium to strong tannins: Thick, dark grape skins result in fairly strong tannins, especially in wines from the Hermitage region of France. If you don't like tannins, reach for Australian versions as the tannins feel softer and smoother due to ultraripe fruit and a whisper of residual sugar in many wines.

Extra Credit Words

Fruit aromas:

> Red fruits—raspberry, cherry
> Black fruits—blackberry, blackberry jam, blueberry, boysenberry, plum

Peppery, spicy: If you want to add spice to your life, Syrah's characteristic white pepper (from cool-climate regions) and black peppery notes (from warmer spots) will do the trick.

Meaty: Think bacon and pancetta. Sounds odd, but when a touch of meaty character shines through, it is delicious in Syrah.

Chocolate, smoky: These deep, intense aromas and flavors usually result from the use of oak barrels. American oak versus French oak often imparts a coconut and chocolate character.

North and South

The Rhône Valley is the wild child of France's wine-growing regions. Bordeaux is grand and aristocratic, like its Cabernet Sauvignon and Merlot-based wines. Burgundy, with gently sloping hillsides planted to Pinot Noir and Chardonnay, is elegant yet informal. The Rhône, on the other hand, is rugged and edgy, characteristics also used to describe wines produced there.

Thousands of years ago Romans settled the valley, which is located in the southeast of France. Towns sprang to life along the Rhône River, which is the lifeblood of the region. Sweeping through the valley at a powerful pace, the mighty waterway curves through the hilly northern Rhône and becomes gentler as it winds its way through the southern Rhône. The two regions are distinctly different in climate, terrain, and ambience, but the river binds them together in a contented marriage of opposites.

If you really want to know your Rhônes, here's a quick geography lesson:

Northern Rhône: The northern Rhône begins south of France's second-largest city, named Lyon, and includes these top appellations:

- **Condrieu**—White wine–growing region planted in Viognier (see the chapter "Viognier, Chenin Blanc, and Sémillon" for more)
- **Côte Rôtie**—Elegant, smoky Syrah produced in small amounts
- **Hermitage**—The home of classic French Syrah
- **Crozes-Hermitage**—Good-value wines from Hermitage's neighboring region
- **St.-Joseph**—Another appellation producing affordable, smoky Syrah
- **Cornas**—Think rustic, rich, and deeply colored Syrah

Southern Rhône: Syrah is the star in the northern Rhône and plays an important supporting role in the red blends of the southern Rhône. Try these:

- **Châteauneuf-du-Pape**—Spicy, medium-bodied reds and full-bodied whites come from this historic region (read more in the chapter "The Other Hot Reds").
- **Gigondas**—Can't afford pricey Châteauneuf wines? My best-buy recommendation is to pick up a wine from the nearby appellation of Gigondas.
- **Côtes-du-Rhône**—Affordable reds and whites are made from grapes grown primarily in the southern Rhône region. Wines labeled *Côtes-du-Rhône Villages* are a notch higher on the quality scale.

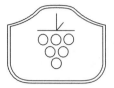
EARTHY AND VIBRANT

These cooler-climate areas produce Syrah with an earthy, spicy character and tightly wound layers of bright fruit and strong tannins. Let's kick off our journey in one of my all-time favorite wine regions—the northern Rhône.

Place: Côte Rôtie, France

Taste: I made my first trip to the Rhône out of pure passion. Years ago these elegant, spicy wines awakened my wine-loving giant, and I had to go see, taste, and feel the place.

As my rental car sped across the Rhône River south of the city of Vienne, I was grinning from ear to ear, like a kid in a candy store. The vertical hills jutting from the riverbed loomed in the distance, and when I got closer I noticed low stone walls terracing vineyards like zigzag stitching. Stubby vines were attached to stakelike poles, making the image almost surreal. Sun beating down on my back snapped me back to reality, however, and I suddenly understood why *Côte Rôtie* means "roasted slope." There is a unique intensity of flavor and finesse in Côte Rôtie wines: inky-black with smoky aromas underscored by intoxicating perfume scents and bright berry flavors. Such distinctiveness comes not only from the setting but also from the tradition of adding the white grape Viognier to fermenting Syrah. The result transcends logic. Instead of making the red wine lighter in color and flavor, cofermentation with the Viognier intensifies the wine's deep hue and adds floral, spicy notes.

Tasting Tip: Two New World producers are adding a touch of Viognier to their Syrah with great success. Try an Aussie Shiraz named The Laughing Magpie from d'Arenberg or the Cuvée Orleans from Washington's McCrea Cellars.

Côte Rôtie is famous for its two hillsides, the Côte Brune and the Côte Blonde. Legend has it that an ancient aristocrat bequeathed these plots of land to his two daughters—one of light hair and the other dark. Fittingly, the soil is quite different on the two hillsides, and wines from the Côte Brune tend toward fullness and power, while the Côte Blonde wines are lighter and more perfumed. That's terroir at work.

Place: Hermitage

Taste: From Côte Rôtie it's a short drive to the appellation of Hermitage, which is named for a dome-shaped hill that dominates the landscape. With just over three hundred acres of vineyards, the hill of Hermitage may be the oldest vineyard site in France and is responsible for producing the greatest wines of the Rhône. The region's cold nights impart deep white pepper spiciness, while the low-yielding old vines planted on the hill's meager soils develop concentrated tannins and deep berry, earthy flavors. Talk about ageworthy wines, these muscular reds can last for decades.

Two famous families—Chapoutier and Jaboulet—rule the hill, and both have massive signs marking their territory. It's a friendly rivalry dating back centuries and illustrated by Hermitage's most famous landmark, La Chapelle. The small white chapel is perched high on the hill of Hermitage, a white speck standing tall and proud, overlooking the vineyards. It housed Gaspard Chevalier de Stérimberg, a crusader of the thirteenth century who, after being injured in battle, built the chapel and became a hermit (hence the name *Hermitage*).

I'll never forget sitting in the winery cafeteria with Michel Chapoutier, the director of Maison M. Chapoutier. After a lunch of pâté paired with his smoky Côte Rôtie and homemade lasagne with a bottle of his classic Hermitage, L'Ermite (made from 120-year-old Syrah vines), Michel suggested we take a trip to see the "real" Rhône. He signaled his helicopter pilot, and in a matter of minutes I was swooping over the hill of Hermitage and neighboring appellations, viewing the region as I could never have imagined—talk about sweeping a girl off her feet.

Place: Crozes-Hermitage, France

Taste: In the shadow of the hill of Hermitage lies Crozes-Hermitage. Though
quite large, the appellation is less well
known than its neighbor and its wines
are better values (though never reach the
greatness of Hermitage). Usually ready to

drink upon release, they are spicy, earthy, and pleasantly rough around the edges. My lasting culinary impression of the northern Rhône lies in a quaint ten-table restaurant in Crozes-Hermitage named Le Bistro des Vins. The owners, a young husband and wife, served a set menu to the small crowd. When offered wine for the meal, I was not given a choice, simply asked, "Marcel's wine, of course?" Not knowing this producer, I said yes. Soon an open jug of wine arrived at the table. Fresh and fruity, it was drawn from a cask provided by the next-door neighbor and paired with eggplant terrine and slowly roasted pork. I can't remember when a bottle of wine cost so little and tasted so good.

Place: Columbia Valley, Washington

Taste: Syrah is a relative newcomer to Washington state, but I think it's poised for greatness. Flying over the Cascades from the rainy
Seattle and Puget Sound region is a total rush.
Snowcapped peaks appear out the window of
the plane, and you feel you can almost touch

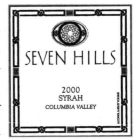

them. They give way to desertlike red earth and flat land, peppered with carpets of green vineyards. This is the Columbia Valley—one of the best places in the world to grow Syrah grapes. A warm, long growing season stretched out by bracing cool evenings lends tightness to the wine while preserving its ripeness. Syrah from Washington state (in particular those from the Yakima Valley, which is part of the larger Columbia Valley) splits the difference for me in style and taste between earthy Rhônes and jammy Australian Shiraz.

Look for these places on the label, too . . .
 Walla Walla, Washington
 Russian River Valley, California
 St.-Joseph, France
 Margaret River, Australia
 Orange, New South Wales, Australia

leslie's label links
Connecting taste to place makes wine buying easy

RICH AND FRUITY

Warmer climates lend a lush ripeness to Syrah grown in these areas. Smooth tannins, powerful fruit, and a bursting-at-the-seams fullness are the hallmarks.

Place: Barossa Valley, Australia

Taste: The succulent texture wraps you in a big bear hug, jammy fruit flavors promise pleasure, and a piquant peppery finish leaves you wanting more. That's Barossa Shiraz, mate.

How does a wine get this fun? I wondered. One step into a dry, sun-baked Barossa vineyard and it's clear. The earth is a reddish hue, the sky vibrant blue, and silvery-green eucalyptus trees tower protectively over the gnarly, century-old bush vines like bodyguards. The Barossa is often dubbed the Napa Valley of Australia since it's home to biggies like Jacob's Creek and Wolf Blass as well as cult wineries such as Rockford, Charles Melton, and Henschke. For all of the valley's fame and high-tech wineries, however, the Barossa's rugged beauty is what I think about when I sip a glass of Shiraz.

Value Tip: Shiraz is Australia's most widely planted red grape, accounting for nearly 40 percent of production. Most of the under $10 Shiraz seen on store shelves will simply say *South Eastern Australia*, which means it's made from grapes grown in the southeastern part of the country. These rank as the most consistently quaffable and affordable reds on the market.

> ### The Buzz on…Grange, the Making of an Australian Classic
>
> Australia's most famous wine is named Penfolds Grange (rhymes with *range*), and I can honestly say there is nothing in the world to compare to its opaque black color, aromas of smoked meat, coconut, and bittersweet chocolate, and its thick, chewy texture. In 1951 Penfolds' winemaker, Max Schubert, made an experimental wine called *Grange Hermitage* (it's now simply called *Grange*). Inspired by a trip to Bordeaux, where he had the opportunity to taste decades-old wines, Schubert vowed to make an ageworthy wine to compete with the best in the world. But he didn't have French oak or Cabernet Sauvignon, so Schubert used the raw materials he did have—Shiraz and American oak barrels. It was a match made in heaven. At first people thought he was crazy, and for years he had to make the wine in secret. After a decade of struggle, however, Grange found the recognition it deserved and went on to redefine Australian wine. A bottle of Grange, if you can find it, will drain your bank account of approximately $150–200. Save this one for a special occasion!

Place: McLaren Vale, Australia

Taste: Sip a Barossa Shiraz next to one from McLaren Vale and you'll notice a difference—the Barossa is thick like velvet, while the McLaren Vale is opulently sleek like satin. This streak of elegance comes from the region's proximity to cooling sea breezes that moderate the warm Aussie sunshine. Located less than an hour's drive south of the city of Adelaide, gently rolling hills  are covered with old-vine vineyards dating back a century or more. Shiraz thrives in this climate because grapes are afforded the luxury of a long time to hang on the vine and slowly develop their flavors while maintaining vibrant acidity. Look for the big producers such as BRL Hardy, but don't miss terrific Shiraz from smaller wineries such as Shingleback, Coriole, and Kangarilla Road. (All range in price from $19–25.)

Place: Chile

Taste: Chile has a reputation for producing easy-to-drink Cabs, and I think its Syrah will soon start upstaging other New World spots. Rich, ripe fruit flavors, soft tannins, and sometimes a hint of mint define these wines.  Syrah is a newcomer to Chile brought by Eduardo Chadwick of Viña Errazuriz in 1994. He suspected it would adapt well to the climate and terrain, and he was right. When planted on flatlands, Syrah vines produce generally affordable, good-quality wine. However, winemakers are now heading for the hills and planting vines on slopes where Syrah is sure to shine even brighter. Keep an eye out for intense, supple Syrah from the Aconcagua Valley. My advice is to grab any Syrah you see from Chile and try it.

Place: Sonoma County, California

Taste: "Shiraz varies from the Barossa to Sonoma yet maintains a common thread of big, rich, ripe fruit all with a friendly approach; an honest wine with great density and integrity," says winemaker Michael Scholz.  He should know since this Barossa-born Aussie and his American wife, Lisa, now make their own coveted Sonoma County Shiraz named Baystone. Sonoma County is one of the top regions for Syrah in the whole state, and from the cooling reaches of Russian River to the warm stretches of Dry Creek Valley, Syrah from Sonoma should serve up a generous mouthful of fruit and spice.

Place: California

Taste: Syrah labeled simply *California* is starting to compete with low-cost versions from Australia. Can it match up? So far these wines are not terribly complex, but the price is right for an easy quaff.

Value Tip: Try the Delicato Family Vineyards Shiraz from California. Tagged at around $5–7, it's one of those rare finds that tastes like it costs twice, maybe even thrice, the price.

Look for these places on the label, too . . .

Dry Creek Valley, California

El Dorado, California

Livermore Valley, California

Cornas, France

Languedoc, France

The Buzz on . . . French Wine Laws, the Birthmother of Them All

The letters *AOC* or *AC* on a French wine label stands for *Appellation d'Origine Contrôlée*—or "controlled place of origin." Beginning around 1936, the French developed a way to delineate and regulate wines by region, and it has become the model for all subsequent classification systems. Within the regions—or appellations—detailed guidelines pertaining to types of grapes that can be planted, production levels, and wine-making techniques are set forth by a government organization. Though it doesn't guarantee that every AOC wine is excellent, the system helps to protect against fraud and keep quality fairly high. The downside is that it's very restrictive. Those who want to experiment can choose to bottle wines under the *vin de pays* category (theoretically a step below those tagged AOC) because the regulations are much looser. Interestingly, vin de pays wine is garnering a lot of attention these days. Much of the wine sold in the United States comes from the massive Languedoc-Roussillon region in southern France. Many good-value bottles, often between $5–8, will indicate the grape variety and can taste better than wines carrying an AC pedigree. Look especially for Syrah tagged *Vin de Pays d'Oc* from Barton & Guestier (known as B&G) and Georges Duboeuf.

A MATTER OF STYLE

Unlike other agricultural products that are heavily fertilized, showered with water, and planted on fertile soils, grapes destined to become wine are subjected to tough love. Many winemakers take a no pain, no gain approach to grape growing. Vines need to "suffer," they say, to produce top-quality grapes.

Syrah: The Virile Vine

In the vineyard Syrah is a stud. It's a prolific vine that propagates with ease, and often winemakers or growers must intervene to restrict the amount of fruit each vine produces. This focuses the vine's energy on developing a small number of flavorful grape clusters instead of many, potentially less flavorful ones.

With Syrah two factors act like saltpeter to keep the vine in check: slope and soil. If Syrah is planted on steep hillsides, the roots struggle to survive and nourish the plant. Naturally the vine will restrict itself and produce less fruit with generally smaller berries. A vineyard's soil also makes a difference. As Eric Dunham, of the hot Washington winery Dunham Cellars, says, "Syrah is definitely a more vigorous plant than most and needs very low-vigor soils to concentrate fruit quality."

Making the vines suffer does produce smaller, more intense grapes, but how does that translate to better wine?

If red grapes are small in size, they have a higher skin-to-juice ratio when they hit the fermentation tanks. More skin and less juice equals deeper color, tannin, and flavor extraction. Think of it as making chicken soup: too much broth and too little chicken and noodles, and the final soup will have less flavor.

The Buzz on...Organic Wines

One of the toughest questions I'm asked is which "organic" wines I recommend. It's difficult to answer, because *organic* can mean so many things. For a finished wine to be considered organic, it must have been produced from organically grown grapes and have been made without additions of yeasts, fining agents, and sulfites, which protect against spoilage. Since most commercial wineries won't take the risk of putting potentially spoiled wines on the market, there are very few purely organic wines. There are, however, many producers worldwide who grow grapes with chemical-free, organic methods, including M. Chapoutier and Château de Beaucastel from the Rhône, Bonterra and Fetzer Vineyards, Robert Sinskey, Marimar Torres, and Frog's Leap wineries in California, Sokol Blosser from Oregon, and New Zealand's Seresin Estate.

Shopping Guide

Stash-Your-Cash Syrah/Shiraz Under $15

	Name of Wine	From	Style Profile	Price Range
PW	Hardys, "Stamp of Australia," Shiraz	South Eastern Australia	Medium-bodied, light tannins, bright and fruity	$5–7
	Rosemount, "Diamond Label," Shiraz	South Eastern Australia	Medium-bodied, light tannins, bright and fruity	$7–10
PF	Penfolds, "Thomas Hyland," Shiraz	South Australia	Medium-bodied, supple tannins, smooth and fruity	$10–13
	Covey Run Winery, Syrah	Washington state	Medium-bodied, light tannins, bright and fruity	$9–11
GW	Jacob's Creek, Reserve, Shiraz	South Eastern Australia	Medium-bodied, light tannins, bright and fruity	$9–11
PW	Barton & Guestier, Syrah	Vin de Pays d'Oc, France	Medium-bodied, light tannins, bright and fruity	$6–8
	McDowell Valley Vineyards, Syrah	Mendocino, California	Medium-bodied, light tannins, bright and fruity	$9–12
PF	Grant Burge, "Barossa Vines," Shiraz	Barossa, Australia	Medium-bodied, supple tannins, smooth and fruity	$9–12
PW	Delicato Family Vineyards, Shiraz	California	Medium-bodied, supple tannins, smooth and fruity	$5–7

Well-Known Winners $15–30

Name of Wine	From	Style Profile	Price Range
Paul Jaboulet Aine, "Les Jalets"	Crozes-Hermitage, France	Medium-bodied, strong tannins, bright and earthy	$15–18

	Name of Wine	From	Style Profile	Price Range
	Alain Graillot, Crozes-Hermitage	Crozes-Hermitage, France	Medium-bodied, strong tannins, bright and earthy	$15–18
GW	Yalumba, Barossa Shiraz	Barossa Valley, Australia	Medium-bodied, supple tannins, smooth and fruity	$17–20
PF	d'Arenberg, Shiraz, "The Footbolt"	McLaren Vale, Australia	Medium-bodied, supple tannins, bright and earthy	$17–20
GW	Caliterra, "Arboleda," Syrah	Colchagua Valley, Chile	Medium-bodied, supple tannins, bright and earthy	$17–20
	Columbia Crest, "Reserve" Syrah	Columbia Valley, Washington	Medium-bodied, supple tannins, bright and earthy	$25–29
	Geyser Peak Winery, Shiraz	Sonoma County, California	Full-bodied, supple tannins, smooth and ripe	$15–18
	Montes, "Alpha," Syrah	Colchagua Valley, Chile	Full-bodied, supple tannins, smooth and ripe	$14–18
	Chateau Reynella, "Basket Press," Shiraz	McLaren Vale, South Australia	Full-bodied, supple tannins, smooth and ripe	$25–28

Luxury Sips

Worth-the-Splurge Wines $30–50+

	Name of Wine	From	Style Profile	Price Range
GW	McCrea Cellars, Syrah	Yakima Valley, Washington	Medium-bodied, supple tannins, bright and earthy	$43–48
	Columbia Winery, "Red Willow," Syrah	Yakima Valley, Washington	Medium-bodied, supple tannins, bright and earthy	$38–42
PF	DeLille Cellars, "Doyenne," Syrah	Yakima Valley, Washington	Medium-bodied, supple tannins, bright and earthy	$38–42

	Name of Wine	From	Style Profile/Price	Price Range
	Stag's Leap Winery, Syrah	Napa Valley, California	Full-bodied, supple tannins, smooth and ripe	$28–32
PF	Wolf Blass, "Platinum Label," Shiraz	Barossa Valley, Australia	Full-bodied, supple tannins, smooth and ripe	$38–42
	Arrowood Vineyards and Winery, Syrah	Sonoma Valley, California	Full-bodied, supple tannins, smooth and ripe	$48–50
PF	Guigal, "Brune et Blonde," Côte-Rôtie	Côte-Rôtie, France	Full-bodied, strong tannins, earthy and ripe	$42–46
CW	M. Chapoutier, "La Sizeranne," Hermitage	Hermitage, France	Full-bodied, strong tannins, earthy and ripe	$75–85
CW	J.L. Chave, Hermitage	Hermitage, France	Full-bodied, strong tannins, earthy and ripe	$95–125

Surprise Sips

Unique Wines Worth Seeking Out

	Name of Wine	From	Style Profile	Price Range
PW	Reynolds Vineyards, Shiraz	New South Wales, Australia	Medium-bodied, light tannins, bright and fruity	$7–10
	Xanadu, Shiraz	Margaret River, Australia	Medium-bodied, supple tannins, bright and earthy	$15–18
PF	Kangarilla Road, Shiraz	McLaren Vale, Australia	Medium-bodied, supple tannins, bright and earthy	$18–20
GW	Novy Cellars, Syrah	Napa Valley, California	Medium-bodied, supple tannins, bright and earthy	$20–22
	Domaine du Monteillet, "Cuvée du Papy"	St.-Joseph, France	Medium-bodied, strong tannins, bright and earthy	$25–28

	Name of Wine	From	Style Profile	Price Range
	Fox Creek, "Short Row," Shiraz	McLaren Vale, South Australia	Full-bodied, supple tannins, smooth and ripe	$26–30
CW PW	Dunham Cellars, Syrah	Columbia Valley, Washington	Full-bodied, supple tannins, smooth and ripe	$45–50

pairing

SYRAH IS THE ULTIMATE COMFORT WINE AND THE ideal companion to anything slow-cooked and rich. Whether it's osso buco, pot roast, or roasted lamb, if it falls apart with the touch of a fork, then I want Syrah.

But you don't need to be a meat eater to enjoy the charms of Syrah. From risotto to ratatouille or mushrooms to mole, this smoky red works beautifully.

The Buzz from … Victoria Angove,
Angove's of Australia

Victoria Angove is the fifth generation involved in one of Australia's largest family-owned wine companies. Their Shiraz-Cabernet blend tips the cash scales at a mere $8 or so, and according to Victoria "goes extremely well with kangaroo with a quince and black pepper glaze accompanied by fresh vegetables." For those of us without regular access to kangaroo meat, she suggests a good steak with a mushroom sauce or gnocchi with a rich tomato and eggplant sauce.

Let's Talk Texture First: Is it medium or full, smooth or chewy?
Syrah is a big wine. These reds need powerful, full-flavored dishes with meat on their bones.

Consider It a Complement: Are there earthy, fruity aromas or spicy, meaty flavors?
Go for the mushrooms and eggplant or head for the plum sauce and pepper shaker. The smoky, meaty notes of the wine augment a hunk of meat off the barbecue beautifully.

It's Tannin Time: Does the wine have noticeable levels of tannins?

If it makes your mouth pucker when you take a sip, serve it alongside a piece of meat or cheese. Keep in mind that French Syrahs from the northern Rhône will be more tannic than Australian or California versions.

Design-a-Dinner

STOCK YOUR SHELVES

Bottoms: Steak, burgers, roasts, lamb, sausages, bacon, ham, prosciutto, chicken, duck, pilaf, pasta, sweet potato

Tops: Mushrooms, olives, dates, plums, zucchini, red bell peppers, eggplant, cheeses (Parmesan, pecorino, smoked Gouda), barbecue sauce, plum sauce

Accessories: Oregano, rosemary, sage, herbes de Provence

GET SAUCY . . . WITH SYRAH

Fruity Plum Sauce: Finely chop several dried apricots and prunes. Combine with 1/4 cup red wine and a 7-ounce jar of store-bought plum sauce. Simmer in a saucepan over low heat until the fruit softens. Use as a topping for pork roasts or chicken or pass at the table as a dipping sauce.

Olive-Pepper Salsa: Roast 1 red bell pepper in the broiler, then peel it and chop into small pieces. Sauté 1 cup small whole mushrooms and 1 minced garlic clove until brown and slightly soft. Let the mixture cool and then mince finely. In a small bowl combine all the vegetables and add them to 1/4 cup chopped pitted Kalamata olives. Marinate the mixture with a dash of olive oil, a shake of hot red pepper flakes, and rosemary, and a squirt of lime or lemon juice. Add salt and pepper to taste and serve on toasted bread or use it to stuff chicken breasts and pork chops or on pizza.

MEAL ENSEMBLES

Bacon-Wrapped Dates: These are so easy and always a hit. Wrap dried, pitted dates in a small piece of bacon. Place on a baking sheet and bake until the bacon is crispy.

Roasted Garlic: Garlic loses its pungency and gains a sweet smoothness when it's roasted slowly, making it a perfect pairing with Syrah. Take a whole head of garlic and trim off $1/2$ inch of the top to expose the flesh inside. Drizzle the whole garlic head with olive oil and oven roast at 375°F for 45–60 minutes until the cloves are soft. Squeeze out each clove and slather on toasted pita bread triangles.

Plum Pork and Sweet Potato Casserole: Generously cover 1 pork tenderloin with Fruity Plum Sauce (page 186) and roast in a 375°F oven until thoroughly cooked.

Sweet Potato Casserole: Grease a casserole pan with butter, and layer peeled rounds of 2 russet and 2 sweet potatoes (slices should be approximately $1/4$ inch thick), alternating the type of potato with each layer. Sprinkle a bit of salt on each layer. Pour milk over the casserole until it almost reaches the top layer. Dot the whole pan with pieces of butter. Bake uncovered in a 375°F oven until the potatoes are tender and the top is crispy. Serve immediately with the roast pork.

Grilled Portobello Sandwich: This is essentially a gourmet grilled cheese. Start by grilling or sautéing a whole portobello mushroom, then slice it into thick strips. Lightly butter one side of each of 2 slices of white or wheat bread. Spread the unbuttered side of 1 slice of bread generously with Olive-Pepper Salsa (page 186) and alternate layers of provolone cheese and portobello mushroom strips. Cover with the other piece of bread, unbuttered side toward the filling, and grill the sandwich until the cheese is bubbly and the bread is golden brown.

Ratatouille with Spicy Sausages: Roughly chop 1 onion, several garlic cloves, 2 or 3 zucchini, 1 red bell pepper, 1 eggplant, and several tomatoes. Sauté the onion, garlic, and bell pepper in olive oil, stirring occasionally, until the vegetables are browning on the outside. Add the zucchini, eggplant, and tomatoes and cook the mixture until extremely soft, adding a dash of wine, if necessary, to keep everything from sticking. When done, the mixture will be almost stewlike in consistency. Stir in 1 or 2 teaspoons of herbes de Provence and black pepper. In a separate pan, cook your favorite sausages and serve alongside the ratatouille.

Rosemary Lamb and Pilaf: Rub lamb chops with salt and freshly cracked black pepper. Place in a dish, drizzle with herb-infused olive oil, and cover with sprigs of fresh rosemary. Let the chops sit, covered, in the refrigerator for several hours or overnight. Cook the lamb chops over a hot grill until they are just pink on the inside. Add ¼ cup each of chopped pitted prunes and sliced almonds to a box of prepared rice pilaf. Serve alongside the lamb.

MELISSA REGULARLY ENTERTAINS CLIENTS AT HIGH-end restaurants. As host for the evening, the selection of the wine inevitably falls to her. "Help!" she said in a recent phone call. Could I give her any surefire tips for navigating a wine list?

Whether faced with a sixty-page tome or a one-page wine list, I said, just remember a few pointers:

○ **Get the lay of the land.** Look at the list to see how it is set up. Most traditional lists organize wines by categories such as grape variety and region. This is helpful if you know you like Merlot, for example. But there is a trend these days to rank wines according to the way they taste. These "progressive" wine lists are helpful because they separate bottles from relatively light-to full-bodied, from mild to strong tasting, and from dry to sweet.

- **Find your price comfort zone.** Don't be pressured into spending more money than you want. Just be open-minded. If $40 is your limit, look for all the wines up to that amount, including unfamiliar ones. Restaurants aren't always the best place to experiment if bottles are really pricey, but if you feel comfortable with the price tag, play around.

- **Consider the markup.** Markups at restaurants cover overhead such as storage of wine, service, and stemware. But, markups are all over the map. Some restaurants charge double what you would pay retail for a bottle of wine while others triple that price! Just to complicate matters even more, lower-priced wines are often marked up the most, while the high-priced beauties have lower price hikes. Luckily some restaurants are getting hip to consumer-friendly pricing strategies. They actually want diners to enjoy wine with dinner and are pricing all wine at $5 or $10 over retail.

- **Think about the food.** Put the list down and decide what you're having for dinner. Meat? Fish? Light, delicate food or heavy, rich cuisine? Don't worry about the perfect match, but remember to consider the weight and texture of the food and the wine.

- **Be a gracious host.** Ask people at the table what they like. Red or white, sweet or dry, light or full? That's part of the fun of wine. Be prudent, though. There's nothing worse than listening to the know-it-all at the table go on and on. As master sommelier, Peter Granoff says, "In more than twenty years of working as a sommelier, I never once saw a woman grab the wine list and show off how much she knew about wine!"

- **Look at half bottle and by-the-glass options.** Half bottles are my favorite option on a wine list. I immediately gravitate toward these .375 ml bottles that contain about two to three glasses. If you're dining alone or on a romantic date, it's the perfect size. Have a group of people with diverse opinions and menu desires? Order a few half bottles. Wine bars and savvy restaurants are beginning to treat wines served by the glass with the credibility they deserve, too. Many establishments even serve tasting "flights" so you can sample several different sips with your meal.

- **Ask for help.** I generally consult the sommelier to compare notes and seek out the hidden gems or great value wines on his or her list. The sommelier of today doesn't wear an old ashtray around his neck or stick her nose in the air when asked questions. On the contrary, sommeliers are usually the ones who put the wine list together and want nothing more than to help you find what you desire. Keep these three things in mind when asking for help: the price you're comfortable with, the type of wine you like, and what you plan on eating.

   If you want to be discreet about the price, point to a bottle on the list in the price range you want and indicate you'd like a comparable wine.

- **Should you really sniff the cork?** There is no need to pick up the cork and smell it. Simply eye it to make sure it's intact and moist. After the taste has been poured for you, feel free to swirl it and take a quick smell and taste. Unless the wine is flawed, say thanks and enjoy your meal.

Pinot Noir/Burgundy
THE "SEDUCTIVE SATIN" RED

buying

THERE'S SOMETHING MAGICAL ABOUT WEARING SATIN. Seductive and compelling, it's not an everyday wardrobe choice. When you want something special, though, the sleek feeling of the fabric is hard to match.

Like satin, a great Pinot Noir is extraordinary. Stunning bottles are elusive, but that's hardly discouraging to true Pinot fanatics. We're a loyal lot and put up with one (or three or five) bland bottles for the promise of a silky, graceful, amazing Pinot Noir the next time.

THE GRAPE STORY

Pinot Noir is not only the temptress of wine, but the diva of grape varieties. Pinot insists everything be perfect—from climate to winemaking—or it won't perform to its potential.

Part of the grape's demanding nature is that it thrives only in select wine-growing regions, which push the climate envelope. Pinot prefers cool places bordering on cold and needs every ray of sunshine to ripen fully. These conditions allow for the maximum time grapes spend on the vine—called *hang time*—to slowly develop their flavors.

Due to their thinner skin, Pinot Noir grapes produce wines that are lighter in tannins and color than other reds. (I think of it as silky sheer panty hose to Cabernet Sauvignon's or Syrah's opaque tights.) Once in the cellar, winemakers have to treat the sensitive grapes gently, or the hard-earned quality gained in the vineyard can be lost. No wonder Pinot Noir is often called the *heartbreak grape.*

THE NAME GAME

Pinot Noir = red Burgundy

When you see the French growing region *Burgundy,* or *Bourgogne,* on a bottle of red wine, you know the wine is made from Pinot Noir grapes. The exception is Beaujolais, which is an area in the southern part of Burgundy planted to the Gamay grape.

Lingo Lesson

Core Words

Dry: Pinot Noir and those labeled red Burgundy are dry wines. Not as dry tasting as Sangiovese-based wines like Chianti, but usually drier tasting than Australian Shiraz, for example.

Bright: A fairly-high-acid grape, Pinot produces wines that exhibit brightness and zip. In New World spots such as California, the wines often seem smoother and fleshier but still with vibrant character.

Light- to medium-bodied: I think of Pinot as the 1940s' red-headed pin-up girl, the slim yet curvaceous Rita Hayworth.

Light to medium tannins: Pinot Noir is inherently less tannic than thicker-skinned grape varieties. If you prefer reds with lighter tannins, Pinot Noir is a wine to try.

Extra Credit Words

Fruit aromas:

Red fruits—cherry, cranberry, raspberry, strawberry

Black fruits—black cherry, blueberry, plum

Spicy: Though not as overtly spicy as Syrah or Zinfandel, for example, Pinot Noir is often described as smelling of clove, nutmeg, and pepper.

Earthy, tea leaves, mushrooms: Characteristic aromas of moist earth, fresh mushrooms, and dry tea leaves define great Pinot Noir for me.

Elegant: When a wine is described as elegant, there's a balance among all the components that contribute to its subtle style. It's not about power but about grace.

Silky: A great Pinot will have all the *nesses*: smoothness, silkiness, and suppleness.

My Pinot Obsession

I was seduced early on by a bottle of Burgundy. Like a first boyfriend, that experience created an emotional connection to Pinot that has only been strengthened over time. Opening each new bottle, I secretly hope to capture that feeling of first love again.

If you're not a Pinot Noir admirer, I understand. Discovering wines you like is often a game of hit or miss. For those fellow Pinot fans, though, you're nodding your head in agreement. Pinot Noir is worth the effort.

In today's world, where so many wines taste the same regardless of their origin, Pinot Noir is distinct and speaks to your soul. An amazing bottle will transport you to its birthplace, if only for a moment, and for me, that's the journey of wine.

leslie's label links

Connecting taste to place makes wine buying easy

BRIGHT AND EARTHY

Pinot Noir's home is the Burgundy region of France. With a cool continental climate and limestone soils, the region produces elegant reds with bright fruit and a savory earthiness. But Burgundy doesn't have a lock on this style of Pinot. Just look halfway across the world to Oregon, which some folks fittingly call *Burgundy West*.

Place: Bourgogne, France

Taste: Affordable wines labeled simply *Bourgogne* are made with grapes grown in the entire Burgundy region. They tend to be the lightest and least complex reds, but in the hands of a good producer they offer freshness, bright cherry fruit, and pleasing earthiness. Start with these on your journey to discover Burgundy.

Somewhere Over the Côte d'Or

No other place in the world has been able to embrace, coddle, and caress the grape like Burgundy, in particular the thirty-mile slice of sloping land called the *Côte d'Or* (or "golden slope"). I think of this tiny patchwork of vineyards as the Judy Garland of wine regions. Just as Judy was a petite thing with a booming, world-famous voice, the Côte d'Or is small but oh-so-powerful in the world of wine.

The Côte d'Or is broken down into two smaller regions roughly separated by the city of Beaune. The Côte de Nuits lies to the north of Beaune, and the Côte de Beaune lies to the south.

Place: Chambolle-Musigny, Côte de Nuits, Burgundy

Taste: The delicate and floral-scented wines of Chambolle are among my favorite red Burgundies. Whenever people ask me how to start exploring wines from the Côte d'Or, I recommend Chambolle-Musigny. It  is a fairly easy one to remember and rarely disappoints. Closing my eyes, I can smell the dusty cherry aromas and moist earth, taste the hints of cocoa powder, and feel the texture of silk. The small commune (*commune* is another name for the village and its surrounding vineyards) is situated between the Côte de Nuits region of Gevrey-Chambertin and Burgundy's largest vineyard, the 125-acre Clos de Vougeot. Though famous grand cru vineyards of Chambolle such as Les Musigny and Les Bonnes Mares are fabulous and expensive, my heart belongs to the premier cru vineyard wines named Les Amoureuses and Les Charmes.

Place: Vosne-Romanée, Côte de Nuits, Burgundy

Taste: It's hard to talk about the red wines of Burgundy without mentioning those velvety, rich wonders from the Côte de Nuits' most famous commune,  Vosne-Romanée. Wines from this minuscule area command some of the highest prices in the wine world.

The first time I saw these world-famous vineyards, I was expecting grandeur. Imagine my surprise when I stood on the small road at the base of the hill and looked up to see gently sloping vineyards that appeared no bigger than several baseball fields. That's when it dawned on me: This is it for the entire world. That's all, folks! No wonder each bottle of the highly limited amount of wine produced from these vineyards each year costs hundreds, and sometimes thousands, of dollars.

Value Tip: *Value* is a relative term here, considering the average tag of these wines, but to taste the uniqueness of the place, search for moderately priced village wines labeled simply *Vosne-Romanée*. You can usually find a delicious wine starting around $30.

Place: Volnay, Côte de Beaune, Burgundy

Taste: When I first had the courage to spend money on Burgundy, I stumbled upon the well-priced reds of Volnay. They are more earthy and penetratingly tart than Chambolle but with the same perfumed floral aromas, lightness, and  elegance. Don't be disappointed if you find Volnay a little lean upon opening. Take a bite of food, and it will change. Once while dining at a family-run eatery in the rustic hills above the city of Beaune, I had a date with a bottle of Volnay from the premier cru vineyard named Les Caillerets. At first the wine seemed tight and rather uninspired, then a steamy plate of *boeuf à la Bourguignonne* arrived, and the wine expanded in the glass to challenge the savory stew head-on. The result was a culinary match made in heaven.

Place: Oregon

Taste: If you find the earthiness of some Burgundies too much, jump over the pond to Oregon. Pinot Noir is the state's most widely planted grape and has become Oregon's signature wine. Bright and a  touch earthy, Oregon Pinot Noirs are so easy to sip because they overflow with fruit. I consider them the "girl-next-door" versions of

Pinot Noir since just about everyone enjoys their friendly, approachable style.

Place: Willamette Valley, Oregon

Taste: The Willamette Valley is located about an hour's drive southwest of Portland. While driving there through forests of pine trees and huge fruit orchards, you definitely get the impression this is fertile land. The maritime climate with its long, cool growing season is ideal for growing grapes, but it wasn't until the late 1960s and 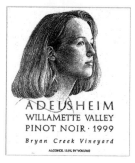 early 1970s that founders of Oregon's wine industry—people like David Lett, Dick Ponzi, and Susan Sokol Blosser—suspected this was the Promised Land for Pinot Noir. They were right. Top wines capture the beautiful black cherry quality of the grape, while maintaining a sense of underlying earthiness and structure. The Willamette Valley is sometimes called *Burgundy West* because so many Burgundians have come to live and work there. It's quite a fitting moniker, too, since many of the wines emerging from the largest wine-growing region in the state are reminiscent of the elegance of top Burgundy.

Look for these places on the label, too . . .

Mercurey, Burgundy

Casablanca, Chile

Yarra Valley, Australia

Tasmania

The Buzz from . . . Susan Sokol Blosser,
Sokol Blosser Winery, Oregon

In the Willamette Valley is a special place called the Red Hills of Dundee. Some of the most highly regarded Pinot producers in the state—including Domaine Drouhin, Archery Summit, Domaine Serene, and Sokol Blosser—call this unique spot home. "The Dundee Hills, with its distinctive red clay–loam soil, has become the epicenter of the finest Oregon Pinot Noir. Why? I can't point to just one thing. It's how it all comes together on these hillsides to create the perfect place for growing Pinot Noir grapes with complex and wonderful flavor," muses Susan.

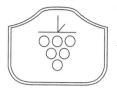
JUICY AND RIPE

Less earth, loads of spiciness, and explosive fruitiness make up Pinot's profile in these New World spots. Sure, some might be a bit warmer than Burgundy, but essentially they are still cool-climate regions with a long growing season, perfect for the diva grape.

Place: Marlborough, New Zealand

Taste: Marlborough is not just for Sauvignon Blanc anymore. Unlike Burgundy and Oregon, where harvest rains can be an issue, Marlborough is dry in the fall, allowing the grapes to ripen gradually during the long, cool growing season. I think Marlborough will ultimately prove to be one of New Zealand's top spots for Pinot.

Value Tip: One of my favorite Marlborough-based wineries is Villa Maria. Their well-crafted wines are widely available and span the price spectrum from zesty Sauvignon Blanc for a cool $12 to complex Pinot Noir for around $25.

Place: Martinborough, New Zealand

Taste: Add the elegance of a Chambolle-Musigny to the supple tannins of an Oregon bottling and the pure fruit of a top California Pinot, and what do you get? Martinborough Pinot Noir. While up-and-coming South Island regions like Central Otago and Marlborough get attention, the home of Pinot Noir in New

Zealand is the North Island spot of Martinborough in the Wairarapa region. It has Pinot Noir roots dating back to the late 1880s, but only in the past two decades has it again taken center stage. Vines are planted on an ancient riverbed with well-drained soils, and the cool

climate tends to be more like Burgundy since Martinborough rests inland from the water. Warm sunny days coupled with cold nights helps to develop rich, fruity Pinot with hints of cocoa powder and exotic spice notes.

Place: Russian River Valley, California

Taste: To complete our worldwide Pinot Noir tour, we need to cross another ocean and land in California. With their intensity of fruit and velvety texture, wines from northern California's Russian River Valley offer one of the best expressions of Pinot Noir in the world. Oddly enough, it was not a tasting trip that made me fall in love with this region; it was a camping jaunt. As I drove about an hour and a half north of San Francisco's urban congestion, I hit rural paradise. Taking a walk through the small town of Guerneville tucked in along the river's wooded banks, I was sure I was going to spot a weathered lumberjack resting his ax in a saloon because the feel of the place is still so laid-back. When I woke up the next morning and my tent was shrouded with fog, I realized this cool, coastal climate is the reason redwoods and Pinot Noir flourish in the Russian River Valley.

MERRY EDWARDS
2000
RUSSIAN RIVER VALLEY
PINOT NOIR
KLOPP RANCH
MÉTHODE À L'ANCIENNE
ALCOHOL 14.4% BY VOLUME

Although the valley has been an important wine-growing region for more than a century, Pinot Noir really took off in the 1960s. Today the Russian River boasts a high concentration of recognized

---

The Buzz from...Kate MacMurray, MacMurray
Ranch in Russian River Valley

When Kate's dad, actor Fred MacMurray of "My Three Sons" television fame, and her mom, actress, June Haver, entertained at their ranch in Russian River Valley, Kate remembers wine as an integral part of every meal. "Growing up, we'd have John Wayne and Jimmy Stewart over for dinner, and there was always great food, wine, and conversation. My parents both loved to cook, and we raised our own cattle, had fresh milk and garden vegetables and canned fruit from our trees. My dad particularly enjoyed Pinot Noir, and now we make it from grapes on the property. He would be just thrilled."

producers such as Williams Selyem and Gary Farrell and rising stars such as Sapphire Hill and MacMurray Ranch.

Place: Anderson Valley, California

Taste: In my never-ending search for the Pinot Promised Land, I've added Anderson Valley to the short list. One of California's coolest growing regions (the average temperature is fifty-six degrees), it's home to the best Gewurztraminer outside Alsace

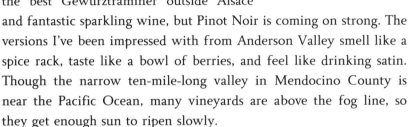

and fantastic sparkling wine, but Pinot Noir is coming on strong. The versions I've been impressed with from Anderson Valley smell like a spice rack, taste like a bowl of berries, and feel like drinking satin. Though the narrow ten-mile-long valley in Mendocino County is near the Pacific Ocean, many vineyards are above the fog line, so they get enough sun to ripen slowly.

Place: Santa Lucia Highlands, California

Taste: I predict great things for this coastal California hot spot, a fairly new region in terms of popularity and recognition. Located in Monterey County, the Highlands are actually a little band of vine-

yards perched on mountainous slopes that block the warm Salinas Valley from the cold Monterey Bay winds. Grapes planted here take in the sun and thrive in the fog. This combination produces spicy, rich, and, above all, velvety Pinot Noir. Keep your eye out for wines from the Pisoni vineyard, such as my favorites from Testarossa and Siduri.

Place: Santa Maria Valley, California

Taste: Part of the larger Santa Barbara area, Santa Maria is a unique appellation. Warm spring days give the coastal region a distinctly Mediterranean feel, but cool, foggy summers create an extremely long growing season. Pinot Noir is in heaven

here, and it shows in the bottle, with silky, fruit-driven Pinots. Wines produced in this region include those from the world-famous Bien Nacido vineyard.

The Buzz on…Julia's Vineyard, Santa Maria Valley's Rising Star

Santa Maria Valley wine producer Cambria is well known for its Chardonnay, but its Julia's Pinot Noir has captured my heart. "My husband, Jess Jackson, and I named the vineyard after our daughter because we thought Pinot Noir was like Julia—elegant, dramatic, somewhat persnickety, but capable of great beauty," says owner Barbara Banke. Other Pinot Noir beauties from Julia's vineyard are made by Lane Tanner, Hitching Post, and Benjamin Silver.

Look for these places on the label, too . . .
Carneros, California
Santa Barbara, California
Sonoma Coast, California
Central Otago, New Zealand

A MATTER OF STYLE

Place is paramount when it comes to the taste of Pinot Noir. As Maison Louis Jadot's winemaker, Jacques Lardière, says, "The wine is a key to the place where it comes from." Only when top-notch grapes come in from the vineyard can gentle wine-making techniques unlock and amplify that quality in the final wine.

In the Vineyard: The Big *T*

The way the place expresses itself in the glass is what the French call *terroir*, and there is no other wine region in the world where it has as much meaning as in Burgundy.

Inches separate grand cru vineyards from premier cru ones. One row of vines might be planted in limestone soil, situated on a slope gradient that drains properly and benefits from the optimal amount of daily sunshine, while a neighboring row's conditions change slightly. Each row produces a different quality of grape.

How in the world would someone figure out that minute amount of detail? She would need the patience of a saint! Well, in Burgundy it was as close as you can get—monks. Beginning in the twelfth century, Cistercian monks planted vineyards in Burgundy and began recording the particulars on places that made the best wines. Over time the monks (and subsequent winemakers) narrowed down each plot of land row by row to find the premier spots. This is why Burgundy is so wonderful and so complicated at the same time.

What's a Winemaker to Do in the Cellar?

The heartbreak grape should also be called the *hands-off grape* when it comes to winemaking. So-called "Burgundian" techniques are employed to preserve fragile Pinot Noir's character. From soaking the grapes in cold water for a few days to gently extract color before fermentation begins, to keeping temperatures low during fermentation, everything is done with a delicate touch.

There are two other important techniques worth mentioning that affect the ultimate taste of Pinot Noir.

Go Wild . . .

Many winemakers choose to ferment their wines naturally. Instead of adding cultured yeasts to kick off fermentation, they allow the wine to begin fermenting with the yeasts that live naturally on the grape skins. Wild yeasts are less reliable than inoculation (or adding cultured yeasts), but winemakers take the risk because they believe it results in a more complex wine.

. . . But Don't Strip

Ever see the word *unfiltered* or *unfined* on a wine label? Both filtering and fining are simply processes used to remove sediment and particles from the wine to make it more stable in the bottle. Because Pinot is so delicate, winemakers often decide not to filter or fine their wine because they feel it may strip out flavor.

Shopping Guide

Stash-Your-Cash Wines $20 and Under

	Name of Wine	From	Style Profile	Price Range
GW	Louis Latour, Pinot Noir, Bourgogne	Burgundy, France	Light-bodied, light tannins, bright and earthy	$8–12
	Boisset, Bourgogne Rouge	Burgundy, France	Light-bodied, light tannins, bright and earthy	$8–12
PW	Beaulieu Vineyards, "Coastal," Pinot Noir	California	Light-bodied, light tannins, bright and fruity	$7–10
PW	Robert Mondavi, "Private Selection," Pinot Noir	Central Coast, California	Light-bodied, light tannins, bright and fruity	$9–11
	Villa Mt. Eden, "Coastal," Pinot Noir	Central Coast, California	Light-bodied, light tannins, bright and fruity	$9–11
PF	Turning Leaf, "Coastal Reserve," Pinot Noir	North Coast, California,	Light-bodied, light tannins, bright and fruity	$9–11
	Echelon, Pinot Noir	Central Coast, California	Light-bodied, light tannins, bright and fruity	$9–13
	Erath, Pinot Noir	Oregon	Light-bodied, light tannins, bright and earthy	$13–15
PW	Chateau St. Jean, Pinot Noir	Sonoma County, California	Medium-bodied, light tannins, bright and fruity	$15–18
	Charles Krug, Pinot Noir	Carneros, California	Medium-bodied, light tannins, bright and fruity	$15–18
	Kenwood, Pinot Noir	Russian River Valley, California	Medium-bodied, light tannins, bright and fruity	$15–18
GW	Artesa, Carneros, Pinot Noir	Carneros, California	Medium-bodied, light tannins, bright and fruity	$17–20

Well-Known Winners $20–35

	Name of Wine	From	Style Profile	Price Range
PF	Adelsheim, Pinot Noir	Oregon	Medium-bodied, light tannins, bright and fruity	$20–22
	Au Bon Climat, Estate, Pinot Noir	Santa Maria Valley, California	Medium-bodied, light tannins, bright and fruity	$20–25
	Navarro Vineyards, "Méthode à L'Ancienne," Pinot Noir	Anderson Valley, California	Medium-bodied, supple tannins, bright and earthy	$22–25
	Marimar Torres, "Don Miguel Vineyard," Pinot Noir	Russian River Valley, California	Medium-bodied, light tannins, bright and fruity	$25–29
	Byron, Pinot Noir	Santa Maria Valley, California	Medium-bodied, supple tannins, smooth and fruity	$20–25
	Sokol Blosser, Pinot Noir	Willamette Valley, Oregon	Medium-bodied, supple tannins, bright and earthy	$26–30
PF	Handley Cellars, Pinot Noir	Anderson Valley, California	Medium-bodied, supple tannins, smooth and fruity	$23–26
	Gary Farrell, Pinot Noir	Russian River Valley, California	Medium-bodied, supple tannins, smooth and fruity	$29–33
PF	Louis Jadot, Chambolle-Musigny	Chambolle-Musigny	Medium-bodied, supple tannins, bright and earthy	$30–35

Worth-the-Splurge Wines $35–50+

	Name of Wine	From	Style Profile	Price Range
GW	Domaine Drouhin, Pinot Noir	Willamette Valley, Oregon	Medium-bodied, supple tannins, bright and earthy	$35–40

	Name of Wine	From	Style Profile	Price Range
CW	Anne Gros, Vosne-Romanée	Vosne-Romanée, France	Medium-bodied, supple tannins, smooth and fruity	$35–45
	Michel Lafarge, Volnay	Volnay, France	Medium-bodied, supple tannins, bright and earthy	$45–55
CW	Jean-Jacques Confuron, Chambolle-Musigny	Chambolle-Musigny, France	Medium-bodied, supple tannins, bright and earthy	$45–55
	Rochioli Vineyard, "Estate," Pinot Noir	Russian River Valley, California	Medium-bodied, supple tannins, smooth and fruity	$50–60
CW	Georges Roumier, Chambolle-Musigny, "Les Amoureuses"	Chambolle-Musigny, France	Medium-bodied, supple tannins, smooth and fruity	$100–120
	Cristom, "Jessie Vineyard," Pinot Noir	Willamette Valley, Oregon	Full-bodied, supple tannins, earthy and ripe	$35–45
GW	Goldeneye Winery, Pinot Noir	Anderson Valley, California	Full-bodied, supple tannins, smooth and ripe	$45–50
PF	Merry Edwards Wines, Pinot Noir	Russian River Valley, California	Full-bodied, supple tannins, smooth and ripe	$45–55
GW	Hartford Court, "Velvet Sisters," Pinot Noir	Anderson Valley, California	Full-bodied, supple tannins, smooth and ripe	$45–55

Surprise Sips

Unique Wines Worth Seeking Out

	Name of Wine	From	Style Profile	Price Range
	Mount Riley, Pinot Noir	Marlborough, New Zealand	Medium-bodied, light tannins, bright and fruity	$18–22
GW	Seresin Estate, Pinot Noir	Marlborough, New Zealand	Medium-bodied, supple tannins, smooth and fruity	$25–30

	Name of Wine	From	Style Profile	Price Range
	Martinborough Vineyard, Pinot Noir	Martinborough, New Zealand	Medium-bodied, supple tannins, smooth and fruity	$30–35
	Palliser Estates, Pinot Noir	Martinborough, New Zealand	Medium-bodied, supple tannins, smooth and fruity	$25–28
GW	MacMurray Ranch, Pinot Noir	Russian River Valley, California	Medium-bodied, supple tannins, smooth and fruity	$27–32
CW	Alex Gambal, Volnay	Volnay, France	Medium-bodied, supple tannins, bright and earthy	$32–38
PF	Brogan Cellars, Pinot Noir	Russian River Valley, California	Medium-bodied, supple tannins, bright and earthy	$45–50
PF	Testarossa, "Pisoni Vineyard," Pinot Noir	Santa Lucia Highlands, California	Full-bodied, supple tannins, smooth and ripe	$45–50
CW	Siduri Wines, "Pisoni Vineyard," Pinot Noir	Santa Lucia Highlands, California	Full-bodied, supple tannins, smooth and ripe	$45–50

Five Simple Steps to Buying and Enjoying Burgundy

Exploring the wines of Burgundy is not an easy or cheap task. But where there's a will there's a way. Take a refresher course in "Burgundy 101" (page 29) and then try this.

1. Start with affordable versions named *Bourgogne blanc* (white) and *rouge* (red). Most bottles cost less than $15. You can't go wrong when buying Burgundy from the following large wine shippers known as *négociants*:
   ○ Louis Jadot
   ○ Joseph Drouhin
   ○ Bouchard Père et Fils
   ○ Louis Latour

2. Then branch out and explore a particular regional or village wine, such as these:

Whites (see Chardonnay chapter for more)
- Chablis—crisp
- Pouilly-Fuissé—fresh
- Puligny-Montrachet—rich
- Meursault—full

Reds
- Mercurey—light
- Volnay—elegant
- Chambolle-Musigny—aromatic
- Vosne-Romanée—full

Tasting Tip: Host a Terroir Tasting Party by selecting one bottle from each region listed above. Sip them side by side to see if you detect the differences place makes in taste.

3. Once you've narrowed down your preferences to a few areas, it's time to uncork wines from several different producers. Here are some of my preferred négociants and small growers:

Whites
- Verget
- Antonin Rodet
- Prosper Maufoux
- Olivier LeFlaive
- Domaine Laroche
- Colin-Deléger
- Louis Carillon

Reds
- Henri De Villamont
- Georges Roumier
- Frédéric Esmonin
- Domaine Dujac
- Robert Arnoux
- Joseph Faiveley
- Anne Gros

4. By now you should have had a good time exploring regions and producers without spending a fortune. If you have the money, choose one or two producers and buy several wines from their portfolios. Then note the differences from various vineyards.

5. Finally, if you really get into Burgundy and want to cellar some wines, it's worth it to research vintages. Because Burgundy is susceptible to rain and hail, one vintage may vary significantly from another. With that said, my problem with vintage predictions is that they are simply guidelines. I've had excellent wine from so-called "bad" vintages and just OK wine from "great" vintages. The bottom line is to find a Burgundy producer whose wines you enjoy drinking, read several sources to get vintage information, and then make your own decision. Remember, each vintage will be a new experience. And isn't that the fun of it all?

pairing

PINOT NOIR IS THE ULTIMATE FOOD WINE. IT SWINGS both ways in culinary circles and works equally well with fish and meat. If I were stranded on a desert island, Pinot Noir would be my beverage choice. What else goes perfectly with wild boar, freshly speared fish, and roasted coconut?

The reason Pinot is such a natural with a wide range of food is its ability to fill in the gaps. Due to its bright acidity, elegant texture, and earthy spiciness, Pinot Noir subtly melds itself to the dish at hand while not overpowering its flavors.

Let's Talk Texture First: Is the wine light- or medium-bodied and silky?

Pinot Noirs are generally light- to medium-bodied wines, so don't overpower their delicacy with heavyweight dishes. I enjoy Pinot with beef stew but feel a huge slab of steak pummels the wine.

Consider It a Complement: Do you get spicy, earthy aromas and flavors?

All I can say is *mushrooms, mushrooms, and mushrooms.* (If you don't like mushrooms, many of the recipes still work. Just leave them out.) Being a fungus lover, I think there is nothing better than an earthy Pinot echoing the flavor of mushrooms in a dish. Another winner is to highlight the wine's black cherry kick with chopped dried cherries tossed in a sauce.

About Acid: Is the wine bright or smooth?

Pinot Noir's affinity for food has much to do with its bright, racy levels of acidity, which counteract the heat of mildly spicy foods, slice through rich cheeses, and complement the fruity tang of cranberries or dried cherries.

It's Tannin Time: Are there light or medium tannins?

Most Pinots will fall on the light-tannin side of the scale, which makes it an ideal choice for fleshy fish such as salmon and tuna. It has the richness and mouth-filling texture of those fish but doesn't make fish taste funky the way a more tannic wine does.

Design-a-Dinner

STOCK YOUR SHELVES

Bottoms: Beef, veal, pork, chicken, turkey, duck, salmon, tuna, swordfish, sweet potatoes, brown/wild rice

Tops: Mushrooms, beets, cranberries/dried, cherries/dried, cheeses (Brie, goat cheese, Gruyère, Swiss), red wine sauces, mustard sauces

Accessories: Dijon mustard, walnuts, caramelized onions, tarragon, pepper, clove

Merry Edwards is a wine industry pioneer and the queen of California Pinot Noir. Under her namesake wine label, she produces Russian River Pinots that rank among my favorites. "Pinot Noir is complex, elusive, fickle, seductive, frustrating, and fabulous," jokes Merry. What is her recommendation for pairing Pinot? A simple mushroom lasagne whipped up in minutes. Layer lasagne noodles with various types of sliced mushrooms and creamy white béchamel sauce. "Complement the flavors and textures of wine and food, and you can't go wrong."

GET SAUCY . . . WITH PINOT NOIR

Pinot Noir Sauce: In olive oil, sauté 1/2 cup finely diced onion with a handful of sliced mushrooms and 1/4 cup chopped dried cherries or cranberries. Cook until the onions and mushrooms are lightly browned. Pour in 2 cups Pinot Noir, 1 teaspoon each sugar and dried oregano, and simmer for approximately 30 minutes. Add salt and pepper to taste and pour over pork or chicken,

Maple Glaze: In a small saucepan, heat 1 cup maple syrup over low heat. Add 1 tablespoon honey, 2 tablespoons apple juice, and 3 tablespoons balsamic vinegar. Simmer for 5 to 10 minutes. Use as a glaze after grilling or cooking fish and pork. It's also delicious poured over mashed or baked sweet potatoes.

MEAL ENSEMBLES

Pinot Pork and Potatoes: This is one of my staple party meals because it looks so elegant yet takes so little time to prepare. Slice pork tenderloin into 1-inch medallions. Brown the medallions in butter, salt, pepper, and chopped fresh or dried tarragon and cook thoroughly. Top with Pinot Noir Sauce (above) and serve with Sweet Potato Casserole (page 187).

Maple-Glazed Salmon: Drizzle a fillet of salmon with Maple Glaze (above) and roast in a large pan until still slightly pink in the center. Serve over brown rice or pilaf, with a simple green salad, and pass additional Maple Glaze at the table. Works beautifully with pork, too.

Nutty Turkey Sandwich: This is a terrific sandwich to make with holiday leftovers. Slice a crusty loaf of French bread in half lengthwise and warm in the oven. Meanwhile, stir together ½ cup cream cheese and ¼ cup toasted chopped pecans. Spread the mixture on one side of the bread, and on the other side spread chunky cranberry sauce. Layer with roasted turkey and lettuce leaves. Sprinkle with salt and pepper. Squeeze together the halves and slice into hearty portions.

Burgundian Beef Stew: In a Dutch oven, heat a bit of butter and olive oil and add approximately 2 pounds cubed beef (stewing meat). Quickly sear the meat over high heat and remove. Brown 1 diced onion and 1 carrot, several minced garlic cloves, and 1 tablespoon of herbes de Provence in the same pot. Return the meat to the pot and add 2 cups each Pinot Noir and beef broth. Cover the pot and let it simmer for several hours. Uncover the pot and add 1 cup quartered mushroom caps and ½ cup brandy or Cognac. Cook for another hour or so to reduce the liquid. Season with salt and pepper and serve over white rice or noodles.

The Buzz from…Jack Czarnecki, Chef and Owner,
Joel Palmer House, in Oregon's Willamette Valley

The menu at Joel Palmer House in Dayton, Oregon, revolves around mushrooms. Owners Jack and Heidi Czarnecki forage for the wild fungi themselves and then bring them back to prepare fabulous dishes paired with—what else? Pinot Noir. "When I bite into an earthy truffle or chanterelle, then sip the chewy, palate-gripping sweetness of a fine Oregon Pinot Noir, I understand in a brief instant that life is good," Jack says. I couldn't agree more.

---

sharing

MY FRIEND BOBBIE IS HOSTING THANKSGIVING DINner for the whole family. What wine could she serve to please everyone—from her beer-drinking son to her wine-savvy daughter? The best option, I suggested, was to offer a variety of wines, including sparkling, red, and white, and let the guests pick for themselves. The only joint decision of the day should be which football game to watch.

PILGRIMS UNCORKED

The original Thanksgiving revelers washed down their roast goose and duck with potent brew made from wild grapevines. Modern turkey tables, however, resound with a cacophony of flavors. My advice for when sweet candied yams meet tart cranberry sauce and savory sausage stuffing? Stay away from whites with too much oak and reds with strong tannins.

Recommended Sips

Bubbly
Crémant de Loire
Prosecco
Brut Champagne

Whites
Viognier
Gewurztraminer
California Chenin Blanc
Riesling

Reds
Rosé
Beaujolais
Pinot Noir
Zinfandel

Sweeties
Don't forget capping off the meal with dessert wines that can take on pumpkin and apple pie:

Tawny Port
Muscat

Thanksgiving isn't the only holiday when wine is a must. Here are
ideas for other celebratory days.

DECEMBER 25: CHEERS, SANTA

Whether your Christmas feast is turkey, ham, or roast beef, the season
calls for celebrating with impressive bottles.

Recommended Sips

> White Burgundy
> White Bordeaux
> Aged Cabernet Sauvignon
> Rhône Valley Syrah
> Italian Chianti Classico
> Sauternes

FEBRUARY 14: SPARKLING SWEET

My preference on Valentine's Day is to be swept off my feet and taken
out to eat, but when that doesn't happen, I make a honey-glazed ham
for my honey and top it off with decadent chocolate cake. What to
serve with it?

Recommended Sips

> Burgundy from Chambolle-Musigny
> Sparkling Shiraz
> Rosé Champagne
> Late-Bottled Vintage Port
> Late-Harvest Zinfandel

The Buzz on...Be My Terra Valentine

Want a special holiday wine? Try Cabernet Sauvignon from Napa Valley's Terra Valentine ($35). The winery honors the importance of the land, hence *terra,* as well as co-owner Margaret Wurtele's father-in-law, who was born on Valentine's Day and named—what else? Valentine.

JULY 4: ALL-AMERICAN DRINKS

Picnics and barbecues are typically the order of the day on the Fourth of July, so go for All-American, inexpensive red, white, and pink:

Sauvignon Blanc
Riesling
Rosé
Zinfandel
Sangiovese

The Buzz on...The Ultimate Women's Wine List

Chef Anita Lo, of annisa restaurant in New York City, says she and co-owner Jennifer Scism have built their restaurant around a central theme—women. "The name of our restaurant, annisa, is found in many cultures: In English it means 'gracious,' and in Arabic it means 'women.' As two women in the restaurant business we felt compelled to make our statement this way. We've also gone out of our way to celebrate women in the wine industry as most all our bottles are either made by female vintners or from vineyards owned by women."

Sangiovese/Chianti
THE SLEEK "ITALIAN HEELS"

buying

WHILE SOME SAY CLOTHES CAN MAKE THE PERSON, I say, what about shoes? Many of us consider footwear the ultimate fashion necessity, especially when it carries the discreet badge of honor "Made in Italy."

I gravitate toward stylish Italian heels that miraculously seem to make any outfit look elegant. Granted, it may take time to break them in, but it is a small price to pay for beauty. That's the same way I feel about Sangiovese, the grape responsible for producing Italy's classic Tuscan reds. These tightly wound wines often need time in the glass to soften up but show their true beauty when paired with food.

Unlike other reds that pummel you with power, Sangiovese-based wines seduce with style. Just like a pair of Italian heels.

THE NAME GAME

Sangiovese = Chianti and Chianti Classico

Chianti is a region in Tuscany located in the central part of Italy. Chianti and Chianti Classico are made primarily with the Sangiovese grape. In the Tuscan town of Montalcino, a wine named *Brunello di Montalcino* is produced from a clone of the Sangiovese grape named *Brunello*.

You won't find a more Tuscan grape than Sangiovese. It rules this central part of Italy like a powerful king. Like many monarchs, however, Sangiovese has an attitude.

While Cabernet Sauvignon and Syrah both globe-trot with ease and generate good wines from France to Chile, Sangiovese needs everything to be "just so" to be happy. The soil, the climate, the type of Sangiovese planted, and the wine-making technique all need to work in harmony before we're blessed with a top-notch wine.

If one of those factors is off, the naturally tart grape can produce wines that are thin and lean. But when the confluence of the four is successful, the wines can be positively regal.

While you may never have heard of Sangiovese, I would venture to guess you have tasted it as the main grape in Chianti. If your experiences with Chianti have been more peasant than royal, it's time to revisit these Tuscan wines. Over the past several decades, nothing short of a renaissance has occurred within the great Tuscan region. The image of a straw-covered bottle containing a lackluster red has all but disappeared, in its place a vision of innovation.

How did such a transformation happen? It's a saga worthy of a monarch.

Under the Super Tuscan Sun

The time was the early 1970s, and Chianti was becoming a victim of its own popularity. As Americans quaffed the inexpensive wine, quality began spiraling downward. High-volume clones of Sangiovese were planted to keep up with demand, and legally approved white grapes—which up until then had comprised a small percentage of the Chianti blend—were used to further stretch the already-diluted Sangiovese. Mass production had taken over, and things looked bad in Tuscany—very bad.

Instead of Superman swooping in to save the day, it was Super Tuscans that instigated change.

Led by Piero Antinori, a member of one of Tuscany's most revered winemaking clans (whose family has been making wine for more than six hundred years), a group of winemakers began turning the tide of mediocrity in the region by turning away from Sangiovese.

Though Antinori jokes that "Sangiovese is part of our DNA in Tuscany," he was inspired by his uncle, Mario Incisa della Rocchetta, to add Cabernet Sauvignon to Sangiovese and use innovative wine-making techniques for the time (like aging wine in small French oak barrels) to produce a new type of wine. It was called *Tignanello*.

By the late 1970s, other producers had followed suit, and within a decade international varieties such as Cabernet Sauvignon and Merlot were helping to create a luxury class of wines unofficially dubbed *Super Tuscans*.

Oddly enough, taking the focus off Sangiovese for a short time raised the quality bar in Tuscany. Pretty soon that innovative spirit and wave of modernization spread throughout the region, especially in Chianti Classico. Today winemakers have returned to their signature grape, and just about every Sangiovese-based Tuscan wine—from affordable reds labeled *Toscano* to glorious Chianti Classico Riserva—is reaping the benefits.

The king is back, and Sangiovese is helping to make Tuscany one of the most exciting wine regions in the world.

The Buzz on... Super Tuscan Stars

When I can afford to drink Super Tuscans, my favorites include Ornellaia, Sassicaia, Solaia, Tignanello, and Castello Banfi's Summus, but many others are on the market. How do you know if a wine falls into the Super Tuscan realm? It's not an official category, but generally these are the top wines coming from a winery in Tuscany. Prices are high, usually $50–100+ per bottle, and most of the wines contain grape varieties other than Sangiovese, including Merlot, Cabernet Sauvignon, Cabernet Franc, and Syrah. These wines are often labeled with an *IGT* classification (see page 51 for more information).

Cal-Ital Revolution

While it's true that Sangiovese flourishes in Tuscany, it has found a home away from home in California.

If you're put off by the tight sleekness of Chianti, it's time to try a California Sangiovese, which captures the grape's softer side. Think of it as trading in those superpointy heels for ones with a slightly rounder toe.

Sangiovese is not a new grape in the Golden State. Originally planted by Italian immigrants at the turn of the twentieth century, most Sangiovese vines died from disease or were ripped out. In the mid-1980s, however, Sangiovese in California was resurrected by none other than Tuscany's Piero Antinori.

On a jaunt to Napa Valley, Antinori discovered an idyllic location named Atlas Peak. Craggy hillsides located fifteen hundred feet above the valley floor reminded him of home, so he brought over cuttings from his Tuscan estate and founded Atlas Peak Winery.

Was this the beginning of another Sangiovese renaissance? The promise fizzled when winemakers couldn't quite figure out how to deal

Lingo Lesson

Core Words

Dry: Most Italian reds taste very dry. In fact, some people say they don't like Italian reds because they're "too" dry. Usually that drying, astringent feeling comes from the combination of strong tannins and high acidity, not simply the lack of sweetness in the wine.

Bright: The acidity is definitely zesty, which gives Sangiovese-based wines a bright, vibrant quality. These wines are also referred to as having firm acidity. Think of bouncing a penny off a drum. There is a ping and sense of tautness that translates to the firmness of many Italian Sangiovese.

Medium-bodied: Mostly medium-bodied and elegant (more akin to Pinot Noir than Syrah, for example), but wines blended with other grapes such as Cabernet Sauvignon have a medium-full body.

Medium to strong tannins: Italian wines generally have more noticeable tannins than California Sangiovese. Wines with too much tannin are said to be hard.

Extra Credit Words

Fruit aromas:
>   Red fruits—tart cherry, raspberry
>   Black fruits—black cherry, plum

Floral aromas: Rose petals and violet are typical with these wines.

Dusty and tobacco: Sangiovese to me smells of fresh, warm earth and sweet pipe tobacco.

Licorice: Another one of the signature aromas in Sangiovese. Sometimes it's red, other times black.

with the particular grape, and consumers were slow to embrace the less-than-distinctive wines.

Luckily, a number of die-hard producers of Cal-Itals (hip term for Italian-style wines made in California) stuck by Sangiovese, taking the time to discover ways the grape best expresses itself outside its Tuscan home. As Jack Stuart, winemaker at Napa's Silverado Vineyards, says, "We can produce tasty wines in the style of Tuscany but with California flair. This makes Sangiovese a really terrific alternative to the mainstream varieties."

Eclectic Sangiovese-based wines have developed a devoted following of wine drinkers who covet elegance. As Patrick Llerena, owner of Sangiovese-producing Viña de la Cruz, observes, "Most of our customers are professional women in their thirties to forties looking for unique yet food-friendly wines."

> ### The Buzz on...Wine Is Like a Child
>
> One of the richest rewards of my travels around the world has been meeting amazing women with unique perspectives on wine. Giovannella Stianti Mascheroni, owner of Tuscany's Castello di Volpaia, believes, "Wine agriculture is a very important feminine experience. The maternal feeling that any woman has can be devoted to grapes, so wine becomes more like a child, not just business-producing money."

leslie's label links
Connecting taste to place makes wine buying easy

Wines originating in Tuscany generally have a brighter, tighter character, while California versions tend toward the softer, riper side.

Place: Chianti, Italy

Taste: Chianti is one of my top picks for value and food-friendliness. The fresh berry flavors, zesty acidity, and black pepper kick tackle everything from cheese pizza to fried chicken. The characteristic

brightness comes from Chianti's unique combination of sandy soils and ruggedly rolling hills.
Flushed with daytime sun and cooling evening
breezes, Sangiovese thrives in this land. On a map,
Chianti looks like one big region in central Tuscany,
but it's actually made up of seven smaller zones with
myriad soil types and climate variations. The two
most familiar to American wine drinkers are Chianti Classico and Chianti Rufina. Other zones, such

as Colli Senesi, Colli Fiorentini, and Colline Pisane, are named for
hillside areas that surround the main towns of Siena, Florence, and
Pisa.

The Buzz on...The "Red" Barone's Blend

The year was 1861, and the man was Barone Bettino Ricasoli. In a move
that would define Chianti for generations, the barone devised a standard for-
mula to produce Chianti's red wine. His blend would consist of Sangiovese and
Canaiolo (a red grape), but for wines meant to be consumed immediately, the
white grapes Malvasia and Trebbiano would be added. Over time, the white
grapes undermined the quality of Chianti, and today top-quality producers
have abandoned the use of white grapes altogether.

Place: Chianti Classico, Italy

Taste: These classic wines are complex yet
elegant, with bright fruit notes and a pleasing tannic bite that softens with age and
food. Generally *classico* means the heart of
the wine-growing district, and this elon-
gated strip of land situated between Flo-

rence and Siena is truly the filet mignon of Chianti. By 1716, wines
from this area were already so famous that the grand duke of Tuscany
declared the renowned growing region needed to be protected from
imposters calling their wine Chianti. Thus was born the first official
European wine region. Beautiful and rich in history as it is, Chianti
Classico is also the epicenter of innovation that is rocking Tuscany.
On a recent visit, the juxtaposition of rusticity and technology came

into focus. After visiting the state-of-the-art Fontodi Winery, I returned to the rustic farmhouse where I was staying. Perched high on a hill above the town of Greve in Chianti, it afforded me an unparalleled view of neighboring vineyards planted on the craggy hillsides, olive orchards, and several nearby castles. When I taste a top Chianti Classico, I can taste its rugged character polished by impeccable winemaking.

Tasting Tip: You'll often see the word *Riserva* on a bottle of Chianti Classico. Riservas are the best of Chianti Classico and undergo extended periods of aging lasting more than two years. These wines typically cost $5–10 more than regular Chianti Classicos.

The Buzz on... The Women of the Rooster and Beyond

Ever wonder what that rooster logo is atop a bottle of Chianti Classico? It is a seal of quality awarded by the Chianti Classico Black Rooster Wine Consortium. Interestingly, this formerly male-dominated organization has recently been overrun by the fairer sex, led by Emanuela Stucchi Prinetti of the highly regarded Badia a Coltibuono. She is the first women to be elected the president of such an important Italian wine association. As Tiziana Frescobaldi of Tuscany's famous Frescobaldi family says, "The role of women in the Tuscan wine world is growing steadily, and we have very important tasks, from the offices to the cellars and the vineyards. This was not the case just a few years ago."

Place: Brunello di Montalcino, Italy

Taste: Wines named *Brunello di Montalcino* give true meaning to the phrase *iron fist in a velvet glove*. These are the Italian stallions of Tuscany and some of the most coveted, ageworthy wines in the world. Due to their scarcity and resulting high prices, these are not wines I drink regularly. But whenever I do get the chance to sample one,  I think back to the day I spent with the famous Dr. Franco Biondi-Santi. An aristocratic gentleman with a twinkle in his eye, he proudly showed me the Biondi-Santi cellars replete with wines dating back to 1888. His relatives propagated the dark-skinned Sangiovese grosso clone, whose local nickname is *Brunello* or "little dark one." In doing so, they created Brunello di Montalcino. Other producers followed suit and planted Brunello on rugged hillsides surrounding the small, picturesque town of Montalcino. Looking at the steep slopes planted in vines, it's easy to understand why Brunello di Montalcino tastes so hearty and concentrated. Grapes, protected by the nearby mountain named Monte Amiata, bask in the warm Tuscan sun and get extremely ripe, tannic, and full. Brunellos aren't even released for four to five years to give them a chance to soften up and start showing their true potential.

Value Tip: Though Brunello is not an everyday wine, its younger sibling should be. Called *Rosso di Montalcino*, these juicy reds are usually priced around $15 and ready to drink upon release. My favorites include Col d'Orcia and Altesino.

Place: Amador County, California

Taste: Whenever I drink Sangiovese from Amador, I think of Italy. The hot region—located several hours from the San Francisco Bay Area on the way to the Sierra Nevada mountain range—reminds me of Tuscany (but with a Wild West flair). You can almost taste the robust ruggedness of the place in a bottle of dusty Amador Sangiovese.

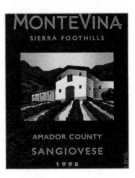

Place: Napa Valley, California

Taste: Napa is certainly Cabernet country, but Sangiovese has found a home on the valley's hillsides. Lacking the weather variations that often make growing Sangiovese such a challenge, grapes bask in the California sun and get ripe and juicy. This translates into Sangiovese with softness and elegance.

Look for these places on the label, too . . .
   Vino Nobile di Montepulciano, Italy
   Umbria, Italy
   Columbia Valley, Washington
   Mendocino, California

A MATTER OF STYLE

While it's true that the grape expresses itself quite differently in Tuscany and California, it still takes great care in the vineyards and cellar to make primo vino from Sangiovese. Three of the biggest factors affecting the ultimate taste of the wine are clones, yields, and blends.

The Cloning Question

Grape clones are simply different versions of the same grape variety. While these vines essentially share similar genetic material, each one has adjusted to its environment and developed slightly different strengths and weaknesses. Clones are selected and propagated to highlight certain qualities in a vine, such as resistance to disease or adaptability to a particular climate.

Sangiovese has a high propensity to mutate and therefore has many clones. Choosing the right clone for the vineyard's soil and climatic conditions makes a huge difference in the final quality of Sangiovese-based wines.

The Smaller the Better

Sangiovese is a prolific variety, and vines love to go wild and produce a large amount of fruit. Although this is good for table grapes, it's bad for wine grapes. When you have high yields (measured in tons of fruit per acre), the resulting wine is often less concentrated and complex. Growers strive to restrict the number of grapes on each vine so the vine puts all of its energy into making those few grapes more flavorful.

As with Syrah, planting on hillsides and in poor soils helps restrict the growth of the vine. Another common technique used to maintain low yields is called *green harvesting*. When the grapes are just developing, workers will go through the vineyards and chop off clusters on each vine, leaving only a few to grow to maturity. This gives more intensity and concentration to the final wine.

It's All in the Blend

Whether using white varieties in old-time Chianti or Super Tuscans with Cabernet Sauvignon, Syrah, Cabernet Franc, and Merlot, Sangiovese has historically been blended with other grape varieties. Blending is such an important part of the final wine's taste that current regulations put into place in 1996 allow for up to 15 percent of virtually any grape variety to be blended with Sangiovese in Chianti. The grapes blended with Sangiovese will make a difference in what you taste in the glass. Since most labels won't indicate the blend, its best to explore various producers to find ones you like.

Shopping Guide

Bargin Sips

Stash-Your-Cash Wines $15 and Under

	Name of Wine	From	Style Profile	Price Range
PF	Monte Antico, Rosso	Toscana, Italy	Light-bodied, light tannins, bright and earthy	$7–10
PW	Frescobaldi, "Rèmole"	Toscana, Italy	Light-bodied, light tannins, bright and earthy	$6–10
	Castello di Fonterutoli, "Badiola"	Toscana, Italy	Light-bodied, light tannins, bright and earthy	$11–14
	Pepi, Sangiovese	California	Light-bodied, light tannins, bright and earthy	$13–15
	Montevina Winery, Sangiovese	Amador County, California	Medium-bodied, supple tannins, bright and earthy	$10–12
GW	Chappellet, Sangiovese	Napa Valley, California	Medium-bodied, supple tannins, bright and earthy	$12–14
	Atlas Peak Vineyards, Sangiovese	Atlas Peak, Napa Valley, California	Medium-bodied, supple tannins, bright and earthy	$11–14

Well-Known Winners $15–25

	Name of Wine	From	Style Profile	Price Range
	Vino Noceto, Sangiovese	Amador County, California	Light-bodied, light tannins, bright and earthy	$15–18
	Bonny Doon Vineyard, "Ca'del Solo," Sangiovese	California	Light-bodied, light tannins, bright and earthy	$16–18
	L'Uvaggio di Giacommo, Sangiovese	California	Light-bodied, light tannins, bright and earthy	$17–20
GW	Flora Springs, Sangiovese	Napa Valley, California	Medium-bodied, supple tannins, bright	$15–18
	Silverado Vineyards, Sangiovese	Napa Valley, California	Medium-bodied, supple tannins, bright	$15–18
PF	Luna Vineyards, Sangiovese	Napa Valley, California	Medium-bodied, supple tannins, bright	$17–20
	Seghesio, Sangiovese	Alexander Valley, California	Medium-bodied, supple tannins, bright	$20–24
	Badia a Coltibuono, Chianti Classico	Chianti Classico, Italy	Medium-bodied, strong tannins, bright and earthy	$15–18
PF	Tenuta Caparzo, Rosso di Montalcino	Tuscany, Italy	Medium-bodied, strong tannins, bright and earthy	$15–18
GW	Castello di Volpaia, Chianti Classico, Riserva	Chianti Classico, Italy	Medium-bodied, strong tannins, bright and earthy	$23–25

Worth-the-Splurge Wines $30–50+

	Name of Wine	From	Style Profile	Price Range
GW	Ferrari-Carano, "Siena"	Sonoma County, California	Medium-bodied, strong tannins, bright	$25–29
	Kuleto Villa, Sangiovese	Napa Valley, California	Medium-bodied, strong tannins, bright	$29–32

	Name of Wine	From	Style Profile	Price Range
CW	Barone Ricasoli, Castello di Brolio, Chianti Classico	Chianti Classico, Italy	Medium-bodied, strong tannins, bright and earthy	$35–45
	Ruffino Riserva Ducale, "Gold Label," Chianti Classico	Chianti Classico, Italy	Medium-bodied, strong tannins, bright and earthy	$42–46
CW	Frescobaldi, "Montesodi"	Chianti Rufina, Tuscany, Italy	Medium-bodied, strong tannins, bright and earthy	$40–46
CW	Marchesi Antinori, "Tignanello"	Toscana, Italy	Medium-bodied, strong tannins, bright and earthy	$69–75
PF	Borgo Scopeto, "Borgonero"	Toscana, Italy	Full-bodied, strong tannins, bright and ripe	$31–35
CW	Col d'Orcia, Brunello di Montalcino	Tuscany, Italy	Full-bodied, strong tannins, bright and earthy	$40–45
CW	Altesino, "Montosoli," Brunello di Montalcino	Tuscany, Italy	Full-bodied, strong tannins, bright and earthy	$100–110
CW	Biondi-Santi, Brunello di Montalcino	Tuscany, Italy	Full-bodied, strong tannins, bright and earthy	$125–150

The Buzz on… Buying Wine from the Back Label

Just as the back of a piece of china or silver reveals its pedigree, the back label of a bottle of imported wine will often tell you the name of the person or company that brought it to these shores. As a rule of thumb, top importers bring only in good wines so find a first-rate importer, and chances are their wines will taste delicious. Here are my top picks of importers to seek out (web addresses of these and other importers are in the Checkout Counter: Resources at the back of the book):

Billington Imports
Cape Classics
Frederick Wildman and Sons, Ltd.
Marc De Grazia Selections
Palm Bay Imports
Paterno Imports

Via Pacifica Imports
Vineyard Brands
W. J. Deutsch & Sons Ltd.
William Grant & Sons
Wilson Daniels, Ltd.
Winebow/Leonardo LoCascio

pairing

WHEN I MARRIED AN ITALIAN, THE FIRST THING MY mother-in-law did was buy me a hand-crank pasta machine and teach me the family recipe for ravioli. Every year since we tied the knot, our Christmas Eve tradition is to make ravioli and uncork a bottle of Chianti Classico.

Though Sangiovese is by no means a wine to drink only with Italian food, we think of Tuscan fare as its natural complement. Slices of crostini rubbed with oil, salads and soups made thick with doughy bread, rare grilled steak, pasta noodles dripping with a rich meat sauce, herb-infused beans, polenta, and olive oil, olive oil, olive oil.

As Pat Kuleto, well-known restaurateur and Napa Valley Sangiovese producer, notes, "Sangiovese is such a food-friendly wine because it cleanses your palate with bright acidity and makes food taste so much better." How true.

Let's Talk Texture First: Is the wine light, medium, full, and elegant or rich?

Chiantis are generally lighter than Chianti Classico or California Sangiovese bottlings, and Brunellos are the real big boys. Lighter wines are delicious with lighter dishes such as pasta and beans, while bigger, more full-bodied versions are top choices for meat and pungent cheese.

About Acid: Is the wine bright or smooth?

Food loves acidity, and Sangiovese-based wines have it in spades. That's the reason these wines have such an affinity for tangy tomato sauce. California versions of Sangiovese tend to be smoother than their Italian brethren, with more ripe fruit and less tartness.

It's Tannin Time: Does the wine have noticeable tannins?

Most Sangiovese-based wines have apparent tannins. If the wine you're sipping is overly drying, take a bite of protein to counteract the effect of the tannins.

Design-a-Dinner

STOCK YOUR SHELVES

Bottom: Steak, sausages, salami, prosciutto, chicken, duck, squab, polenta, pasta, beans, bread

Tops: Zucchini, red bell peppers, tomatoes, cheeses, (Parmesan, fontina, ricotta, goat cheese, Asiago), crème fraîche, tomato sauces, olive oil

Accessories: Oregano, rosemary, sage, fennel

GET SAUCY . . . WITH SANGIOVESE

Simple Red Sauce: Sauté 2 chopped garlic cloves and ½ onion, chopped, in a pot with olive oil until translucent, then add a small can of tomato paste and stir. Pour in 1 16-ounce can diced tomatoes, 1 28-ounce can plain tomato sauce, 2 cups water, and loads of dried basil, fennel, and oregano. Simmer the sauce (the longer the better), and when ready to serve, remove from the heat and stir in 2 or 3 spoonfuls of crème fraîche for a creamy texture.

Herb-Infused Olive Oil: Place fresh rosemary, sage, or thyme and dried fennel seeds in an empty screw-top glass bottle. Pour extra-virgin olive oil over the herbs and let sit for several hours. Drizzle on pasta noodles, soups, and meats or use as a dipping sauce for breads. Note: Because the oil will keep for only a few days, make an amount you can use up quickly.

MEAL ENSEMBLES

White Bean and Prosciutto Crostini: Drizzle slices of baguette or other crusty bread with Herb-Infused Olive Oil (see above) and toast until crispy. Smash stewed white beans into a rough paste using a fork. Spread the paste thickly on each piece of bread and drape with a thin slice of prosciutto.

Tomato Bruschetta: Chop several red tomatoes into small chunks and place in a large bowl. Stir in a generous drizzle of olive oil, salt, pepper, 1 pressed garlic clove, and a bunch of chopped fresh basil and/or parsley leaves. Stir this mixture together and let it sit for about 10 minutes. Meanwhile, slice thick pieces of baguette or other crusty bread, then rub them with Herb-Infused Olive Oil (page 227) and toast. Top with the tomato mixture and serve.

Minestrone and Grilled Cheese: This version of the classic soup is one of my most frequently requested dinner items. It's so easy and delicious! Sauté in olive oil ¹/₂ onion, chopped, 2 chopped carrots, and 2 cups frozen green beans. When the vegetables are lightly browned, add 1 16-ounce can diced tomatoes, 4 to 5 cups chicken broth, and 2 cups beef broth. Cook for half an hour or until the carrots are soft. Add 1 chopped zucchini, 1 16-ounce can white beans, ¹/₂ stick (4 tablespoons) butter, several teaspoons dried oregano, and 1 cup small-shaped pastalike macaroni. Cook until the noodles are al dente. Serve with grilled cheese made with mozzarella or fontina.

Polenta Casserole: My family loves lasagne made with my red sauce, but I enjoy substituting a lasagnelike casserole every once in a while. Buy polenta mix and make according to the directions. Pour the warm mixture (like a thick cake batter) into the bottom of an oiled casserole dish. It will set in a few minutes and be springy to the touch. Add a layer of washed spinach leaves and sautéed mushrooms, then cover with red sauce. Top with grated cheeses such as mozzarella and Parmesan. Bake in a 375°F oven until the casserole is warmed through and the cheese is melted and bubbly. Serve immediately.

Stuffed Veal Chops with White Beans: Sauté 1 diced onion, 1 diced carrot, and 1 diced celery rib in olive oil. Add 2 chopped garlic cloves and 1 16-ounce can drained cannellini beans. Douse the mixture with olive oil, salt, and several sprigs of rosemary. Cover and simmer until the beans are heated through, which will take 30 to 45 minutes.

For the chops, make a quick stuffing with soft goat cheese, chopped fresh herbs (rosemary, sage, parsley, and thyme), bread crumbs, and black pepper. Slice gently into the middle of each chop and stuff the incision with the filling, then broil or panfry. Serve with the white beans.

Tuscan-Style Bread Salad: This is a great salad to make in the summer, when tomatoes are abundant. Start by slicing a loaf of crusty bread into cubes. Toss the bread cubes with Herb-Infused Olive Oil (page 227), salt, and minced garlic. Spread the cubes out on a baking sheet and bake until golden brown. While they're cooling, combine several chopped tomatoes with a hearty drizzle of olive oil, salt, pepper, and several tablespoons each of drained capers and chopped fresh parsley. Toss in the cubed bread and one round of young goat cheese, crumbled. Stir together well and let sit for a few minutes before serving.

The Buzz from…The Star-Making Lungarotti Sisters, Umbria, Italy

Sangiovese plays as important a role in red wine in Umbria as it does in neighboring Tuscany. Umbria's top producer is Lungarotti Winery, and currently sisters Teresa Severini-Lungarotti and Chiara Lungarotti and their mother are the first all-women team to own and operate a major winery in Italy. Teresa was the first woman in Italy to achieve a degree in enology from the University of Perugia, and Chiara holds a master's degree in agriculture. So, what do these Italian wonder-women do to entertain at home? "In Italy we say 'The first impression is what counts,' so there is nothing better than to prepare tempting appetizers. Usually I like to offer home-made dried black olives with diced orange skins, a little bruschetta (toasted bread with our extra-virgin olive oil and a pinch of salt), just simple or with some fresh diced tomato over it; crostini with liver pâté and sliced dried sausage together with pieces of a sharp pecorino cheese."

sharing

WHAT TO DO WITH LEFTOVER WINE IS ONE OF THE questions I am asked most often. It's also one of my favorite sharing tips since there are many creative solutions.

First, there is no definitive answer for how long a wine will keep. As with food, each wine's shelf life is different. Delicate whites deteriorate more quickly than big reds, while fortified wines such as port last for months. I've even left bottles of open Champagne on the table overnight and come back twenty-four hours later to find them still fizzy and wonderful.

Most wine will last several days if you simply recork it and store it in the refrigerator. If you want the wine to last longer, give it a squirt of wine-preserving gas (see page 85). You can find this in most wine shops.

What if you still don't finish the bottle?

Cooking with leftover wine is a top way to utilize the last splash in a bottle. My only rule is that I don't cook with a wine I wouldn't drink. Try these creative tricks for cooking with wine.

○ Pour the leftover wine into ice cube trays for later use. You just pop out a cube or two at a time, depending on what you need for a sauce or dish. Freezing sparkling wine in ice cube trays works, too. Not only do they make a flavorful addition to sauces, but bubbly cubes make Sunday morning mimosas a breeze.

○ My favorite wine to cook with is leftover dessert wine. It imparts a delicious layer of flavor to savory sauces or when basting meats.

Still can't finish the bottle? Make homemade vinegar. When the wine comes into contact with the air, it begins the natural process of oxidation, which makes the wine taste dull and flat. Exposed wine is what turns into vinegar, so I say why not outsmart the enemy and turn leftover wine into vinegar yourself? It's easy to get started, and it's a tradition that can go on for a lifetime. I have a friend who started her crock of red wine vinegar more than twenty years ago.

Each Christmas, I give bottles of my homemade vinegar. I save dessert wine bottles (or buy simple ones with a closure), pour in vinegar, add a homemade label, and voilà, gourmet gifts on a budget.

Steps for Making Wine Vinegar

1. Get a large glass or pottery container, preferably one with a spout on the bottom and a fairly wide mouth to expose the wine to the air.
2. Decide whether you want to make red wine or white wine vinegar (don't mix the two) and gather up your half-empty wine bottles. Never use a corked or otherwise tainted wine to make your vinegar. It will spoil the entire batch.
3. The only other thing you'll need is a starter culture, called the *mother*. What turns wine into vinegar is a bacterium called *acetobacter*, and it is contained in the mother. You can buy them at home brew stores, or I've found the easiest way to get the ball rolling is to buy an unpasteurized, unfiltered vinegar. (At the grocery store, simply look for the vinegar that has particles floating in it. Sounds unattractive but works wonderfully.)

The Buzz on...Women and Wine—Let's Get Organized

Italian women started one of the first female organizations in wine, Le Donne del Vino. Founded in 1988, it boasts hundreds of members whose goal is to encourage and promote women's growth in the Italian wine industry. Women in Wine has recently launched in New Zealand, and in the United States groups such as Wine Brats, Les Dames d'Escoffier, and Women for Wine-Sense are devoted to education and enjoyment of wine. Women for Wine-Sense is the premier grassroots organization dedicated to spreading the word that wine enhances and enriches everyday life. Want to join up? Check the Checkout Counter: Resources at the back of the book for contact information.

---

4. Pour in equal parts of the starter culture, or store-bought vinegar, and wine. Cover the opening of the glass container with a piece of porous fabric, like cheesecloth, and secure it with a rubber band.

5. Store the glass container in a dark place, and in three to six months you'll have delicious vinegar. The best part is, the longer it ages, the more intense the flavors become.

6. Keep adding leftover bottles to your vinegar container to replace what you have used. As long as the "mother" is there, you'll continuously produce vinegar.

Zinfandel
THE "LOVE 'EM LIKE LEATHER" REDS

buying

EVERY TIME I PULL THE BLACK LEATHER PANTS FROM my closet, I feel a little wild. It doesn't matter if they're paired with a demure sweater or classic jacket, just wearing them brings out the "biker" in me.

If you own some, you know what I mean. Even if you've only been tempted to buy a pair, you get the picture. For us leather lovers in the group, the wine to choose when you want to walk on the wild side has to be Zinfandel.

A powerhouse red serving up full-frontal fruit and alcohol followed by a piquant, peppery chaser, Zinfandel's brazen decadence inspires legions of devoted fans to have a good time. Why else would winemakers dub their creations Wild Thing, Sin Zin, and ZaZin?

Beware, though . . . sipping this inky elixir just might encourage you to don leather and jump on the back of a Harley.

THE GRAPE STORY

Zinfandel is red, but it might as well be red, white, and blue since it is considered America's heritage grape. While Bordeaux can brag of Cabernet Sauvignon and Burgundy has dibs on Pinot Noir, Zinfandel is firmly rooted in our wine culture. As noted Zin-maker Carol Shelton jokes, "There's no European counterpart to Zinfandel, so we don't have a pretentious standard to live up to. Zin is all about big and bold with a good-natured, dirty edge, and it's as unpretentious as they come!"

How does Zinfandel come by its robust, juicy character? Blame it on the berries. Zin is what we call an *uneven ripener*, which means the same cluster of grapes may contain unripe green berries mixed with ones that look like raisins. Though it is often a wine-making challenge to determine exactly when to pick the grapes, Zin's off-kilter clusters give the final wine a unique spectrum of flavors. A bright hit of acidity is delivered by green grapes, while raisiny ones saturate the juice with sugar. This sugar is turned into high levels of alcohol during fermentation. The heady fullness, followed by a peppery kick, is what gives Zin its signature one-two punch.

The Buzz from…Joel Peterson, Cofounder, Head Winemaker, Ravenswood Winery

Sonoma California's Ravenswood Winery stamps its hearty Zinfandels with a well-deserved slogan, "No Wimpy Wines." As Joel says, "While we take our winemaking seriously, we don't take ourselves too seriously. Wine needs to be removed from its pedestal and placed on people's dining room table, where it belongs." That's the attitude.

The Renegade Red

Zin thrives in warm regions, so the grape has found its primary home in California. Vines were originally brought to the state in the early 1850s, and European immigrants coveted rustic Zin for their home brew. While fortifying fortune seekers during the California Gold Rush, Zinfandel's popularity grew even more, and by the 1890s it had become the state's most widely planted grape.

Over time, however, other red varieties claimed the heart of Californians, and Zinfandel suffered as a result. That is, until the past twenty years, when the "modern era" of Zinfandel began. California wineries such as Ridge Vineyards, Joseph Swan, Ravenswood, and Rosenblum embraced Zin and helped to create a fanatical underground following during the wine-heady 1980s. When Zinfandel got "zapped," however, the wine's recognition exploded aboveground.

In 1991, a group named Zinfandel Advocates and Producers (ZAP) held its first tasting in San Francisco. The event began quietly with a hundred people sipping and swirling, but in the past decade it has mushroomed into the largest tasting of one grape variety in the world. I've gone every year, and it's amazing to see the devotion wine drinkers have to this raucous red. The annual Zinfandel festival now draws more than nine thousand Zinophiles who come to pay homage to their favorite wine.

The Mysterious One

In addition to the boost from ZAP, the mystery of the grape's origin fueled Zin frenzy. As I discovered my passion for Zinfandel, I was swept into the saga. The search for the origins of Zin became the wine world's equivalent of the television series "*Unsolved Mysteries*."

A widely held belief was that Zinfandel originated in Italy and was transported to California during a wave of Italian immigration. This theory gained momentum when a southern Italian grape named Primitivo was proven to be the same variety as Zinfandel. Mystery solved, right? Wrong. Researchers discovered Italy was not the original home of Zinfandel. Essentially, Primitivo is an interloper in southern Italy, transported there most likely by eighteenth-century Croatian monks. Post-Primitivo, the plot thickened. The question remained, where did Zinfandel originate?

Historical records were soon uncovered that showed the grape variety was probably brought to America in 1829 from the Imperial nursery collection in Vienna. Included in the collection were "all the grape varieties grown throughout the Austro-Hungarian Empire. At that time, Croatia

---

The Buzz on...A "Primo" Zin

Have you noticed wines labeled *Primitivo* on store shelves? You will definately see more in the future as value-conscious drinkers search for alternatives to Zinfandel's escalating prices. Primitivo and Zinfandel are the same variety (simply called different things, as with Syrah/Shiraz) and do share a similar earthy, spicy character. I've found most Italian Primitivos lack the overt fruitiness of California Zins, but with price tags hovering in the $8 range they just might find their niche.

TERRALE

2000

PRIMITIVO

PUGLIA

INDICAZIONE GEOGRAFICA TIPICA

was part of the Austro-Hungarian Empire," said Carole Meredith, a professor at the University of California at Davis and lead Zinfandel sleuth. All roads were leading back to Croatia, and the trail was hot.

When Meredith and her colleagues at the University of Zagreb in Croatia found a grape that looked similar to Zinfandel called Plavac Mali, they thought the case might be closed. Drat, the researchers were foiled again. Plavac Mali was not the same variety as Zinfandel, but its offspring! In December of 2001 the mystery was finally solved by Meredith and her team.

Drum roll, please . . . Zinfandel did originate in Croatia, and in its homeland it goes by the tongue-twisting name *Crljenak Kastelanski* (*CK* for short).

Lingo Lesson

Core Words

Dry: Though they are generally considered dry, Zinfandels can taste sweeter than other red wines due to their high alcohol levels, ripe fruit, and often residual sugar. If you like the juicy quality of Australian Shiraz, Zin is for you.

Smooth: Unlike Sangiovese, which is a high-acid grape variety, most Zins will fall on the smoother side of the acidity scale.

Medium- to full-bodied: I use the term *medium-bodied* in relative terms since Zinfandels can range from an average 12–13 percent alcohol to a whopping 16 percent. These are some of the most full-bodied reds you will encounter.

Medium tannins: Zinfandel is not generally meant to age, so tannins play a supporting role. Tannins also feel suppler in many ultraripe Zins because as the grape ripens, the tannins soften.

Extra Credit Words

Fruit aromas:

> Red fruits—strawberry jam, raspberry
> Black fruits—plum, blackberry jam, boysenberry
> Dried fruits—prune, raisin

Spicy: Think freshly ground black pepper and brown spices such as nutmeg, allspice, and clove.

Elegant: Not all Zins are huge wines. Some are crafted in a more restrained, elegant fashion and are dubbed "claret-style" Zins.

Big, chewy: The way the alcohol, fruit, and tannins meld together makes you think you might need a knife and fork to cut through the "big boy" versions.

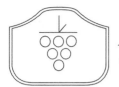
Zinfandel is crafted in a range of styles from relatively medium-bodied and vibrant to portlike powerhouses. Let's take a cruise around California to visit some of my favorite Zin haunts and discover some Zins you may enjoy. Your leather pants and a Harley might come in handy here.

Place: Dry Creek Valley, California

Taste: I think of Zinfandel from Dry Creek as leaning toward the elegant side of the style scale. Juicy fruit flavors are supported by a streak of vibrancy and luscious spice notes that come from the valley's rollercoaster climate (hot days/cool nights), which traps the bright fruit character gained during long hours of sunshine. I'm definitely biased when it comes to Zins from Dry Creek because that's where my husband and I spent many hot days and cool nights while dating. (Or was it the other way around?) With a strong Italian influence still apparent throughout the valley—wineries carry names such as Teldeschi, Rafanelli, and Pedroncelli—it really brought out his romantic Italian side.

Place: Mendocino County, California

Taste: Floral aromas and a bright cherry character waft from the glass and are chased with Zin's sinful spiciness. Beginning about ninety miles north of San Francisco, the Mendocino region encompasses miles of dramatic Pacific Ocean coastline and steep coastal mountains covered with towering redwoods. (It reminds me more of the Pacific Northwest than California.) Logging and organic farming are important in the region, and though there is a laid-back feel to the place, innovation and tradition go hand in hand. Old-vine Zinfandel vineyards, dating back nearly a century, share the landscape with emerging Rhône and Italian varietals such as Syrah and Barbera. A wide-ranging group of subregions make up Mendocino, from ultracool, Pinot-Noir-loving Anderson Valley to the warm Redwood and Ukiah valleys. These warmer inland valleys beget Zinfandel with power and elegance.

Place: El Dorado County, California

Taste: The epicenter of California's Gold Rush, El Dorado County is truly a golden spot to grow Zinfandel. Because of its proximity to the Sierra Nevadas, distinctive volcanic soils help the vines develop concentrated flavors, while the high altitude lends coolness to the growing season's warm daytime temperatures. At Sierra Vista and Lava Cap wineries, you can actually walk through vineyards while admiring snowcapped peaks in the distance. Sometimes I find it hard to separate the place and the taste, and whenever I pour a glass of spicy, vibrant El Dorado Zin, I imagine gazing at the pristine, snowcapped mountains in the background. That's why you visit a wine region—to return there every time you take a sip.

Place: Paso Robles, California

Taste: If Mendocino reminds me of the Pacific Northwest, then Paso Robles is pure California. Located smack in the middle of the state's Central Coast region, Paso Robles sits inland from the Pacific and produces Zins with sun-baked fullness. While driving around in the flatlands of the region (though there are numerous canyons and steep hillsides), the sun beats down on the car, inviting short sleeves and bottles of cold water. You can feel that warmth when you taste Zin from the region. By the way, Paso is also a terrific spot to go wine tasting if you prefer the down-home feel to Napa Valley's glitz and glamour. Bikers welcome here!

Place: Lodi, California

Taste: Lodi Zin is a bodybuilder of a wine with a benevolent streak. The powerful, jammy character is tinged with hints of dried fruit aromas and a supple, smooth texture and soft tannins. Century-old vineyards pack the place—located between the Sierra foothills and the San Francisco Bay—helping winemakers rediscover the high-quality wines that can be produced from the region. Stay tuned: Lodi is sure to get hotter and hotter among Zin lovers.

2000
OLD VINE
ZINFANDEL
LODI
LAUREL GLEN VINEYARD

ALC. 14.5% BY VOL.

Look for these places on the label, too . . .

Napa Valley, California

Sonoma County, California

Russian River Valley, California

The Buzz on . . . Three Tastes, One Place

As a founder of Women for WineSense and a winery owner herself, Julie Johnson is one of Napa Valley's most prominent women. Recently, Julie decided to tackle a unique project called Tres Sabores, or "three tastes." With one small vineyard planted in seventy-six-year-old Zinfandel vines, she hired three different winemakers to craft their expression of Zin. As Julie says, "I adore the personalities involved in winemaking, and I wanted to celebrate my vineyard site with tastes beyond terroir." I have tasted all three side by side, and though there is a commonality to them, clearly the decisions each winemaker made had quite an impact on the final taste.

A MATTER OF STYLE

If you're a Zinfandel drinker, you may have picked up a bottle that said "old vines." Due to Zin's history in California, many of the vineyards have survived for more than a hundred years. Why are old vines so special, and how do they affect the final taste of Zinfandel?

Time in a Bottle: Old Vines

By the time the vines hit old age—anywhere from forty to a hundred-plus years—they can eke out only enough energy to produce minimum clusters with small, intensely flavored grapes. This fruit can make wine of depth, power, and complexity. "I'm look-ing for a slap on the head, not a gentle kiss, with my Zinfandel, so I find vineyards that give me that character," says Ray Coursen of Napa Valley's Elyse Wine Cellars. Old vines naturally give you that slap. When you're a hundred years old, you can do anything you want, too.

All About Structure
PART IV

Zinfandel is defined by its ripeness and alcohol level. A portlike Zin can sport alcohol levels reaching 16 percent, while a claret-style version tips the scales at 12–13 percent. That may not seem like a huge difference, but it affects the final style greatly. How? Let's go back and visit Brut to get the details on why alcohol is such an important component in wine.

Light-, Medium-, and Full-Bodied = Alcohol Level

Alcohol is the reason we drink wine. It makes us feel good and, in moderation, is good for us. But we don't "taste" alcohol; we sense it. Wines with less alcohol feel lighter in body, and those with more alcohol have a fuller body and give a heavier impression in the mouth. If a wine has too much alcohol, you detect a hot sensation in the back of your throat.

How does wine come by its level of alcohol? Sunshine.

Brut and his other buddies in the cluster love to soak up the sun. As they do, those energy rays create sugar in grapes. Sugar is what gets converted to alcohol in the wine-making process. So if Brut is full of sugar, he'll have more alcohol by the time he becomes wine. That's the reason wines from warmer regions are more full-bodied than ones from cooler regions (think ripe California Zinfandel versus racy German Riesling).

The Buzz on...Brix

When winemakers want to test a grape for ripeness, they measure the degrees Brix, or sugar content. Most grapes destined for wine will be picked at about 22–25° Brix, which roughly equals a wine with 12–14 percent alcohol. Due to Zinfandel's uncanny ability to produce raisined grapes, measurements can reach up to 30° Brix, which explains its high levels of alcohol and fuller body.

Shopping Guide

Bargain Sips

Stash-Your-Cash Wines $15 and Under

	Name of Wine	From	Style Profile	Price Range
PF	A-Mano, Primitivo	Puglia, Italy	Medium-bodied, light tannins, bright and earthy	$7–10
PW	Cline Cellars, Zinfandel	California	Medium-bodied, light tannins, bright and fruity	$8–10
PW	Trinity Oaks, Zinfandel	California	Medium-bodied, light tannins, bright and fruity	$8–12
PW	Rosenblum, Vintner's Cuvée, Zinfandel	California	Medium-bodied, light tannins, bright and fruity	$8–12
	Dunnewood, Zinfandel	Mendocino County, California	Medium-bodied, light tannins, bright and fruity	$9–11
	Sebastiani, Zinfandel	Sonoma County, California	Medium-bodied, supple tannins, smooth and fruity	$9–12
GW	Rancho Zabaco, "Dancing Bull," Zinfandel	California	Full-bodied, supple tannins and ripe	$9–12
	Benson Ferry Vineyards, Old Vine, Zinfandel	Lodi, California	Full-bodied, supple tannins and ripe	$9–11

	Name of Wine	From	Style Profile	Price Range
	Bogle Vineyards, "Old Vine," Zinfandel	California	Full-bodied, supple tannins and ripe	$9–13
	EOS, Zinfandel	Paso Robles, California	Full-bodied, supple tannins, ripe and earthy	$15–18
GW	Francis Coppola, "Diamond Series," Zinfandel	California	Full-bodied, supple tannins and ripe	$12–15

Classic Sips

Well-Known Winners $15–25

	Name of Wine	From	Style Profile	Price Range
PF	Lava Cap, "Reserve," Zinfandel	El Dorado, California	Full-bodied, supple tannins, ripe and earthy	$21–25
	Sierra Vista, Zinfandel	El Dorado, California	Medium-bodied, supple tannins, bright and earthy	$16–20
	Sobon Estate, "Rocky Top," Zinfandel	Shenandoah Valley, California	Full-bodied, supple tannins, ripe and earthy	$15–18
PF	Nalle Winery, Zinfandel	Dry Creek Valley, California	Medium-bodied, supple tannins, bright and spicy	$20–25
	Alderbrook, "OVOC," Zinfandel	Dry Creek Valley, California	Medium-bodied, supple tannins, smooth and spicy	$20–23
GW	Fife, "Whaler Vineyard," Zinfandel	Mendocino County, California	Medium-bodied, supple tannins, smooth and fruity	$20–23
	Lolonis Winery, "Estate," Zinfandel	Redwood Valley, Mendocino, California	Full-bodied, supple tannins and ripe	$20–23
	Eberle Winery, "Sauret," Zinfandel	Paso Robles, California	Full-bodied, supple tannins, ripe and earthy	$15–19
GW	Norman Vineyards, "The Monster," Zinfandel	Paso Robles, California	Full-bodied, supple tannins, ripe and earthy	$16–22

Worth-the-Splurge Wines $30–50+

	Name of Wine	From	Style Profile	Price Range
	Edmeades, "Eagle Point Ranch," Zinfandel	Mendocino Ridge, California	Full-bodied, supple tannins and ripe	$25–26
PF	Elyse, "Morisoli Vineyard," Zinfandel	Napa Valley, California	Full-bodied, supple tannins and ripe	$25–28
PF	Carol Shelton Wines, "Wild Thing," Cox Vineyard, Zinfandel	Mendocino County, California	Full-bodied, supple tannins and ripe	$28–32
	Ridge, "Lytton Springs" Zinfandel	Dry Creek Valley, California	Full-bodied, supple tannins and ripe	$29–35
	St. Francis, "Old Vines," Zinfandel	Sonoma County, California	Full-bodied, strong tannins and spicy	$25–26
	Miner Family Vineyards, Zinfandel	Napa Valley, California	Full-bodied, strong tannins and spicy	$25–26
	Jessie's Grove Winery, Old Vine, "Westwood Vineyard," Zinfandel	Lodi, California	Full-bodied, strong tannins and spicy	$25–26
	Ravenswood, "Monte Rosso," Zinfandel	Sonoma Valley, California	Full-bodied, strong tannins and spicy	$29–34
GW	Mayo Family Winery, "Ricci Vineyard," Zinfandel	Russian River Valley, California	Full-bodied, strong tannins and spicy	$35–38
PF	Sineann, "Old Vine," Zinfandel	Columbia Valley, Oregon	Full-bodied, strong tannins and spicy	$36–38

The Buzz on…Give Me an *R*!

The cry for lovers of big, bold Zin has always been to buy one of the classic Rs: Ravenswood, Ridge, Rosenblum, Renwood. These producers are responsible in many ways for beginning the Zinfandel craze of the past twenty years and still craft some of the best bottles today.

pairing

ZINFANDEL IS AS AMERICAN AS APPLE PIE WHEN IT comes to food. Grilled beef is an ideal match for its full-bodied character. Fear not, though; you don't need to be a meat eater to appreciate Zinfandel.

Pizza, pasta, and even chocolate desserts pair well with the various styles of Zinfandel. And there aren't too many red wines that take on the heat of spicy foods as well as this red-wine wonder.

To discover a Zinful food and wine match made in heaven, ask yourself a few questions:

Let's Talk Texture First: Is the wine medium-bodied or full, elegant, or big?

The only problem with Zinfandel is that occasionally the wine is too full-bodied. High alcohol can overpower many dishes and amplify the spice in spicy foods. Keep an eye on the alcohol content if you have a lighter-styled dish.

Consider It a Complement: Do you get deep berry fruit or lots of spiciness?

Barbecue sauces complement the juicy tang of fruit in Zinfandel, while spicy foods echo the black pepper kick of the wine.

It's Tannin Time: Are the tannins noticeable in the wine?

If your mouth puckers up with a drying sensation, the Zin leans toward the tannic end of the scale. In that case, decrease their effect by pairing the wine with steak. Since Zinfandel has so much fruit, however, tannins tend to be less apparent.

Design-a-Dinner

STOCK YOUR SHELVES

Bottoms: Steak, ribs, burgers, sausage, bacon, pork, chicken, pasta, beans

Tops: Sweet potatoes, zucchini, red bell peppers, tomatoes, plums/prunes, figs, cheeses (aged goat, strong Cheddar, blue cheeses), barbecue sauces, tomato sauces, mustard

Accessories: Creole spices, ginger, allspice, oregano, black pepper, chocolate (the ultimate food accessory)

GET SAUCY . . . WITH ZINFANDEL

Sweet Meat Marinade: Combine 1 cup ketchup and ½ cup each of sherry, soy sauce, and olive oil. Add 2 teaspoons Worcestershire sauce and 2 to 3 crushed garlic cloves. Use to marinate flank steak and/or ribs (see page 246).

Balsamic Dipping Glaze: Reduce 2 cups balsamic vinegar to the consistency of thick syrup by simmering it over low heat for about 30 minutes. Drizzle the glaze on sandwiches and meats or use as a dipping sauce for fries and even strawberries.

MEAL ENSEMBLES

Burgers with Sweet Potato Fries: To make Sweet Potato Fries peel and slice several sweet potatoes into long sticks. Toss with olive oil, sea salt, and cracked pepper and bake until soft inside and lightly browned and crispy outside, 30 minutes at 375°F. For the hamburgers, mix 1 to 1½ pounds lean ground beef with 3 tablespoons barbecue sauce and form into patties, then cook. For cheeseburgers, place a small cube of Cheddar cheese in the center of the meat patty as you're forming it. The meat should completely surround the cheese.

As the patty cooks, the cheese will melt inside. Serve with the fries and pass Balsamic Dipping Glaze (page 245) at the table.

Red Beans and Rice: Here's a simple way to spice up your favorite canned red beans. Sauté 1 chopped green bell pepper, 1 onion, and 1 chopped tomato. Add 1 teaspoon cayenne pepper and 1 16-ounce can red beans. Add rice and water (two parts water to one part rice) to the bean mixture and cook on the stove, following the rice package directions, until the rice is tender. Serve with hot links or sausages.

BLT with Baked Beans: You can't find a better match with Zinfandel than a BLT. Simply cook thick-sliced bacon and drain it. Slice tomatoes and slather white bread with mayonnaise. Layer the bread with Iceberg lettuce, tomatoes, bacon, and freshly cracked black pepper. Meanwhile, heat your favorite brand of baked beans and stir in a few spoonfuls of Sweet Meat Marinade (page 245).

Sweet Marinated Ribs: Use baby back pork ribs if you're using the dish as an appetizer or longer beef ribs if they will be a main course. Marinate ribs in Sweet Meat Marinade (page 245) overnight and grill or broil until crispy. Serve with a salad topped with Retro Green Goddess Dressing (page 59).

sharing

My friend Linde and I were enjoying a girls' night out, away from husbands and kids, when she asked me about the health issues around red wine and heart disease. I'm not a doctor, but because my father died of a heart attack when he was very young, it's a subject I have always followed closely.

Ever since 1991, when news of something called "the French paradox" hit the airwaves, there has been a buzz surrounding the health benefits of drinking wine. Morley Safer of CBS's "60 Minutes" broadcast the results of work completed by several esteemed scientists, who showed that despite a high-fat diet, the French population's incidence of heart disease was comparatively lower then in other Western countries. They concluded that the health benefits were tied in part to the regular consumption of wine, in particular red wine.

Though many studies have since followed—some supporting the added benefit of red wine and others questioning it—all have demonstrated that alcohol can aid in keeping your heart healthy.

To help explain the issue in more detail, I turned to Dr. Michael Apstein, an assistant professor of medicine at Harvard Medical School, who, in his off-hours, is a James Beard Award–winning wine writer. Dr. Apstein notes that experts are generally in agreement on the role of alcohol in reducing the risk of coronary heart disease. Considering that heart disease is still by far the leading cause of death among women in this country, it is an extremely important subject.

"Looking at the big picture, we can safely say that moderate alcohol consumption is good for the heart. Some people insist that there is an added protective effect of wine, particularly red wine, but that has yet to be proven positively," says Dr. Apstein.

The Buzz on…How Come *He* Can Drink More?

According to Dr. Apstein (who is also a member of the division of gastroenterology at Beth Israel Deaconess Medical Center in Boston, where he is a liver specialist), the amount of alcohol consumed is not only about differences in body weight between the sexes.

"Women are more susceptible to the effects of alcohol than men—good and bad—because they have less of an enzyme in the lining of the stomach, which is needed to metabolize alcohol efficiently. This means that they absorb more alcohol than men. This stomach enzyme also explains why drinking wine with food raises blood alcohol more slowly than drinking on an empty stomach, for both men and women. Food slows the rate at which things leave the stomach; hence the alcohol remains in the stomach longer in the presence of food, giving the stomach enzyme more time to metabolize alcohol."

Red wine had been touted as providing an extra benefit over other forms of alcohol because of chemical compounds known as *phenolics* in the skins and seeds of red grapes. Tannins fall into this category, as do pigments in dark-skinned grapes, which are called *anthocyans*. These antioxidants may possibly help to protect the heart against the action of "bad cholesterol," thereby lowering a person's chances of developing coronary heart disease.

The most important argument for the health benefits of wine versus other forms of alcohol, however, may lie in the way we consume wine.

How Much and When?

Moderation is important in everything we do from eating to working, and certainly in drinking. Too much alcohol, like anything, can be dangerous. According to the current federal dietary guidelines, one glass, or five ounces, of wine is the daily recommended limit for women and two glasses for men.

The key word there may be *daily*. That's because regular, moderate alcohol consumption is where the benefits lie. As Dr. Apstein jokes, "You can't save up your drinks and binge on the weekend!" The fact that we enjoy wine slowly over several hours with food, he says, may be why wine could have additional protective heart benefits over other forms of alcohol.

See, those French (and Italian, and Spanish . . .) really do know something. The joys of uncorking wine with a daily meal are actually good for you.

Other Hot Reds

IT'S RAINING REDS, HALLELUJAH!

buying

WE HAVE COVERED FAMILIAR REDS, BUT WHAT ABOUT other fun bottles—from Beaujolais to Rioja—vying for your attention as you pass through the wine aisles? There is a flood of hot wines just waiting to be discovered, so while it might not be raining men (as in the Weather Girls one-hit wonder), it is raining reds . . . hallelujah!

EVERYDAY WINES

BEAUJOLAIS: LIGHT AND FRUITY

THE NAME GAME
Gamay = red wines from Burgundy's Beaujolais region in France

Buying

Beaujolais is my Ray Romano of reds—friendly and fun, and there's something more there than meets the eye.

The fun side of Beaujolais makes its annual appearance on the third Thursday of November, when inexpensive Beaujolais Nouveau is released. Nouveau, or "new" wine, is bottled mere months after the Gamay grapes are harvested and captures a fresh-from-the-vine character. This earns Beaujolais my title as "Kool-Aid for adults." But Beaujolais is far more than nouveau.

To take a step up the quality ladder, search for wines called Beaujolais-Villages, which indicates the Gamay grapes come from vineyards planted near the slopes of the hilly Beaujolais region. No need to stop there, though. Several more rungs up the ladder lie the cru wines of Beaujolais. These bright, juicy, and spicy reds are complex yet quaffable.

There are ten crus named after the villages where the hillside vineyards are located. Look for wines carrying place names such as *Morgon*, *Fleurie*, *Chiroubles*, *Saint-Amour*, *Chénas*, *Juliénas*, *Brouilly*, *Côte de Brouilly*, *Régnié*, and *Moulin-à-Vent*. Here are my three favorite regions in order from lighter to fuller:

- **Brouilly:** juicy, light tannins, fresh
- **Morgon:** medium-bodied, bright cherry, peppery
- **Moulin-à-Vent:** spicy with loads of deep berry fruit

Tasting Tip: Do a comparative tasting with these recommended wines to see if these appellations are really different in the glass (prices are approximate):

- **Château de La Chaize** from Brouilly ($14)
- **Jean Descombes** from Morgon ($10)
- **Château des Jacques** from Moulin-à-Vent ($15)

How do you know if you're getting a Beaujolais cru? The price will be slightly higher, you will see the *cru* mentioned, and the vintage will normally be a year or two older than current-year nouveau releases.

Price: Bargains! Most fall between $8 and $15.

Favorite producers: Maison Louis Jadot, and Georges Duboeuf.

Pairing

Beaujolais wines are top summertime picks because they taste delicious after a few minutes in the ice bucket and are the perfect match with burgers and sausages off the grill. These seasonless sippers are also a top pick on the turkey table to tackle fruity cranberry sauce and candied yams.

RIOJA: SPICY AND SMOOTH

THE NAME GAME

Tempranillo and Garnacha (or Grenache) = red wines of Spain's Rioja region

Buying

I think of Rioja reds as the vinous version of Antonio Banderas: spicy, smooth, and sexy. What makes Rioja so special? A unique combination of grapes and years of aging—mostly in American oak barrels—gives Rioja reds a vanilla- and strawberry-scented character wrapped in smoothness.

Located in northern Spain, the wine-growing region is tucked away behind a range of mountains protected from the harsh Atlantic Ocean weather. Rioja's extremely warm yet temperate climate allows Tempranillo and Garnacha grapes to ripen slowly and develop ripe and concentrated flavor.

To attain the wine's soft tannins, Rioja is aged for a set period of time in accordance with government regulations. Just as in France and Italy, where regions are controlled, Spain's DO and DOC (or Denominación de Origen and Denominación de Origen Calificada) system regulates grape varieties and wine-making procedures. The Spanish take the additional step of setting timetables for aging many wines. This affects not only the taste, but the price, with Gran Reservas costing more than those labeled Crianza.

Crianza—the basic level of wine, with up to twelve months of aging in oak casks to impart some softness.

Reserva—minimum of three years aging with at least one of those years in cask. These wines taste ultrasmooth.

Gran Reserva—These wines are made only in exceptional years and require a minimum of five years of aging with two years in cask. Mellow, suave, and classy.

Tasting Tip: Try other Spanish reds made with Tempranillo from the Ribera del Duero region and dry red Portuguese wine from the Duoro River Valley (where the grape is called *Tinta Roriz*).

Price: Generally affordable. Most fall between $10–25

Favorite producers of Rioja include: CVNE, Marqués de Cáceres, Marqués de Murrieta, Marqués de Arienzo, Conde de Valdemar, and Ramón Bilbao.

Pairing

Uncork Rioja with traditional Spanish cuisine from paella to chorizo sausages, but don't forget casual American fare such as burgers and ribs. A simple meal idea is store-bought rice pilaf doctored up with chopped roasted red peppers and olives. Served with grilled flank steak and a bottle of reserva Rioja, it's a crowd pleaser.

MALBEC: DEEP AND BROODING (OR IS IT?)

Buying

Argentina's star grape is named *Malbec*. It reminds me of the soulful singer Aaron Neville, who looks like a tough guy but sounds like an angel. When I first tasted Malbec, I thought it was going to do a tango on my tongue. Deeply-hued, the wine smelled of licorice, tar, and deep berry fruit. I was sure one sip and I'd be reaching for a knife and fork to cut through this chewy wine. Wrong! Malbec is bright and zesty and ever-so-stylish.

Argentina's top wine-growing regions are essentially high deserts with rocky soils, loads of sunshine, and dramatic differences in day and night temperatures. Malbec flourishes in these conditions, getting ultra-ripe but maintaining vibrant levels of acidity and developing smooth, almost sweet tannins.

Tasting Tip: Malbec is a traditional component in the blends of red Bordeaux and is famous as part of the "black wine" of France's Cahors region (though rarely found in this country). Save for a few brave California and Chilean winemakers, Malbec is rarely bottled alone outside of Argentina.

Price: Generally affordable. In the $8–20 range

Favorite Argentinean producers: Catena Alamos, Tapiz, Altos las Hormigas, Susana Balbo, Ben Marco, Bodega Norton. The classic Napa Valley winery Pine Ridge bottles an inky-black Malbec-based wine named Onyx. It's pricey ($45–50) but definitely a "wow" wine.

Pairing

Malbec is like a cross between the intensity of Syrah and the finesse and brightness of Sangiovese. Its natural companion is beef, but I've found Malbec to pair as easily with tomato dishes like chicken cacciatore.

> ### The Buzz from...Laura Catena, Vice President, Bodega Catena Zapata in Argentina
>
> Laura Catena's family emigrated from Italy to Argentina in 1902, and in the past century the Catena clan has become one of the country's most famous producers. I asked Laura—a petite, elegant young mom—what her top nosh is with Malbec. "Pork, lamb, and Argentine beef are ideal, but I also like Malbec with Indian food that is not too spicy. To end it all, dark chocolate is my favorite."

CARMENÈRE: HERBAL AND EXOTIC

Buying

For those enological adventurers out there, there's a special wine to seek out called Carmenère. Exotic and smooth with a touch of herbal aromas, I think of it as Carlos Santana in a glass. Just as Santana has made a comeback in recent years, Carmenère has too.

An obscure red Bordeaux grape, Carmenère was planted in Chile in the late 1800s and, until fairly recently, was confused with Merlot. It can have the velvety but sometimes herbal quality of Merlot but serves up a spicy edge like Zinfandel. Now that the vines have been identified correctly, Chile is embracing Carmenère as its signature grape. Versions are beginning to trickle into this country, so you'll definitely be seeing more of this spicy sipper.

Price: Bargains! In the $8–15 range.

Favorite producers: Arboleda, Caliterra, Calina, Primus Veramonte, Baron Philippe de Rothschild, Maipo Chile, Santa Rita

Pairing

Carmenère goes anywhere a Merlot or Zinfandel treads. But, because it often expresses an even more green herbal character, it's my top choice with any dish that has olives or fresh veggies (think pizza and pasta).

WEEKEND WINES

BAROLO: MAJESTIC AND EARTHY

THE NAME GAME

Nebbiolo = Barolo from the Piedmont region of northern Italy

Buying

Say it slowly: Barolo. It rolls off the tongue like Pierce Brosnan purring "Bond . . . James Bond." In true Bond fashion these wines can be dangerously powerful, but that's not the point. Barolo wins you over with its suave elegance. If you've yet to explore Barolo, I encourage you to splurge the next time you're looking for an impressive bottle.

Barolo hails from vineyards planted around the historic hillside town of Barolo in northern Italy's Piedmont region. *Piedmont* means "foot of the mountains," and it is the towering, snowcapped Alps cupping the region like a gentle giant hand that give it a majestic feel and unique environment to grow grapes. Often referred to as the Burgundy of Italy, Piedmont is a patchwork of small vineyards planted mostly on sloping hillsides. Fog shrouds many of the vineyards in the Barolo area, and it is there that a red grape named Nebbiolo—*nebbia* is "fog" in Italian—thrives and produces wines named *Barolo*. As wine importer Marc De Grazia told me, "Barolo is the place where the grapes meet the fog, producing truly expressive wines."

It wasn't too long ago that you had to wait decades to open a bottle of Barolo because they were typically so tannic and tight upon release. Times have changed, however. Producers are now crafting Barolo in a more approachable style, with softer tannins, while maintaining the powerful fruit component and telltale perfumed, trufflelike aromas that make Barolo unique. With a string of classic vintages kicked off in 1996, now is the time to begin exploring Barolo.

Price: Expensive wines, no doubt about it, ranging from $40 to hundreds of dollars.

Favorite producers:

In the $40–50 range: Fratelli Revello, Marchesi di Barolo, Attilio Ghisolfi

In the $50–80 range: Paolo Scavino, Luciano Sandrone, Pio Cesare, Aldo Conterno

One California producer that has found success with Nebbiolo is Napa Valley's L'Uvaggio di Giacomo ($20–25 per bottle)

Tasting Tip: Nebbiolo is also the grape responsible for the great reds named Barbaresco after the nearby Piedmontese zone of the same name. Though in the same general price category as Barolos, Barbarescos are often more approachable when young.

Pairing

Barolo is unique because it has the elegance of Pinot Noir, with the backbone and tannic structure of Cabernet Sauvignon. With its unique musky, earthy character, Barolo is ideal with game, stews, mushroom dishes, and pungent cheeses.

If you really want to taste heaven on earth, drink Barolo with white truffles. Considered aphrodisiacs, nuggetlike white truffles are a specialty of Piedmont and are available generally from October to December each year. I was lucky enough to hunt for white truffles one year. Specially trained dogs sniff the ground (dogs are used in Piedmont, not pigs) and indicate where a truffle may be. The dog's owner quickly digs to find the elusive fungus, and when you smell one pulled straight from the ground, the scent is deliciously overwhelming. You need only a small piece shaved over homemade pasta or risotto paired with a glass of Barolo.

CABERNET FRANC: FRUITY AND AROMATIC

THE NAME GAME

Cabernet Franc = one of the important grapes of Bordeaux reds and France's Loire Valley wine named Chinon

Buying

Cabernet Franc is my Jon Bon Jovi of reds—what a face, and can he ever sing. This "pretty boy" wine has backbone and fruit intensity highlighted by aromatic delicacy. Part of the traditional blend in Bordeaux—especially important in the wines from the region of Saint-Émilion—Cabernet Franc has always played a supporting role. But this stylish red grape variety has lived under the shadow of its famous offspring, Cabernet Sauvignon, for too long.

Planted in California, Washington, and Virginia (where it ranks as the third-most-planted variety), Cabernet Franc is starting to be bottled all by itself. Though it tends to lack the overall complexity and tannic power of Cabernet Sauvignon, delicious versions of this blueberry, lead pencil, and rose-petal-scented red are sneaking onto store shelves near you.

For refreshing lightness and affordability, seek out wines from . . .

Chinon, France: If you like Pinot Noir or Beaujolais, you'll gravitate toward the cherry-red wines from Chinon in France's Loire Valley. Cabernet Franc grapes are grown along the limestone cliffs of the river Loire and, in that cool-climate region, produce refreshing reds that are bright and earthy.

For impressive elegance, seek out wines from ...

Saint-Émilion, France: I'm not one to covet superexpensive wine (there are too many good values in the world), but the select times that I've tasted the Cabernet Franc–based wine, Château Cheval-Blanc, I was convinced one of the priciest wines in the world was worth it. Needless to say, it's just one of the many wonderful reds from Saint-Émilion where, along with Merlot, Cabernet Franc expresses itself beautifully.

For intensity of fruit and power, seek out wines from ...

California: From Napa to the Sierra Nevada foothills, Cabernet Franc is starting to get attention. In the California sunshine the grapes—which can have a fairly herbal character in cooler regions—tend to get riper. This results in full-bodied wines with lovely blueberry, mineral, and floral aromas.

Price: Ranges from less than $10 to $60 for top California versions to outrageously expensive French bottlings from Saint-Émilion costing hundreds of dollars per bottle.

Favorite producers
  California
    In the $6–10 range: Pepperwood Grove, Ironstone Vineyards
    In the $20–30 range: Lang & Reed, Crocker & Starr
    In the $40–60+ range: Pride Mountain, Chappellet
  Chinon
    Values $10–$16: Marc Brédif, Couly-Dutheil, Olga Raffault, Langlois-Château
  Saint-Émilion (these wines are Cabernet Franc-based blends)
    Luxury wines $60–80: Château Figeac, Château Angélus
    Dream wine costing several hundred dollars: Château Cheval-Blanc

Pairing

Wines from Chinon are ideal alternatives to lighter-styled Pinot Noir, which makes them a top pick for everything from pork tenderloin to salmon and honey-glazed ham. Riper versions go well with dark-meat chicken, burgers, and other beef dishes.

CHÂTEAUNEUF-DU-PAPE: EARTHY AND PEPPERY

THE NAME GAME

Primarily Grenache but up to thirteen varieties including Syrah = Châteaneuf-du-Pape reds from France's southern Rhône Valley

Buying

Want to start a weekend with a visit from Gerard Depardieu? Then open a bottle of earthy, rustic, and embracing Châteauneuf-du-Pape. It will transport you to the south of France in style.

Châteauneuf-du-Pape, the place, is the picture of Provence. Driving from the southern Rhône Valley city of Avignon, you pass fields brimming with lavender, rows of tall cyprus trees, and olive groves. The houses are painted Provençal pastels with vibrant purple shutters and white lace curtains; wrought iron is used for gates, furniture, and fences; and the feel is distinctly Mediterranean. In fact, Châteauneuf-du-Pape means "new castle of the pope" because in the fourteenth century the popes of nearby Avignon used it as a summer residence.

What's unique about Châteauneuf-du-Pape from a wine perspective, however, are the rocks. I'd seen pictures of the area's abundant *cailloux* but couldn't believe my eyes when I saw them. Rocks the color of rust and the size of large grapefruits covered the vineyards, and it seems nearly impossible that grapes could grow.

Not only do they have to contend with rocks, but winds—the famous mistrals—blow so fiercely across this portion of southern France that you feel like the Flying Nun, ready to take flight at any moment. Despite these conditions, the grapes thrive. In fact they love it. The vines are pruned short to deal with the gusts, while the rocks act as solar panels, soaking up daytime heat and sealing it in for the cool nights. A vineyard visit makes it easy to understand how the wine's sun-baked character originates.

Tasting Tip: Grenache vines thrive in the Mediterranean climate of southern France and comprise not only the backbone of Châteauneuf-du-Pape and Gigondas reds but also the affordable red wines named Côtes-du-Rhône. These popular bottlings share the same spicy, earthy character as their more expensive brethren. To explore Grenache further, taste the hot wines coming from Spain's Priorat region (where it's known as *Garnacha*) or the complex Australian versions produced from some of the world's oldest Grenache vines.

Price: Affordable to expensive. Châteauneuf-du-Pape generally falls in the $20–50 category, while delicious Côtes-du-Rhône reds and ones from the neighboring region of Gigondas can be found from $10–20.

Favorite producers in Châteauneuf-du-Pape and Côtes-du-Rhône include: Château de Beaucastel, Château la Nerthe, Château du Vieux Télégraphe, Château Fortia, M. Chapoutier, E. Guigal, Perrin/La Vieille Ferme, Paul Jaboulet Aîné

Australia's top picks include: Charles Melton's Nine Popes and Grant Burge's Holy Trinity, also d'Arenberg, Simon Hackett, and Tim Adams versions of Grenache

Pairing

Echo the earthy, rustic character of Grenache-based wines by pairing with spicy dishes that include mushrooms and sausages, and dark-meat turkey.

Pink, Bubbly, and Sweet

Rosé

THE "BEACHWEAR" WINE

buying

HEADING TO THE BEACH IS ALL ABOUT FUN WITH A capital *F*. You're there to relax and unwind. When the ensemble calls for shorts, T-shirt, and a straw hat, I think of rosé, my beachwear of wines. Refreshing rosé isn't about serious complexity—it's just serious fun.

Most bottlings are light enough to replace white wine, but because they're made from red grapes, rosés are substantial enough sippers to take the place of a juicy red. Besides quaffability and versatility, though, the best thing about pink wines is their affordability.

> ### The Buzz from . . . Milla Handley, Winemaker, Handley Cellars, California
>
> "Rosé is a remarkably flexible wine with food. It can go anywhere a Chardonnay can go and possibly do it better. But by the same token, it can go where a light Pinot Noir can go. It's ambidextrous."

THE PINK STORY

Europeans embrace rosé with a passion. During summer in the south of France, café tables are dotted with pink wine on white table-cloths—my favorite kind of polka dots. In Spain, where it's called *rosado*, the infatuation is no less intense, and even Italians get into the act with *rosato*. Americans seem to have a split personality when it comes to pink wines, however.

On the one hand, there are those who adore sweeter-styled blush wines such as white Zinfandel. Sutter Home, inventor of this American favorite, estimates there are nearly ten million consumers of white Zinfandel. That's about 21 percent of the wine-drinking population indulging in blush wine.

On the other hand are those who think blush is a beginner's wine and wouldn't be caught dead with it in their glass. They eschew all pink wines without realizing there are dry versions on store shelves, too. Luckily, dry rosés do have a small and devoted cadre of followers.

The Buzz on…What's in a Name? Blush Versus Rosé

Wines with some sweetness, such as white Zinfandel, are called *blush wine*, while dry pink wines are referred to as *dry rosé* or simply *rosé* (which means "pink" in French).

Crush Me, Squeeze Me (Just Not Too Hard!)

Rosé is interesting because in wine terms it goes both ways. It's essentially made like a white wine but with red grapes. To make white wine, grapes get crushed and the juice is removed immediately from the skins. For reds, grapes get crushed and the juice is left in contact with the red grape skins for weeks to soak in the color and tannins. To make rosé, red grapes are crushed gently and the juice has a brief rendezvous with the skins, lasting from several hours to several days. This short-lived interaction imparts the appealing pinkish hue. Sweeter wines contain various levels of residual sugar, while dry versions are fermented completely.

Color and flavor, however, have to do with grape variety as well. Rosés can be made from a host of red grapes, including Zinfandel, Merlot, and Cabernet Franc. Rhône varietals such as Syrah, Mourvèdre, Cinsault, and Grenache are included, and even Burgundian Pinot Noir, Spanish Tempranillo, and Italian Sangiovese are responsible for delicious rosés. But, because these varieties have their own characteristics—from light, fresh, and fruity to deep, rich, and spicy—the resulting wine can vary in final taste and color.

Sweeter Versus Drier

Keep in mind that we are a nation of soda drinkers, so sweetness in a wine is an appealing taste. That's the reason blush wines are so popular. If the label says *white* anything, such as white Zinfandel or white Merlot, it will have a healthy dollop of residual sugar and fall into the slightly sweet, blush wine category. When served nice and cool, the sweetness will be less apparent and more integrated. So, if you're uncorking a blush, get the ice bucket ready.

Rosés can also be very dry, and with your eyes closed you would swear you were sipping a dry white wine. Dry rosés are produced in France, Italy, and Spain, and domestic producers often use the word *dry* on their wine's label to indicate a lack of sweetness.

The Buzz on…From Pink Wine to Pink Ribbons

America's most famous blush wine, Sutter Home white Zinfandel, was initially a dry rosé and became a sweet wine by accident. "A stuck fermentation in the 1975 vintage left some residual sugar in the wine," says Roger Trinchero, president of Sutter Home. They decided not to worry about unsticking the fermentation and bottled the wine anyway. People loved it, and that's when white Zin really took off.

Interestingly, if you buy a bottle of Sutter Home white Zinfandel, you're contributing to breast cancer awareness and research. Several women at the company are breast cancer survivors and have transformed personal challenge into corporate action. In addition to donating money to research, during the months of September and October, Sutter Home white Zinfandel uses pink corks and sports the pink ribbon of awareness on the front label to remind women to get breast exams.

Bigger Versus Lighter

It's fairly easy to tell if the wine you're choosing is more delicate or more powerful in nature simply by looking at its color intensity and alcohol level. Lighter-colored wines—pale salmon and pale pink—with a lower level of alcohol (11–12 percent) will be more delicate than those that are darker and higher in alcohol (around 13–14 percent).

Besides its lovely color, the beauty of rosé lies in its ability to refresh and rejuvenate. Meant to be consumed chilled and young, these wines don't strive for greatness but offer pure enjoyment.

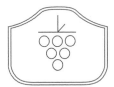

leslie's label links
Connecting taste to place makes wine buying easy

Place: Côtes de Provence, France

The Name Game: Main red grape varieties include Grenache, Cabernet Sauvignon, Cinsault, Mourvèdre, and Carignane.

Sweetness: Dry

Taste: With floral aromas, touches of spice, and a veritable fruit bowl of strawberry, cherry, and peach flavors, these wines are as bright as the famous Mediterranean sunshine. They invite

relaxation and lounging in a beach chair. When I travel to Provence, I feel my stress melt away. Moving south from the steep hillside vineyards of the northern Rhône Valley toward Nice and the Mediterranean Sea, the landscape flattens out and vineyards and lavender fields blanket gently rolling hills. Houses are painted terra-cotta with bright purple doors, markets overflow with local fare that makes having countryside picnics a snap, and everything seems laid back and languorous. It's rosé country. The Côtes de Provence produces more than 100 million bottles of wine per year, with 80 percent of it falling into the rosé category. Americans are beginning to discover the joys of Provençal pink wine, too. Statistics show a jump in sales of nearly 200 percent since 1997.

Place: Bandol and Tavel, France

The Name Game: Main grape varieties are Mourvèdre, Cinsault, Grenache.

Sweetness: Dry

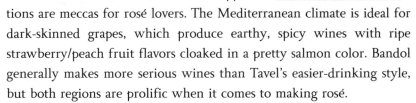

Taste: These warm, southern French appellations are meccas for rosé lovers. The Mediterranean climate is ideal for dark-skinned grapes, which produce earthy, spicy wines with ripe strawberry/peach fruit flavors cloaked in a pretty salmon color. Bandol generally makes more serious wines than Tavel's easier-drinking style, but both regions are prolific when it comes to making rosé.

Place: Anjou, Loire Valley, France

The Name Game: Main grape varieties are Cabernet Franc, Cabernet Sauvignon, and Grolleau.

Sweetness: Medium-dry

Taste: From the sometimes mediocre but enjoyable Rosé d'Anjou (usually made with Grolleau grapes) to the more intense and complex Cabernet d'Anjou (made with Cabernet Franc and Cabernet Sauvignon), wines from this Loire Valley region are lighter and cranberrylike in nature, often with a dash of sweetness. The soil is limestone and the climate mild, so the wines sport a zesty mineral character. They're especially good when the temperature heats up and you want a crisp, thirst-quenching quaff.

Place: Rioja and Navarra, Spain

The Name Game: Main grape varieties are Tempranillo and Garnacha.

Sweetness: Generally dry

Taste: If you don't drink Spanish wines, start with rosé from this Iberian wine paradise. I adore the pure wallop of strawberry/watermelon fruit flavors, appealing rose-petal aromas, and spicy kick in pink wines from Rioja and Navarra. These neighboring appellations in the northeastern part of Spain are warm, and nothing goes down quite as easily here as refreshing rosé.

Place: California

Sweetness: Dry, medium-dry, and medium-sweet

Taste: From Santa Barbara and Temecula in the south to Mendocino and the Livermore Valley in the north, pink wine is made in all parts of the Golden State. Some are dry, while blush wines will be medium-dry to sweeter, so it's hard to pin down a typical taste profile. One thing you can expect is loads of fruit. Many labels will also say *dry*, so keep an eye open if you're interested in that style. As French-born winemaker Marketta Fourmeaux of Napa Valley's Château Potelle says, "We're French and felt we needed to make our rosé 'Riviera' because we missed real dry rosé—you know, the kind you get in France that has complexity and personality but is still refreshing."

Shopping Guide

Uncork one of my favorite dry rosés. All except one are priced $15 or less, making it easy to drink pink.

California
- Solo Rosa, Rosé
- Fife, "Redhead Rosé," Mendocino
- Zaca Mesa, "Z Gris," Santa Ynez Valley
- Montevina, "Nebbiolo Rosato," Amador County
- Château Potelle, "Riviera Rosé," Napa Valley
- Concannon Vineyards, "Righteously Rosé," Livermore Valley
- McDowell Valley Vineyards, "Grenache Rosé," Mendocino

France and Spain
- Marqués de Cáceres, Rosé, Rioja, Spain (Usually around $5)
- Château Routas, "Rouvière," Côteaux Varois, France
- Delas Frères, Tavel, "La Comballe," Tavel, France
- Domaine de Curebéasse, Rosé, "Angelico," Côtes de Provence, France
- Domaine Tempier, Rosé, Bandol, France ($20–22)

Other Spots

- Wölffer Estate, dry Rosé, The Hamptons, Long Island, New York
- McCrea Vineyards, Vin Rosé, Yakima Valley, Washington
- Lawson's Dry Hills, Pinot Rosé, Marlborough, New Zealand
- Charles Melton, Rosé, Barossa, Australia
- Fairview, "Goats Do Roam," Rosé, South Africa

pairing

JUICY FRUIT FLAVORS KISSED BY HINTS OF SPICE MAKE rosé the consummate summer wine—indeed anytime wine. Fresh-from-the-garden spring fare partners well with pink wines, but so do hot-weather standards like ribs and burgers. Comfort foods of fall, from chili to meat loaf, make the grade. When Thanksgiving rolls around, pull out rosé for a stellar match. It sports enough guts to stand up to spicy sausage stuffing and has plenty of fruitiness to complement cranberry sauce and sweet potatoes.

The Sweet Side: Does the wine taste sweet to you?

When the wine has some sweetness, it goes well with sauces that share that sweetness, such as barbecue, ketchup, peanut sauce, and teriyaki. A dash of sweetness also offsets the heat of piquant fare from burritos to Kung Pao chicken.

Consider It a Complement: Is the wine fruity? Are there spicy aromas and flavors?

These wines are like a fruit bowl in a bottle, so it makes sense to complement that by serving it with fruit salsas or chutneys. What about pairing its spicy qualities with spicy Thai or Indian cuisine? Works beautifully.

It's Tannin Time: Do you detect any tannins?

Though some rosés (usually darker ones) can have noticeable tannins, they are not usually something to contend with when thinking about a food match.

Design-a-Dinner

STOCK YOUR SHELVES

Bottoms: Ribs, burgers, steak, ham, pork, sausages, chicken, turkey, couscous

Tops: Red bell peppers, sweet potatoes, olives, strawberries, cranberries, citrus fruit, raspberries, cheeses (Monterey Jack, Parmesan, goat and cream cheeses), teriyaki sauce, peanut sauce, barbecue sauce

Accessories: Curry seasonings, tapenade, chili powder, crumbled bacon, garlic, black pepper, fennel

GET SAUCY . . . WITH ROSÉ

Try Sweet Meat Marinade (page 245), Zesty Blueberry Sauce (page 165), Red Pepper Honey Mustard (page 103), and Olive Pepper Salsa (page 186).

MEAL ENSEMBLES

Sweet Potato Chili and Corn Bread: Roughly chop 1 yellow bell pepper, 1 white onion, several carrots, and several celery ribs, then sauté in olive oil until the veggies are slightly browned. Add 1 16-ounce can chopped tomatoes, 1 16-ounce can black beans, and some chili powder (to taste), a dash of cumin, and a sprinkle of cloves. Here's the kicker—microwave 1 sweet potato until soft, then peel and puree with a ricer or in the blender. Add it to the chili for a luscious layer of texture. Serve with corn bread.

Flank Steak and Strawberry Salad: Use butter lettuce and top with cooked crumbled bacon, sliced strawberries, and Creamy Mustard Dressing (page 42). If strawberries aren't in season, substitute dried cranberries. The sweet/savory quality is ideal with rosé. Serve with thinly sliced flank steak marinated in Sweet Meat Marinade (page 245) and fresh rolls.

Orange Juice Chicken: Combine 1 cup orange juice with ¼ cup soy sauce and 2 teaspoons apricot jam. Pour over 3 to 4 chicken breasts and cook in a 350°F oven for 30–40 minutes. Serve with rice.

Spicy Sausage Sandwich: This is a favorite at my house (especially when made with chicken-apple sausage). Cook the sausages and slice lengthwise in half. Cut warm, crusty bread into sandwich-size pieces, then layer with Red Pepper Honey Mustard (page 103), sausage, and caramelized onions. Serve with Sweet Potato Fries (page 103) and Balsamic Dipping Glaze (page 245).

sharing

IT WAS MY TURN TO HOST THE EXTENDED FAMILY FOR Mother's Day. The weather is usually nice in California in May, so I thought about doing a barbecue. Then it dawned on me, one of the best Mother's Days I had ever spent was in the south of France. In the city of Avignon we stocked up on local cheeses, fresh olives, sausages, bread, and several bottles of rosé, then headed to the countryside for a picnic.

With very little effort, I re-created that Provençal picnic party in my backyard.

WINE IDEAS

Serve rosé wines and offer a selection of regions and styles. If you want to augment the wine selection with reds, look for wines from France's Rhône Valley (either northern or southern Rhône wines), which are generally made from the Syrah and Grenache grapes.

Make rosé punch by mixing several bottles of rosé with a big bottle of lemon-lime soda and then adding a dash of Grand Marnier and Grenadine to taste. Fill ice cube trays with rosé and in each cube put a few sprigs of culinary lavender. Freeze and add to the punch. As the ice cubes melt, the aroma will transport you to Provence.

FOOD IDEAS

Olive oil, garlic, tomatoes, eggplant, and herbs such as thyme, rosemary, and lavender are signature foods of Provence. Here are food ideas that showcase the region's culinary bounty.

APPETIZERS AND NIBBLES

Olive Platter with Tapenade: Offer a selection of olives as well as tapenade, a traditional Provençal olive paste, to spread on crostini.

Pepper Rolls: Spread roasted and peeled strips of red pepper (an inch or so wide) with a thin coating of goat cheese or cream cheese. Sprinkle with herbes de Provence and roll them into pinwheels.

Baba Ghanoush and Pita Bread: Buy this eggplant spread at the store and serve with toasted pita bread triangles.

Bacon-Wrapped Dates: Simply wrap pitted dates with a small piece of bacon and broil until crispy.

Olive Oil Bar: Offer three or four types of olive oil to taste with slices of freshly baked bread.

Spicy Sausages with Aïoli: Aïoli is the Provençal mayonnaise made with olive oil and loaded with garlic.

Roasted Potatoes with Rosemary: Drizzle potatoes with olive oil and crumble either fresh or dried rosemary or culinary lavender on top, and then bake until browned.

Ratatouille: A delicious cooked mixture of eggplant, tomatoes, zucchini, and bell peppers (page 188).

Olive-Pepper Pizza: Top prepared pizza crust or cheese bread with tomato sauce, Olive Pepper Salsa (page 186), and Parmesan cheese.

Champagne/Sparkling Wines
MAKE MINE "SEQUINS AND SUEDE"

buying

OPENING A BOTTLE OF BUBBLY IS THE VINOUS EQUIV-
alent of dressing up. As you wiggle into lingerie and zip
up a slinky ensemble, your mood meter immediately
accelerates from zero to sixty.

It's the same sensation with sparkling wine. The
satisfying "pop" and festive bubbles signal celebration and pleasure. But
why wait for a special event to sip a sparkler? Sparkling wine can be
found in all prices ranges and styles, pairing as easily with potato chips
as caviar.

As Lily Bollinger, of the famed Bollinger Champagne house, once
remarked, "I drink Champagne when I'm happy and when I'm sad.
Sometimes I drink it when I'm alone. When I have company, I consider
it obligatory. I trifle with it if I'm not hungry and drink it when I am.
Otherwise, I never touch it unless I'm thirsty."

THE SPARKLING STORY

Sparkling wine is seductive, and one sip makes you want more—and
more and more. Its allure lies with the tiny bubbles. How do they get
all those bubbles in the bottle? Though it may seem like magic, the process of making sparkling wine is fairly straightforward—start with
wine and create the sparkle.

The world's best sparkling wines are made from three primary grape
varieties: Chardonnay, Pinot Noir, and Pinot Meunier. The first is a

From the women behind the bubbles to the ones drinking them, women have a fondness for fizz. Throughout history, we have played an important role in the business of bubbly. The most legendary is Madame Clicquot of Champagne Veuve Clicquot. Nicole Ponsardin Clicquot became a widow, or *veuve* in French, in 1805, when she was still in her twenties. A master marketer and hands-on owner, Madame Clicquot is credited with helping to make Champagne famous throughout Europe. In 1816 she cut holes in her kitchen table because she suspected it would be a better way to anchor bottles so the sediment would gather at the top. This stroke of brilliance evolved into the now-standard process of *riddling* still used by every producer of sparkling wine. The company named its famous Champagne in her honor, "La Grande Dame."

In 1941 Lily Bollinger took over the helm of Champagne Bollinger upon the death of her husband and ran it for thirty years. Her panache helped make *Bolly* a household name (its appearances in James Bond films helped, too). Today women are involved in running other famed Champagne houses, such as Laurent-Perrier, Gosset, and Mercier.

In California, bubbly and women have an ongoing love affair. Just about every big-name wine producer has had females at the helm, including Dawnine Dyer formerly of Domaine Chandon, Jamie Davies of Schramsberg Vineyards, Eva Bertran of Gloria Ferrer Champagne Caves, Joy Sterling of Iron Horse Vineyards, and Judy Jordan of J Wine Company.

A male professor once tried to discourage Eileen Crane from entering the wine business because he believed she wasn't strong enough to move barrels. She ignored his advice and today is the winemaker and president of Napa's Domaine Carneros, which is owned by the French firm Champagne Taittinger. Making sure this type of chauvinism remains under a cork, Eileen has made it a goal to mentor women. "Before Prohibition in this country, nearly 10 percent of winemakers were women. It's taken until 1998 to reach those numbers again," she notes. Along with Claude Taittinger, she recently founded Le Reve Foundation to help young women enter the wine business. Now *that's* girl power.

white grape. The other two are red. To make white wine, the juice is immediately drained from the skins, then turned into wine through fermentation. These are called *base wines*, and when a number of them are blended together, it's called the *base blend*, or *cuvée*.

Now comes the bubble part. A mixture of yeast and sugar is added to the cuvée, and this is put in tightly sealed bottles. As the yeast eats the sugar, it produces gas, which gets trapped in the bottle. Voilà; the sparkle is born. (See page 285 for more details on the sparkling process.)

Unlocking Other Label Clues to Find a Bubbly You Like

Dry Versus Sweet

These are terms you'll see on labels that indicate the sweetness level:

Natural—Very dry (sometimes called *extra brut* or *ultra brut*).

Brut—Dry.

Extra-Dry—Oddly enough, extra-dry bubbly is slightly sweeter than brut.

Demi-Sec—It literally means "half-dry," so wines labeled *demi-sec* tend to fall on the sweeter side. If you want bubbly to drink with dessert, look for a demi-sec.

Tasting Tip: One of my absolute favorites is the demi-sec from Laurent-Perrier. I've poured it for people who say they don't like Champagne because it's too dry and tart. They fall in love with this one, though, because it is soft and lightly sweet.

Lighter Versus Fuller

Just as Paris is the center of the fashion world, the Champagne region of France is the epicenter of the sparkling wine world. These folks have spent nearly three hundred years tweaking the art of making bubbly to get it just right.

Since it's a gamble to ripen grapes properly in the region's cold climate, the Champagne winemakers blend together wines from different grape varieties and various years for consistency. One year's juicy grapes offset another year's tart ones, and the fullness that comes from one grape variety balances the leanness of another.

Each producer has developed its own recipe, which gives her a unique signature or house style. Some Champagne houses go for elegance and a light-bodied style, others for a medium-bodied style with finesse, and still others opt for full-bodied power.

For elegance and light to medium body, look for wines from Billecart-Salmon, Pommery, Lanson, Laurent-Perrier, and Moët & Chandon.

For more fullness and richness, look for wines from: Pol Roger, Mumm, Veuve Clicquot Ponsardin, Bollinger, and Krug.

Grape varieties: Sparkling wines can be made with a variety of grapes, but the three famous ones used in top-notch bottles from Champagne and California are Chardonnay, Pinot Noir, and Pinot Meunier. Labels often indicate these grapes, which gives you an idea of style.

For elegant and crisp sparkling wine, look for **Blanc de Blancs,** which means it is white wine from white grapes. These wines are made from Chardonnay and taste fresh and crisp, like biting into a crunchy apple. Try them with oysters or salted nuts.

For soft and creamy sparkling wine, buy **Blanc de Noirs,** which is white wine made from red grapes. Made from Pinot Noir and Pinot Meunier, they range in color from pale yellow to light pink and are an excellent choice to serve throughout a meal.

For spicy and rich sparkling wines, look for a **rosé.** Ranging from pale salmon to deep pink, these rare wines are usually made by adding a dash of red wine to the base blend but can be crafted like tradi-

tional still rosé, where the pink hue comes from contact with red grape skins. It is the ideal bubbly to sip with your sweetie on Valentine's Day.

The Buzz on…Sparkling Red Wines

Many Australian vintners craft redder-than-red bubbly. Made primarily from the inky purple Shiraz grape, it is full, fizzy, and fun. Seek out Yalumba's "D" Black, "Vixen" by Fox Creek, Rumball Sparkling Shiraz, and Peter Lehmann's "Black Queen." In a nod to its winemaker's Australian heritage, California's Geyser Peak Winery also makes a delicious red sparkler.

Affordable Versus Pricey

When it comes down to it, price is a big factor in buying sparkling wines. You can spend big bucks on special wines or buy bubbly for everyday drinking. Here are a few places to start once you hit the store aisles:

Sequin Sippers: $25–100+

Champagne will usually start around $25 for nonvintage versions and go up for top vintage and prestige bottles.

What is nonvintage? Due to the fact that producers blend many years together to achieve a desired style of wine, most Champagne labels will not designate a vintage. These are known as *nonvintage (NV)* wines.

What is vintage? If you see a year written on the label of a bottle of Champagne, the quality of the grapes harvested in that year was exceptional and the winemaker chose to bottle wine highlighting that particular vintage. These wines are generally higher priced than nonvintage versions. Top California producers often vintage-designate much of their sparkling wine.

What is prestige cuvée? ($90–150+) Champagne houses often produce a specialty wine known as their *prestige cuvée*. You might recognize these names, but unless you're ready to part with serious cash, you probably won't drink them too often (I don't). I recommend these when splurging is in order:

Louis Roederer, "Cristal"

Veuve Clicquot, "La Grande Dame"

Moët & Chandon, "Dom Pérignon"

Perrier-Jouët, "Fleur de Champagne"

Laurent-Perrier, "Grand Siècle"

Pommery, "Cuvée Louise"

Sequins and Suede, California Style: $15–30+

Most high-quality California sparklers are priced in the $20–30 category, with a few winners in the $15–20 range and a handful of the best bottles in pure sequin territory. (See the Shopping Guide for a list of favorites.)

Simply Suede: $15 and Under

Look for these alternatives to Champagne and California sparkling wine for everyday sippers.

Spanish Cava—Spain is churning out loads of delicious fizz for a fraction of the price of other sparklers, generally $6–12.

Italian Prosecco—This typically low-alcohol bubbly made from the Prosecco grape is affordable and fun. Falls in the $9–15 range.

Crémant de Loire—It's bargain time when you uncork Crémant from the Loire region of France as most wines cost around $10–12.

The Buzz from… Eric Benn, Co-owner of the Bubble Lounge

The Bubble Lounge in New York and San Francisco are temples to bubbly. "We open more than a hundred thousand bottles per year, and much of that is sipped and enjoyed by women," notes the charming Mr. Benn. "Sparkling wine is seductive and sensual, and so it attracts women. But women attract men, so we have a healthy mix of both."

Core Words

Dry, medium-dry, and sweet: Look for brut if you want dry wines, extra-dry, and demi-sec for sweeter bubbly.

Crisp: Most wines will be vibrant and refreshing with high levels of acidity.

Light-, medium-, and full-bodied: Sparkling wines can run the gamut from light-bodied Prosecco to full-bodied vintage Champagne. Think chiffon, silk, and satin.

Extra Credit Words

Fruit aromas: apple and pear and red fruits such as strawberry, cherry, and cranberry

Yeasty: When Champagne and the best sparkling wine ages in the bottle and marinates with the yeast from the secondary fermentation that causes the bubbles, it gains a nutty, yeasty character reminiscent of freshly baked bread. The longer the time in contact with the yeast, the more complexity it gains and the smaller the bubbles.

Mousse: The mousse, or effervescent feel in your mouth, should be creamy and smooth, not harsh, and the bubbles should be tiny and stream from the bottom of the glass to the top for a long period of time.

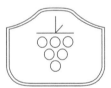

leslie's label links

Connecting taste to place makes wine buying easy

Place: Champagne

The Name Game: Grapes include Char-donnay, Pinot Noir, and Pinot Meunier.

Taste: The playful snap of acidity mixes with a seductive, come-hither creaminess to create a party in your mouth. The best

wines have toasty aromas and flavors that remind me of fresh bread and fruitiness that hints of my mother's baked apples. But to me Champagne is more than just delicious, festive wine. Taking a sip is like drinking history.

That first struck me while visiting Veuve Clicquot's caves located far beneath the streets of Reims, Champagne's main city. Mesmerized by tool marks on the cave's limestone walls, I recognized that I was gazing into the past. Myriad interconnected tunnels, nearly as large as the city above, were created millennia ago when the Romans settled in northern France. Workers dug deep pits in gathering materials to build their settlements, and here I was, two thousand years later, gazing at the handiwork of a long-dead Julius or Marcus.

Later inhabitants of Reims took the Romans' lead and carved hundreds of miles of tunnels underneath the city, where the magic of Champagne takes place. As millions of bottles rest in these ultracool caves, they slowly develop their famous bubbles. At the same time aboveground, vines are digging their roots deep into this chalky soil and struggling to get ripe in the marginal climate. (Champagne is the northernmost grape-growing region in France.) Miraculously, the combination of grapes, soil, and climate is perfect for making Champagne. Slow, cool ripening makes these grapes naturally high in acid, which when the second fermentation takes place in the bottle allows the final drink to be crisp yet balanced.

The Buzz on…Champagne, the Making of a Classic Wine

Contrary to popular belief, Dom Pérignon, the seventeenth-century monk who worked in Champagne, didn't invent bubbly. He was responsible, though, for improvements in grape-growing and winemaking that made modern Champagne possible. At that time no one really understood why the wine sparkled. Winemakers all believed it was a flaw because pressure caused by the bubbles made many bottles explode. However, when the British and others started to embrace this fizzy wonder in the early 1700s, the ever-crafty Champagne makers decided to go with the flow. Capitalizing on its popularity, they utilized stronger bottles and powerful corks, making bubbly the drink of the day. Champagne houses hired flamboyant traveling salesmen who were legendary for getting their products in the hands of famous revelers from Russian czars to French kings and American presidents such as Thomas Jefferson. Champagne became synonymous with celebration, and in the span of a few hundred years Champagne had become the most famous wine in the world.

Place: Crémant de Loire, France

The Name Game: Primary grape varieties include Chenin Blanc and Cabernet Franc.

Taste: Softer and usually lightly sweet, these affordable sparkling wines from the Loire Valley in France are an ideal alternative to more expensive Champagne. Believe it or not, the Loire is actually the second-largest region in France for production of bubbly, and in the early days Champagne producers used to get some of their wines from the Loire and bottle them as Champagne.

Tasting Tip: Crémant ("creamy") wines are made with the same method as Champagne. But, because of slightly less gas pressure in the bottle, the mousse is less fizzy and creamier than Champagne. Try Crémant-style wines from other areas of France, such as Crémant d'Alsace and Crémant de Bourgogne.

Place: Northern California

The Name Game: Main grape varieties include Chardonnay, Pinot Noir, and Pinot Meunier.

Taste: How does California bubbly compare to Champagne? The quality of top bottlings are certainly in the same league as Champagne, but sparkling wines from the sunny Golden State taste, well, like they've seen more sunshine. Though the grapes and the process are the same, California is warmer than Champagne. As a result the grapes get riper and the flavors tend to reflect a juicy opulence. Not that elegance and crispness you'd expect from a good bubbly is lacking. Au contraire. Cool-climate regions of northern California such as Napa's Carneros region, parts of Sonoma, and Mendocino's Anderson Valley produce excellent sparkling wines. In fact many French Champagne firms have set up outposts in these areas, including Mumm Napa, Domaine Chandon, Domaine Carneros, and Roederer Estate.

California settlers, however, were making bubbly long before the French arrived. In 1882 the Korbel brothers founded their famous winery in the foggy Russian River Valley of Sonoma County. Jack and Jamie Davies knew they had struck liquid gold when they abandoned life in southern California to relocate to Napa in 1965 and restore the historic winery founded by Jacob Schram in 1862. Today the Californians are certainly giving the Champenoises a run for their money.

Place: Spain

The Name Game: Grapes include mainly native varieties such as Macabeo, Parellada, Xarello, and Chardonnay.

Taste: If the sometimes piercing crispness of Champagne is not to your liking, try **Cava.** *Softness* is the key word. Sometimes I get a pleasant earthy aroma, and other times I just taste a wallop of ripe fruit flavors. It makes sense when you think of how warm it is in Spain's Catalonia region, where most of the Cava is produced. The nice thing about Cava, besides its unique taste, is the affordable price.

Place: Conegliano and Valdobbiadene, Italy

The Name Game: Grape variety is Prosecco.

Taste: For a great summer sipper or partner for spicy fare, uncork affordable Prosecco. It's fruity, fizzy, and usually sports a hint of sweetness. Prosecco is a white grape variety planted throughout the Veneto region of northern Italy, but it reaches its best expression in the areas around the towns of Valdobbiadene and Conegliano. You will often notice one on a label; for example, Prosecco di Valdobbiadene or Prosecco di Conegliano.

Look for these places on the label, too . . .
Washington state
New Zealand
Tasmania, Australia

A MATTER OF STYLE

To illustrate the full process behind sparkling wine, we'll step into the
shoes of a Frenchwoman I'll call Colette. Colette has just been hired to
take over the wine-making helm at the Champagne house of *le Big Deal
Bubbly* and is reviewing a memo from management.

Job Title: Cellar Mistress/Chef de Cave

Goal: Utilizing the méthode champenoise, make our nonvintage
Champagne taste deliciously elegant.

NOTE: Méthode champenoise is the traditional high-quality process of
producing Champagne, in which the secondary fermentation takes
place inside the bottle. (But of course those producers who do not
come from Champagne yet use our method for producing sparkling
wine should call it *méthode traditionelle*.)

Duties:

1. **Make the base wines**—To make the delicate white wine from
   red grapes, great care needs to be taken when crushing the
   fruit so as not to get much color from the skins. The juice will
   be put into large tanks and undergo fermentation to make
   wine. It is your job to make dozens of wines from various
   vineyards and a number of grape varieties.

   NOTE: Due to the fact that the grapes are harvested at high acid
   levels, wines at this stage will taste extremely tart and acidic.
   Please bring your toothbrush to work.

2. **Create the cuvée (or base blend)**—Take the wines you made and blend them with previous vintages to make a base blend or cuvée (have a notepad ready as there are sometimes hundreds of different lots). Memory is a very important skill during the assemblage, as we call it, because you must maintain consistency of taste from year to year.

3. **Begin the process to create bubbles**—To the base blend, add a mixture of yeast and sugar and mix well. Bottle the wine immediately with a tight-fitting closure. This allows a secondary fermentation to take place. The by-product of this fermentation will be carbon dioxide bubbles, which are now trapped in each bottle. If you notice the dead yeast at the bottom of the bottle, have no fear. The bottle will age on its side for years in order for the wine to make contact with these yeasts. This aging process allows the wine to gain complexity and the telltale toasty, yeasty flavors associated with great Champagne. SAFETY NOTE: Be careful when you check the bottles during this stage as a few may explode from the pressure. Check with Human Resources for safety goggles.

4. **Remove the yeast and sediment**—Confer with one of the staff riddlers (also called *remuers*). He or she will put the Champagne in wooden racks with holes, which keep the bottles at an angle. As the riddler turns the bottles slowly over several months, the sediment will move to the neck of the bottle.

   NOTE: Since the management mourns the death of our longtime head riddler, Monsieur Pierre, we have decided to invest in mechanized cages (called *gyropalettes*). Each holds several hundred bottles, effectively speeding up the process of riddling.

   When the sediment has reached the top of each bottle, it is time to remove it. In this process known as *degorgement*, the neck of the bottle will be frozen, the topper taken off, and the frozen sediment will pop out. Again, we recommend wearing safety goggles since the ice chunk can be propelled quite powerfully from the bottle. (Sadly, this is how we lost Monsieur Pierre.)

5. **The final steps**—Quickly add the dosage, which is a sugar mixture that gives the wine its desired level of sweetness, from brut to demi-sec to doux. Then get a big cork inside that small bottle and secure it with a wire cage. Merci.

The Buzz on…Other Ways of Making Bubbly

The méthode champenoise is the process by which the best bubbly is made worldwide, but there is another popular way to produce less expensive sparklers, called the *Charmat process*. This essentially produces the bubbles in a big vat instead of inside each bottle. Once the tank is full of frothy wine, it is bottled.

Shopping Guide

Bargain Sips

Stash-Your-Cash Sparklers $20 and Under

	Name of Wine	From	Style Profile	Price Range
PW	Domaine Ste. Michelle, "Extra Dry," Sparkling wine	Columbia Valley, Washington	Light, crisp, slightly sweet	$8–10
PW	Canella, Prosecco di Conegliano	Italy	Light, crisp, slightly sweet	$9–11
	Mionetto, Prosecco di Valdobbiadene	Italy	Light, crisp, slightly sweet	$10–12
PW	Zardetto, Prosecco Brut Conegliano	Italy	Light, crisp, slightly sweet	$10–12
GW	Korbel Brut Rosé— "Artist Series, Whoopi Goldberg"	California	Light, crisp, slightly sweet	$11–13
PW	Cristalino, "Brut," Cava	Spain	Medium-bodied, soft and smooth	$5–9
GW	Willm, Crémant d'Alsace, Blanc de Noirs	Alsace, France	Medium-bodied, soft and smooth	$11–15
	Langlois-Château, Crémant de Loire	Loire Valley, France	Medium-bodied, soft and smooth	$12–14

	Name of Wine	From	Style Profile	Price Range
GW	Mirabelle, Brut, Sparkling wine	North Coast, California	Medium-bodied, soft and smooth	$12–16
	Domaine Chandon, Blanc de Noirs	Carneros, California	Medium-bodied, crisp and elegant	$13–16
	Gloria Ferrer, Sonoma Brut	Sonoma, California	Medium-bodied, soft and smooth	$15–18
GW	Segura Viudas, "Heredad" Brut Reserva, Cava	Spain	Medium-bodied, soft and smooth	$16–20

Well-Known Winners $15–40

	Name of Wine	From	Style Profile	Price Range
	"J" Sparkling wine	Sonoma County, California	Medium-bodied, crisp and elegant	$22–26
	Schramsberg Vineyards, Blanc de Blancs	Napa Valley, California	Medium-bodied, crisp and elegant	$22–28
GW	Charles Ellner, "Carte d'Or," Brut	Epernay, Champagne, France	Medium-bodied, crisp and elegant	$27–33
GW	Pommery, Brut Royal	Reims, Champagne, France	Medium-bodied, crisp and elegant	$33–38
	Domaine Carneros by Taittinger Brut "Cuvée"	Carneros, California	Full, creamy, and rich	$23–25
	Pol Roger, Brut	Epernay, Champagne, France	Full, creamy, and rich	$27–35
GW	Iron Horse Vineyards, "Wedding Cuvée," Blanc de Noirs	Sonoma County, Green Valley, California	Full, creamy, and rich	$29–34
	Veuve Clicquot, "Yellow Label," Brut	Reims, Champagne, France	Full, creamy, and rich	$29–33
PF	Comte Audoin Dampierre, "Cuvée des Ambassadeurs," Brut	Champagne, France	Full, creamy, and rich	$36–38

Special Sparklers More Than $35

Name of Wine	From	Style Profile	Price Range
Laurent-Perrier, Ultra Brut	Tours-sur-Marne, Champagne, France	Medium-bodied, crisp and elegant, very dry	$45–50
Lanson, Rosé	Champagne, France	Medium-full, creamy, and rich	$37–44
Billecart-Salmon, Brut Rosé	Champagne, France	Medium-full, creamy, and rich	$50–58
Gosset, "Millésime," Vintage Brut	Champagne, France	Medium-full, creamy, and rich	$48–52
Roederer Estate, "L'Ermitage," Vintage Brut	Anderson Valley, California	Full, creamy, and rich	$36–38

The Buzz on…Grower Champagnes

The buzz among Champagne aficionados is to buy so-called grower Champagnes. Large producers make so much wine that they can't possibly grow all of their own grapes, so they purchase fruit from more than fifteen thousand different growers in the Champagne region. Today some of these small growers make their own unique Champagnes, which are labeled *Récoltant-Manipulant*, or *RM*.

pairing

IT SEEMS THE BUBBLES IN A BOTTLE OF BUBBLY MAKE us giddy and we forget that sparkling wine is just that— wine. As you would consider the body, texture, acidity, and flavors of other wines when discovering their food affinities, it's no different with a bottle of bubbly.

For example, nothing goes better with crisp sparkling wine than potato chips. The salt and fattiness of chips takes the edge off the wine's snap of acidity. Another match made in heaven is one that complements the briny character of oysters with the mineral character of Blanc de Blancs.

Champagne and its bubbly brethren are wonderful aperitifs, but think outside the cocktail hour to dinnertime. Would you pair a Pinot Noir with pork? Absolutely. What about salmon and Chardonnay? Of course. Since these grapes go into sparkling wine, I recommend serving bubbly at dinner with savory dishes such as these:

Blanc de Blancs

Chèvre Chaud Salad (page 80)
Fish and Flash-Fried Beans (page 103)
Roast Chicken and Squash (page 43)

Blanc de Noirs or Rosé

Nutty Turkey Sandwich (page 210)
Pinot Pork and Potatoes (page 209)
Flank Steak and Strawberry Salad (page 271)

Brut

Fruity Fish Tacos (page 80)
Grilled Teriyaki Chicken and Asparagus (page 80)

Demi-Sec or Extra-Dry

Peanut-Pork Skewers (page 103)
Maple-Glazed Salmon (page 209)

sharing

SHARON CALLED ME WHEN SHE WAS IN THE FINAL stages of putting together her wedding. She had done most of the planning herself and was down to the last details of choosing the wine. That's where I entered the picture.

Since I was attending the wedding, I definitely wanted to help her choose wisely. We burned up the phone lines deciding on the right bottles to go with her menu at a price she could afford. Here are some of the things we considered.

DRINK IDEAS

Sparkling Wine—Not only does everyone expect to sip bubbly at a wedding, but it is the traditional wine for all those toasts. Depending on your budget, you can choose California sparkling wine, Spanish Cava, or impressive Champagne. I also recommended offering one other white and red wine:

Chardonnay or Pinot Grigio—It's hard to go wrong with these popular choices, and delicious versions can be found in all price ranges.

Syrah or Pinot Noir—So much Syrah is available that you're sure to find good-quality choices at various price points, and it pairs with most meat dishes, chicken, and cheeses. In my opinion Pinot Noir is the most food-friendly wine on the planet, but it tends to be a more expensive option.

WITHOUT-A-HITCH PLANNING TIPS

How much to buy: Plan on about three glasses of wine per person over the course of a three-hour event. That includes one glass of sparkling wine per person for the toasts. For example, if we had a hundred guests:

  ○ One bottle equals five to six glasses
  ○ Each guest drinks approximately three glasses, so that's approximately half a bottle per person.
  ○ A hundred guests equals fifty to sixty bottles of wine, or four to five cases
    ○ Bubbly = Two cases (more for a brunch-style event)
    ○ White wine = One case
    ○ Red wine = One to two cases (more for a dinner event)

Corkage fees: Many venues allow guests to bring in their own wine and charge a corkage fee. Fees vary tremendously from place to place—some charging as little as a few dollars per bottle, others charging $20 or more. I ended up using this option for my wedding. I was able to buy high-quality wine at a discount and, even with the corkage fees, came out ahead (I also took home the wine that we didn't drink).

Glasses: Be sure to ask about the stemware. There should be flutes, not saucer-style glasses, for sparkling wines and quality wine glasses.

The Buzz from...Alexandra Pereyre, Champagne Laurent-Perrier

Alexandra Pereyre and her sister, Stephanie Meneux, are part of the family team running Laurent-Perrier. Alexandra encourages all who drink bubbly to look at it, too. "What is important for me is the glass—a nice tall flute. It shows the beauty of the wine, and that is essential, because Champagne is very sensual and touches all your senses: the eyes, the mouth, the nose, and even the ears!"

Sharon ended up choosing wine from the restaurant wine list that included a well-known California sparkler, an affordable white Bourgogne (Chardonnay), and an Australian Shiraz. The event was a smashing success, and she didn't even go over her credit card limit. Now that's a wedding miracle.

The Buzz on...Popping the Cork

1. Remove the outer foil and the wire cage slowly.
2. Hold the bottle with your thumb in the punt (the indent in the bottom of the bottle).
3. Grasp the cork with the other hand and turn the bottle counterclockwise.
4. You should feel the cork move under all the pressure, so be prepared . . . the key to opening bubbly is to go slowly.

Dessert Wines
THE "PAJAMAS" OF VINO

FOR ME, PAJAMAS DEFINE COMFORT. DONNING A PAIR melts away any stress of the day. It doesn't matter whether they're silk or flannel—pajamas are soothing and inviting.

That's why I call dessert wines my pajamas vino. Whether it's silky Sauternes or soothing tawny port, sipping a little "sugar" is the ultimate stress buster. Not only does dessert wine finish your dinner with style, but a glass enjoyed in your pajamas works wonders for your love life. Sweet wines are thought of as aphrodisiacs, you know.

Christian Seely of France's Château Suduiraut jokes, "The best way to drink Sauternes is from a woman's belly button." I assume pajamas are optional in this case.

THE SWEET STORY

My passion for dessert wines is a direct result of my love of a good bargain. Many years ago I stopped by my neighborhood wine shop for a bottle of red wine. The salesperson helped me find an inexpensive Zinfandel and, sensing my interest in wine, offhandedly showed me a wooden box filled with sad-looking bottles.

Their tattered labels were covered with a sticky mixture, making it difficult to pry the bottles apart. Explaining that they were expensive dessert wines damaged in transport, the clerk offered to sell them to me for $10 per bottle. "I'll take a few off your hands," I said, having never been able to resist a bargain.

As one of my all-time defining wine moments, it was an understatement to say I was blown away. The golden elixir that emerged from those bottles smelled of pure heaven and tasted of honey and flowers, orange peel and almonds. It was sweet but not sugary. The very next day I raced down to the store and scooped up the rest. Apparently I'd stumbled on one of the world's best dessert wines: Château Rieussec from the French region of Sauternes.

From then on, I realized how wonderful dessert wines could taste. Sure, I had started at the top and wouldn't be able to afford Sauternes on a regular basis, but there were many sweet wines to choose from, and I was going to find them. My dessert discovery tour continues to this day.

A SEASON OF SWEET TREATS

If you haven't been seduced by the sweet side yet, I encourage you to discover its joys. Here are some ideas for building a seasonal wardrobe of sweeties.

For Spring: Smooth and Sexy Silk Pajamas

Tawny Port

This isn't a drink for stuffy Brits in smoking jackets. Tawny Port is sexy and fun. It's an ideal place to start exploring the wonderful world of dessert wines. A good tawny from Portugal is amber in color and never overly sweet. It captures the essence of honey, nuts, and caramel, which makes it the perfect pairing for cheeses, nuts, fruit tarts, and vanilla ice cream.

Look for these wines from Portugal

The longer a tawny ages in the barrel, the richer and more luscious it becomes, so keep your eyes open for these clues on the label (approximate ranges):

10-year-old tawny: fresh and nutty ($20–30)

20-year-old tawny: rich and caramelly ($35–45)

30- and 40-year-old tawny: decadent, spicy and honeyed ($50+)

The Buzz on…Women and Tawny

Dominic Symington of the famed family that produces Dow's and Warre's attributes an increase in its tawny port sales in part to more women discovering the dessert beverage. In response, the company has introduced the Warre's "Otima," a 10-year-old tawny packaged in an elegant, clear bottle, which it feels appeals to women.

Ice Wine

Imagine making Popsicles of the most flavorful grapes you've ever popped in your mouth. That's what ice wine tastes like. It's so juicy, concentrated, and silky. I enjoy sipping it all by itself as dessert, but ice wine can snuggle up to apple tarts and sugar cookies or sumptuously soft cheeses. Ice wine is difficult to make, so it's pricey. Luckily, you need only a small glass to enjoy its charms. Look for versions from Canada, Washington state, New York, and Germany. ($80–100+)

Value Tip: California and Oregon producers are getting into the ice wine act by cheating ever so slightly. They harvest ripe grapes and then stick them in a freezer—how ingenious. The resulting wines taste delicious and won't break the bank. ($15–25)

For Summer: Light and Airy Cotton Pajamas

Muscat

If dessert wines are all about sensual pleasure, there is nothing to compare to the smell of a Muscat. Known as *Moscato* in Italy, wines made from the varying varieties of the aromatic Muscat family range from light and fresh to darkly colored and elegant. Sip well chilled and paired alongside a juicy fruit tart or a simple poached pear. ($10–30.)

Look for:

Moscato d'Asti—delicate, lightly sparkling wine from Italy

Muscat de Beaumes-de-Venise—stronger and richer than other Muscats, but pretty and floral

Tasting Tip: Try the decadently sinful fortified Muscats from Australia.

German Riesling

Sipping a well-chilled German dessert wine while lounging poolside is like taking the day off on a Tuesday—impulsive and decadent. With freshness and crispness that mimic snappy white cotton, German Rieslings are the epitome of things light and summery.

Look for:

Auslese—lightly sweet to very sweet and citrusy ($20–40)

Beerenauslese and Trockenbeerenauslese—very sweet and rich ($50 +)

For Fall: A Cozy Chenille Robe

Sauternes from France

The most famous dessert wine in the world is liquid gold. Imbibing great Sauternes feels like slipping under a fluffy down comforter. Honey, spice, and sweet fruit combined with a creamy texture make it the ideal foil for pungent blue cheese, decadent foie gras, or aromatic baked apples.

Look for: Make sure you don't buy knock-off versions spelled *Sauterne*, without the *s*. The real stuff—from the Sauternes region of France—is expensive but worth it. ($30 to hundreds of dollars)

Tasting Tip: New Zealand producers are crafting high-quality late-harvest Sauvignon Blancs that won't break the bank, while a number of Napa Valley wineries produce versions rivaling the best from Sauternes. ($15–60)

Gewurztraminer from Alsace, France

When leaves turn glorious fall colors and the air is nipped with cold, warm yourself with a glorious Gewurztraminer from Alsace. Wines from this region of France are generally plush, so it makes sense that dessert versions are wrap-me-in-chenille smooth.

Look for:

Vendange Tardive—rich and elegant with loads of spice ($30–80)

Sélection de Grains Nobles—honeyed and ultrasmooth ($100+)

For Winter: Snuggly Flannel Pajamas

Vintage Port and Late-Bottled Vintage Port

Enjoying chocolate-dipped blackberries by a roaring fire is what it's like to drink inky-purple vintage port. A fortified dessert drink made by adding a dollop of brandy to the fermenting wine, port has power and grace. Just as in Champagne, where each house has its own style, producers in Portugal aim for consistency from year to year. If you want a fuller, more powerful wine, look for port from Taylor Fladgate. If elegance is your thing, find Fonseca or Warre's portos. For sweeter styles, look to Graham's, and for drier wines, pick up bottles from Dow's.

Look for:

Late-Bottled Vintage—Much less expensive than vintage port, late-bottled vintage has the same rich character but is ready to drink upon release. ($15–25)

Vintage Port—The crème de la crème of porto made only in great years, this is a wine to age for decades, although I've drunk many straightaway, and they were delicious. ($50–150+)

Value Tip: Uncork a late-harvest Zinfandel from California. With the same deep berry fruit and spice of port, it's the ideal partner for chewy brownies.

Vin Santo

Tuscany is home to a special dessert wine called *Vin Santo,* or "holy wine." Vin Santo gains its unique nutty and spicy flavors from the grapes' being dried into raisins after harvesting. Each grape then gives a precious squeeze of juice. As the wine ages in barrels, it gains a golden amber color and nutty complexity. The traditional accompaniment is crunchy biscotti, dunked in the wine.

Look for: One way to experience Vin Santo is to order it when you go out to dinner. Good Italian restaurants often serve it by the glass.

Value Tip: I've found an affordable substitute for Vin Santo in a dessert wine called *Passito di Pantelleria*, which comes from the southern Italian island of Pantelleria. The grapes are dried like Vin Santo, and they have a honeyed richness that makes all winter woes disappear. ($13–18)

The Buzz on... The Siroco Twist

Move over, gin and tonic, and make way for a refreshing cocktail named the *Siroco Twist*. I tasted this drink after a laborious morning spent traipsing through steep hillsides in the Douro region of Portugal with Robert Bower of Fonseca Winery. As we shook off the dust of the vineyards and noshed on a local specialty named *bacalhau* (little balls of shredded and fried cod), we cooled off with Siroco Twists. To make Robert's specialty, fill a tall glass with ice cubes and pour in one-third Siroco, a dry white port made by Fonseca. Add two-thirds tonic water and a sprig of mint or slice of lemon.

leslie's label links
Connecting taste to place makes wine buying easy

Place: Porto, Portugal

The Name Game: Grapes that go into making porto include Touriga Nacional, Tinta Roriz (Tempranillo), Touriga Francesa, and Tinta Cão

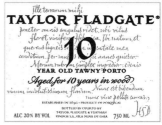

Taste: From nutty, spicy tawny ports to fruity, chocolaty vintage versions, port (or *porto* as Americans call the real stuff from Portugal) has the sweet wine spectrum covered. Every dessert imaginable can be complemented by these wines. What makes them so special? Certainly the unique way in which they are made, but also the combination of the right grapes planted in the right place. That place is the Douro River Valley.

My first visit to these vineyards began on a rustic (read non-air-conditioned) train, which chugged along a precariously perched track beside the snaking Douro River. For three hours I craned my neck to see the terraced vineyards—only a few rows of vines each—dug into the dusty soil of steep hillsides, which rose several thousand feet from the river's banks. With temperatures regularly hitting the hundred-plus degree mark during the growing season, it's no wonder these grapes get ultraripe and loaded with fruit flavors.

The magic of port certainly starts in the upper Douro Valley, but it finishes in Oporto. After harvest and foot stomping to crush some of the grapes (the rest are done by mechanized methods), wines are transported to the coastal city of Oporto, where the river empties into the Atlantic Ocean. In each winery's headquarters—known as *lodges*—great port is made and aged. As tawny ports rest in wooden casks called *pipes*, they gain their telltale nutty qualities. Vintage ports maintain their fruitiness while aging protectively in bottles. This process is what makes port from Portugal taste deliciously distinctive.

The Buzz on…The Birth of Sweet Port

Though we know port as a sweet wine, historically it began as a drier, robust red. By the early 1700s, the British had developed a strong trade link with the Portuguese and were shipping wine from Portugal to Great Britain. But they had problems with such a long journey—spoilage. Winemakers started adding a dash of brandy to the wine to prevent it from oxidizing and turning to vinegar on the sea voyage. Several crafty fellows added the brandy while the red wine was still fermenting, thereby leaving some sugar in the wine. The sweeter versions sold best, and sweet fortified port wine was born. To this day the British descendants living in Portugal are in control of the port business; hence the names on many bottles: Dow's, Warre's, Taylor Fladgate, and Graham's.

Place: Sauternes, France

The Name Game: Grape varieties include Sémillon and Sauvignon Blanc

Taste: Honey, almonds, citrus zest, floral, and spices. I could go on and on when describing the flavors and aromas of Sauternes, arguably the greatest sweet

wine in the world. How the wine gains this complexity is a study in grapes and place. Sauternes is part of the larger Graves region of Bordeaux, and within its boundaries lies Barsac, a smaller appellation known for great dessert wines. I was lucky enough to visit the exclusive and famous winery Château d'Yquem. As I walked this hallowed wine ground, however, it wasn't the historic buildings that impressed me most; it was the view. Standing atop a gentle knoll in the heart of the Sauternes region, I could see flat, lush vineyards stretched out in front of me. What struck me was that mist draped over the vines like airy lace. As the cold waters of the nearby Ciron River spill into Bordeaux's warmer Garonne River, they create a cooling steam bath. Misty autumn mornings give way to sunny harvest afternoons, creating optimal conditions for the development of *Botrytis cinerea*, or noble rot. Because Sémillon and Sauvignon Blanc are particularly susceptible to noble rot, which concentrates the grape's flavors and imparts a honeyed richness to the wine, Sauternes is the ideal place to produce world-class dessert wines.

Place: Australia

Taste: The Aussies call their sweet wines *stickies*, and every one I've ever tasted from down under has a sticky sweetness that makes you want to lick your fingers. That's just what I did one night deep in the cellars of Yalumba, a Barossa Valley winery. After passing through gravel-floored rooms lined floor to ceiling with ancient bottles, the winemaker and I tasted a nearly hundred-year-old fortified Muscat straight from a barrel. Dark amber with aromas of butterscotch and nuts, it tasted like a youthful, twenty-year-old wine. I spilled a bit on my hand and, without any sense of shame, popped my fingers into my mouth to get every drop.

Though Americans are getting familiar with Australian wines such as Shiraz, it was on sweet fortified wines that the 150-year-old Australian wine industry was built. It's been only in the past few decades that dry table wines have taken the focus from these delicious stickies.

A MATTER OF STYLE

Making dessert wine is akin to the fairy-tale story of "Beauty and the Beast." To create the beautiful final product, the grapes are subject to beastly treatment. They are frozen stiff, allowed to shrivel into raisins, devoured by mold, or squashed and then smothered with alcohol. Poor grapes!

Depending on the desired result, the winemaker can use a number of techniques to make dessert wines. Fortified wines such as port, sherry, and Madeira are made by adding brandy or other grape spirit to the fermenting wine. Not only does the spirit give the wine more alcoholic kick, it also kills the yeast before it's completely finished fermenting, which leaves residual sugar in the final wine.

For unfortified dessert wines, the goal is to concentrate a grape's flavors and sugars by removing moisture. There are a number of ways to accomplish this:

Late-harvest wines: Imagine squeezing raisins to make raisin juice. Impossible, right? Only a drop or two may come from each grape. That's pretty much what happens when winemakers make late-harvest wines. They leave the grapes on the vine until they are ultra-ripe and raisiny. This intensifies the flavors but leaves little juice for making wine. What juice is left is so high in sugar that the yeast die from exhaustion before they can convert all the sugar to alcohol.

Botrytis cinerea: If you looked at the shriveled, furry late-harvest grapes affected by *Botrytis cinerea*, you'd think it was a child's science experiment gone bad. This beneficial mold (also called *noble rot*) sends its roots into the fruit, sucking out moisture and concentrating a grape's sugars and flavors. Many dessert wines are made this way, including Sauternes, German Beerenauslese, and Trockenbeerenauslese and Alsatian Sélection de Grains Nobles.

Ice wine: These ultra-late-harvest grapes aren't even picked until December or January. When the grape freezes on the vine, only the water molecules freeze. This pushes the remainder of the sweet juice into tiny pockets within the berry. When the frozen grapes are pressed, the water, in the form of ice, remains in the berry, and only the sweet juice runs out.

Passito-style wines: Instead of letting the grapes hang on the vine to raisin, winemakers harvest them and then hang the bunches from ceiling rafters or lay them out on mats to dry. Again, this concentrates the flavors and sugars by removing moisture. Vin Santo and other Passito-style Italian wines are made with this method.

Shopping Guide

Bargain Sips

Stash-Your-Cash Dessert Wines $20 and Under

Note: Bottle sizes vary greatly with dessert wines. Most come in .375 ml half bottles, but can also be .500 ml bottles or standard-size .750 ml bottles.

	Name of Wine	From	Style Profile	Price Range
PW	Ventana Vineyards, "Muscat d'Orange," white dessert wine	Monterey, California	Light, crisp, and slightly sweet	$12–15
PF	Quady, "Essensia," Orange Muscat, white dessert wine	California	Light, crisp, and slightly sweet	$13–18
	Boony Doon, Muscat "Vin de Glacière," white dessert wine	California	Light, crisp, and slightly sweet	$13–18
GW	King Estate, "Vin Glacé," white dessert wine	Oregon	Light, crisp, and slightly sweet	$16–20
	Lake Chalice, Late-harvest Riesling	Marlborough, New Zealand	Light, crisp, and slightly sweet	$17–20
GW	Angove's winery, "Floreate," white dessert wine	South Australia	Medium-bodied, sweet, and juicy	$17–20
PF	Yalumba, "Museum Muscat"	Victoria, Australia	Medium-bodied, sweet, nutty, and juicy	$17–20
GW	Warre's, "Otima," 10 year Tawny	Portugal	Medium-bodied, sweet, nutty, and juicy	$17–20
	Dry Creek Vineyards, Late-harvest Zinfandel	Dry Creek Valley, California	Full-bodied, sweet, smooth, and rich	$12–15

	Name of Wine	From	Style Profile	Price Range
	Graham's, "Six Grapes" Porto	Portugal	Full-bodied, sweet, smooth, and rich	$13–18
	Quinta do Noval, Late-bottled Vintage Porto	Portugal	Full-bodied, sweet, smooth	$17–20

Classic Sips

Well-Known Winners $20–60

	Name of Wine	From	Style Profile	Price Range
GW	Beringer Vineyards, "Nightingale," white dessert wine	Napa Valley, California	Medium-bodied, sweet, and juicy	$28–35
	Trimbach, Vendanges Tardives, Gewurztraminer	Alsace, France	Medium-bodied, sweet, and juicy	$35–50
PF	Mendelson, Muscat Canelli, white dessert wine	Napa Valley, California	Medium-bodied, sweet, and juicy	$36–42
	Grgich Hills, "Violetta" white dessert wine	Napa Valley, California	Medium-bodied, sweet, and juicy	$40–48
	Château Coutet, Sauternes	Sauternes, France	Full-bodied, sweet, smooth, and rich	$30–40
PF	Château Suduiraut, Sauternes	Sauternes, France	Full-bodied, sweet, smooth, and rich	$35–45
GW	Far Niente, "Dolce," white dessert wine	Napa Valley, California	Full-bodied, sweet, smooth, and rich	$50–60
	Inniskillin, Riesling Ice wine	Niagara Peninsula, Canada	Full-bodied, sweet, smooth, and rich	$65–75
PF	Fonseca, 20 year old Tawny, Porto	Portugal	Full-bodied, sweet, smooth, nutty, and rich	$40–55
CW	Taylor Fladgate, Vintage Porto, "Quinta de Vargellas"	Portugal	Full-bodied, sweet, smooth, spicy, and rich	$50–55

pairing

YOU CAN HAVE YOUR CAKE AND EAT IT TOO BY DRINK-ing dessert. Not only does it satisfy the sweet tooth but a glass has far fewer calories (only around 125) than a piece of chocolate cake.

I enjoy sweet wines sipped by themselves and even cook with them on a regular basis because they add a layer of delicious richness to savory sauces. But these wines also have a love affair with food. Classic dessert pairings include Sauternes and Roquefort cheese, Vin Santo with biscotti, and vintage port with chocolate. Or my top picks: brownies and late-harvest Zinfandel, a fresh pear drizzled with Muscat, and ice wine with ice cream.

The Sweet Side: How sweet is the wine?

Try to find a wine at least as sweet as the dessert, or the wine will be overpowered by the sugary dish.

Let's Talk Texture: Is the wine light-, medium-, or full-bodied, creamy or crisp?

Match the texture of the dessert wine with the dish so you don't pummel a delicate wine with a really decadent dessert.

Consider It a Complement: What color is the wine?

Make a fashion statement and match the color of the wine with the food. Lighter-colored golden wines and amber tawny ports sing with softer cheeses, nuts, dried apricots and figs, fruit tarts with pears, apples or peaches, cookies, and caramels. Darker-colored purple wines are ideal with bittersweet chocolate, hard and blue cheeses, dark nuts, and brownies.

Design-a-Dessert

Chocolate-Dipped Cookies: Melt 2 to 3 quality bittersweet chocolate bars or a bag of dark chocolate chips. Dip store-bought pecan shortbread cookies halfway into the chocolate. Set on wax paper to harden and serve cookies alone or as a garnish for ice cream. The beauty of these cookies is that they are quick to prepare, look elegant, and are not overly sweet.

Easy Apple Turnover: Another easy, lightly sweet winner. Cook 3 or 4 cored, peeled, and sliced apples in butter until lightly browned. Add 1/4 cup brandy and cook until soft. Lay one sheet of puff pastry on a greased cookie sheet and spread out the apple mixture on the puff pastry, leaving an inch uncovered on all sides. Sprinkle with cinnamon and sugar. Cover with another sheet of pastry and squeeze the edges together like a big turnover. Score the top with a knife to release steam and bake in a 375°F oven until golden brown.

Cheese and Nut Platter: My favorite food with dessert wines is simply a platter with cheeses, nuts, and dried fruits. The cheese offers a savory counterpoint to the sweet wine. Some top cheeses to consider are rich blue cheeses, an aged goat cheese, and tangy white Cheddar. My guideline for pairing cheese and wine is simple: the whiter and fresher the cheese, the lighter and crisper the wine; the darker, more aged, and more pungent the cheese, the richer and stronger the wine. Nuts to try include almonds, hazelnuts, or pecans, and my picks for dried fruits are dates, apricots, and quince paste.

sharing

WHEN IT COMES TO BUYING WINE FOR GIFTS, WOMEN are the shoppers. From creative to traditional, affordable to impressive, these ideas are sure to cover all gift occasions.

Under $15
Creative
New Zealand Sauvignon Blanc

California Gewurztraminer

German Riesling

California Syrah

Australian Shiraz

Prosecco

Traditional
Australian Chardonnay

Chilean Cabernet Sauvignon

California Zinfandel

Cava

Under $25
Creative
Sancerre

Gewurztraminer from Alsace

Australian Grenache

Rhône Valley Syrah

California sparkling rosé

Traditional
White Burgundy

Sonoma Chardonnay

Napa Valley Merlot

Chianti Classico

Ten-year-old tawny port

More than $25
Creative

Top German Riesling

Russian River Valley Pinot Noir

Red Burgundy

Vin Santo

Top California sparkling wine

Traditional

Red or white Bordeaux

California Cabernet Sauvignon

Great Italian red

Vintage port

Champagne

The Buzz on...Famous Faces Making Wine

For Sports Fanatics

Greg Norman: The golfing "Shark" shoots and scores with his namesake wines from Australia.

Ernie Els: Not to be outshot, fellow golfer Ernie Els has a label from South Africa under his own name.

Mario Andretti: The famous race car driver wins another one with his wines from Napa Valley simply named Andretti.

For Movie Buffs

Seresin Estate: Filmmaker Michael Seresin crafts star wines from New Zealand.

Niebaum-Coppola Winery: Francis Ford Coppola makes delicious whites and reds from his Napa Valley venture.

Fess Parker: Daniel Boone of television fame has a winery in Santa Barbara with renegade reds.

For Culinary Fans

Emeril Lagasse: Restaurateur and Food Network television star Emeril Lagasse launched a fun white and red in conjunction with Fetzer Vineyards.

Michael Chiarello: Cookbook author and television personality who began Napa Valley's icon Italian restaurant Tra Vigne crafts Zinfandel and Sangiovese.

Pat Kuleto: Known for creating fantastic and whimsical restaurants, Pat Kuleto branched out to create a winery named Kuleto Estate.

Creative Ways to Personalize Wine Gifts

- Wine with mulling spices tied around the neck
- Wine with an invitation to dinner attached
- Tie a small wine accessory around the bottle. For example, a foil cutter, sparkling wine saver, or wine collar

Wine Bundle-Up Ideas

Party of One: Bubble bath, candles, relaxing CD, a mini-bottle of bubbly

Wine and Dine: Wine, a recipe for one of your favorite dishes, and the ingredients to make it

Sweet Treats: Vintage port and chocolate, tawny port with nuts, or Vin Santo and biscotti

Wine Wonders: An accessory basket with solution for cleaning wine
stains (see page 105), wine preserver gas, and a good corkscrew

Honeymoon Heaven: One of my top cocktails is a dash of cognac at
the bottom of a flute filled with Champagne. For wedding gifts I
often give a bottle of cognac, a bottle of Champagne, and two
flutes.

Checkout Counter: Resources

Here are many of my favorite spots to buy wine. I have chosen to highlight stores across the country that sell wine online because there are too many top local and regional wine shops to list here. If you are looking for a particular wine to buy, I suggest comparative shopping on *http://www.wine-searcher.com* (I use this site almost daily), or relying on *http://www.google.com* to locate general information.

Buying Wine

ONLINE/CATALOG ONLY MERCHANTS

Ambrosia
http://www.ambrosiawine.com

Buy Wine Online
http://wine.pippin.us/cart

Geerlings & Wade
http://www.geerwade.com

Wine.com
http://www.wine.com

Winetasting.com
http://www.winetasting.com

RETAIL STORES WITH E-COMMERCE WEB SITES

Best Cellars
http://www.bestcellars.com

Beverages & more!
http://www.bevmo.com

Brown Derby International Wine Center
http://www.brownderby.com

Costco
http://www.costco.com

Dean & DeLuca
http://www.deandeluca.com

D & M Wine and Liquor
http://www.dandm.com

Hi-Time Wine Cellars
http://www.hitimewine.com

K & L Wine Merchants
http://www.klwines.com

Morrell & Company
http://www.morrellwine.com

Sam's Wines & Spirits
http://www.samswine.com

Shop Bin 36
http://www.bin36.com

The Wine Club
http://www.thewineclub.com

The Wine Crier
http://www.thewinecrier.com

Union Square Wine & Spirits
http://www.unionsquarewines.com

Wine Cask
http://www.winecask.com

Wine Exchange
http://www.winex.com

Zachys
http://www.zachys.com

Wine Accessories and Cellars

After 5
http://www.after5catalog.com

International Wine Accessories, Inc.
http://www.iwawine.com

Napa Style
http://www.napastyle.com

Williams-Sonoma
http://www.williams-sonoma.com

Wine & All That Jazz
http://www.winejazz.com

The Wine Appreciation Guild
http://www.wineappreciation.com

The Wine Enthusiast
http://www.wineenthusiast.com

Wine Clubs

Oregon Pinot Noir Club
http://www.oregonpinotnoir.com

The California Wine Club
http://www.cawineclub.com

Wine Club 101
www.wineclub101.com

Bonny Doon Vineyard D.E.W.N. Club
http://www.bonnydoonvineyard.com

Informational Resources

Connoisseurs' Guide
http://www.cgcw.com

Decanter
http://www.decanter.com

Epicurious
http://eat.epicurious.com

Robin Garr's Wine Lover's Page
http://www.wine-lovers-page.com

The Wine Institute
http://www.wineinstitute.org

Wineanswers.com
http://www.wineanswers.com

Wine Business Monthly
http://www.winebusiness.com

Wine Spectator magazine
http://www.winespectator.com

Wine X magazine
http://www.winexmagazine.com

Wine Country Travel

Napa Valley Visitors Bureau
http://www.napavalley.org

Sonoma Valley Visitors Bureau
http://www.sonomavalley.com

Washington Wine Commission
http://www.washingtonwine.org

Burgundy Tourism Bureau
http://www.burgundy-tourism.com

Italian Government Tourist Board
http://www.italiantourism.com

South Australian Tourism Commission
http://www.southaustralia.com

Wellington Tourism Bureau
http://www.wellingtonnz.com

SPAS AND TOUR COMPANIES

The Silverado Country Club & Resort, Napa Valley, California
http://www.silveradoresort.com

Les Sources de Caudalie, Bordeaux, France
http://www.sources-caudalie.com

The Willows Lodge, Woodinville, Washington
http://www.willowslodge.com

The Spa at Pebble Beach, Pebble Beach, California
http://pebblebeach.com

For Bordeaux Saveurs
http://www.classic-wine-tours.com

France in Your Glass
http://franceinyourglass.com

Other Wine Organizations
Around the World for Travel Resources

Indiana Wine Grape Council
http://www.indianawines.org

Michigan Grape & Wine Industry Council
http://www.michiganwines.com

New York Wine/Grape Foundation
http://www.uncorknewyork.com

Ohio Wine Producers Association
http://www.ohiowines.org

Oregon Wine Advisory
http://www.oregonwine.org

Pennsylvania Wine Association
http://www.pennsylvaniawine.com

Texas Wine & Grape Growers Association
http://www.twgga.org

Virginia Wineries Association
http://www.vintagevirginia.org

Australian Wine Bureau
http://www.wineaustralia.com

Champagne Wines Information Bureau
http://www.champagnes.com

Chilean Trade Bureau
http://www.chileinfo.com

Food & Wine From France/SOPEXA
http://www.frenchwinesfood.com

German Wine Information Bureau
http://www.germanwineusa.org

Italian Trade Commission
http://www.italianmade.com

New Zealand Wine
http://www.nzwine.com

Portuguese Trade Commission
http://www.portugal.org

South African Consulate-General
http://www.southafrica.net

Wines from Spain
http://www.wineandfoodassociates.com

For a more complete list, check out www.wineanswers.com

Wine Schools and Classes

Affairs of the Vine
http://www.affairsofthevine.com

Chicago Wine School
http://www.wineschool.com

Copia: The American Center for Wine, Food and the Arts
http://www.copia.org

Court of Master Sommeliers, American Chapter
http://www.mastersommeliers.org

Culinary Institute of America at Greystone, St. Helena, CA
/ Hyde Park, NY
http://www.caichef.edu

Institute of Masters of Wine
http://www.masters-of-wine.org

International Wine Center
http://learnwine.com

Manhattan Wine Seminars
http://www.manhattanwineseminars.com

North Shore Wine Education
http://www.northshorewine.com

Pacific Rim Wine Education Center
http://www.pacrimwine.org

Society of Wine Educators
http://www.wine.gurus.com

University Extension, UC Davis
http://universityextension.ucdavis.edu/winemaking

Wine Organizations

American Institute of Wine and Food
http://www.aiwf.org

Le Donne del Vino
http://www.ledonnedelvino.it

Les Dames d'Escoffiers
http://www.ldei.org

Wine Brats
http://www.winebrats.org

Women for Winesense
http://www.winesense.com

Women in Wine
http://www.womeninwine.com

Wine Events

There are many wine events and tastings around the country. The largest annual consumer wine event in the United States is in Boston.

Boston Wine Expo
http://www.wine-expos.com

An excellent resource to check for events in your area is:

LocalWineEvents.com
http://localwineevents.com

Wine Importers

Billington Imports
http://www.billingtonwines.com

Cape Classics
http://www.capeclassics.com/index.asp

Caravelle Wine Selections
http://www.caravellewines.com

Empson & Company
http://www.empson.com

Frederick Wildman and Sons Ltd.
http://www.frederickwildman.com

Marc De Grazia Selections
http://www.marcdegrazia.com

Michael Skurnik Wines
http://www.skurnikwines.com

Palm Bay Imports
http://www.palmbayimports.com

Paterno Imports
http://www.paternoimports.com

Terry Theise Estate Selections
http://www.skurnikwines.com/wines_by_importer.htm

Via Pacifica Imports
http://www.viapacifica.com

Vineyard Brands
http://www.vineyardbrands.com

W. J. Deutsch & Sons Ltd.
http://www.wjdeutsch.com

William Grant & Sons
http://www.grantusa.com

Wilson Daniels, Ltd.
http://www.wilsondaniels.com

Winebow/Leonardo LoCascio
http://www.winebow.com

DON'T FORGET!

Leslie's monthly newsletter
http://www.lesliesbrocco.com

Index

Barolo, 254–56

Barone Ricasoli, 225

Baron Herzog Winery, 117

Baron Philippe de Rothschild, 162

Barossa Valley, Australia, 34, 74, 96,
106, 121, 138, 151, 177–78

Barton & Guestier, 180, 182

Bâtard-Montrachet, 30

Beaujolais growing regions and wines,
29, 192, 249–50

Beaujolais-Villages, France, 250

Beaulieu Vineyards (BV), 128, 138, 142,
202

Benn, Eric, 279

Benson Ferry Vineyards, 241

Beringer Howell Mountain, 159

Beringer Vineyards, 37, 302

Billecart-Salmon, 288

Biondi-Santi, 225

Biondi-Santi, Franco, 220

Blackstone, 161

Blanc de Blancs, 277

Blanc de Noirs, 277

blending, 73–75, 119, 127, 160–61,
222–23, 276–77

blind tasting, 45

Blosser, Susan Sokol, 196

BLT with baked beans, 246

blush wine, 264

Bodega Catena Zapata, 253

Bogle Vineyards, 242

Boisset, 202

Bolla, "Arcale," 56

Bollinger, Lily, 274–75

Bollini, 56

Bonny Doon Vineyard, 84, 99, 224,
301

Bordeaux, red, 119, 153
classified growths of 1855, 131–32
"cru bourgeois" labels, 132
famous labels, 131–32

growing regions, 72–73, 133–34,
155–56
legendary vintages, 143
shopping guide, 161–63
tips on buying, 130–32
see also Cabernet Sauvignon; Merlot

Bordeaux, white, 65, 76–78
growing regions, 70–71, 72–73
see also blending; Sauvignon Blanc

Bordeaux-style blends, 161

Borgo Scopeto, 225

Botrytis cinerea, 98, 299–300

Botrytis Semillon, 106

bottle collar, 83

bottle sizes, 167

bouquet, 46

Bower, Robert, 297

Brancott Vineyards, 71, 76

Brogan Cellars, 205

Brouilly, France, 250

brunch ideas and wines, 104–7

Brunello di Montalcino, Italy, 214,
220

Buena Vista, 161

burgers with sweet potato fries, 245–46

Burgundian beef stew, 210

Burgundy, France, 27–30

Burgundy, red, 150, 191–95
buying and enjoying, 205–7
growing regions, 193–95
shopping guide, 202–5
terroir, 200–202
see also Beaujolais growing regions
and wines; Pinot Noir

Burgundy, white, 27–30, 42–45
buying and enjoying, 205–7
pairing food with, 40–41
shopping guide, 36–40
see also Chardonnay

butter, sweet sage, 42

Byron, 203

Meritage, 75, 161

Meritage Association, 75

Merlot, 127, 130, 152–59
    fruity and rich, 157–59
    lingo, 154
    pairing food with, 163–64
    recipes, 165–66
    shopping guide, 161–63
    stylish and smooth, 155–57

Merry Edwards Wines, 204

méthode champenoise, 284

Michel Lafarge, 204

Michel Redde, "La Moynerie," 77

Miller, Christian, 151

minerality, 92

Miner Family, 243

minestrone and grilled cheese, 228

Mionetto, 286

Mirabelle, 287

Moët & Chandon, 306

Mondavi, Robert, 66

Monmousseau, 117

Monte Antico, 223

Monterey, Calif., 26

Montes, "Alpha," 39, 183

Montevina Winery, 56, 223, 269

Montlouis, France, 116

Montrachet, 30

Morgan, Jeff, 266

Morgan Winery, 38

Morgon, France, 250

Mosel River Valley, Germany, 89

Mosel-Saar-Ruwer, Germany, 91–92

Moulin-à-Vent, France, 250

Mount Pleasant, 122

Mount Riley, 204

Mouton-Cadet, 155

Müeller, Rudolf, 99

Mulderbosch, 117

Muller-Catoir, "Haardter Herzog," 100

Muscadelle, 70

Muscat wines, 294–95

Nahe, Germany, 98

Nalle Winery, 242

Napa Valley, Calif., 11, 31, 53, 66, 122,
    128, 148, 159, 221, 239

Navarra, Spain, 268

Navarro Vineyards, 99, 203

Nebbiolo grape, 254–55

Neel, Susan, 113

New South Wales, Australia, 33

New York State, 94, 156–57

New Zealand, 53, 66, 71, 75, 84, 92, 94,
    122, 158–59, 197–98, 283

Niebaum-Coppola, 144

noble rot, 98, 299–300

Norman Vineyards, 242

Northstar Winery, 158, 163

Novy Cellars, 184

oak barrels, 11, 35

oak-free wines, 35

Oakville, Calif., 138

Olivier Leflaive, 39

onion tart, 165–66

Orange, Australia, 177

Oregon, 54, 195–96

organic wines, 181

Origin-Napa, "Gamble Vineyard,"
    78

Palliser Estates, 205

Paradigm, 143

Pascal Jolivet, 70, 76

Paso Robles, Calif., 238

Passito-style wines, 301

Ravenswood Winery, 234, 243
ravioli, sweet sage, 43
Recioto della Valpolicella, 308
red beans and rice, 246
red wines, 127–259
Reed, Susan, 44
regional wines, 29
Reuilly, France, 72
Rex Hill, 203
Reynolds Vineyards, 184
Rhône Valley, France, 170–71, 173, 258–59
ribs, sweet marinated, 246
Ricasoli, Bettino, 219
Ridge Vineyards, 234, 243
Riesling, 86–107, 295
   crisp and aromatic, 91–95
   lingo, 90
   pairing food with, 101–2
   recipes, 102–4
   ripe and aromatic, 95–98
   shopping guide, 99–101
   structure, 90–91
Rioja growing regions and wines,
   251–52, 268–69
roasted garlic, 187
roasted leg of lamb with fresh mint
   sauce, 146–47
Robert Mondavi Winery, 77, 202
Robert Sinskey, "los Carneros," 162
Rochioli Vineyards, 77, 204
Rockford winery, 177
Rodeno, Michaela, 81
Rodney Strong, "Chalk Hill," 38, 142
Roederer Estate, 288
Rolland, Dany and Michel, 156
rosé, 263–73
   lingo, 266
   pairing food with, 270
   recipes, 271–72
   shopping guide, 269–70
   sparkling wines, 277–78

rosemary lamb and pilaf, 188
Rosemount Estate, 122, 141, 171, 182
Rosenblum winery, 234, 241
Roussane, 111
Ruffino Riserva Ducale, 225
Russian River Valley, Calif., 26, 32, 73,
   75, 137, 177, 179, 198–99, 239, 283
Rutherford, Calif., 138
Ryan, Phillip, 120–21

Sabourin-Relf, Patricia, 306
Saint-Émilion, France, 152, 155–56, 160,
   257
Saint-Estèphe, France, 133–34
St. Francis, 243
St.-Joseph, France, 171, 173, 177
Saint-Julien, France, 135
St. Supéry Winery, 76, 81
Saint-Véran, France, 30
salads:
   chèvre chaud, 80
   chunky turkey, 60
   crispy corn, 43
   pesto pasta, 81
   Tuscan-style bread, 229
salmon:
   maple-glazed, 209–10
   spicy mango, 43
Sancerre, 65–66, 69–70
   shopping guide, 76–78
   see also Sauvignon Blanc
sandwiches:
   easy chicken, 43
   eggplant and mushroom, 166
   grilled portobello, 187
   sausage, and sweet potato fries, 103
   spicy sausage, 272
Sangiovese, 214–18
   leftover wine, 230–32
   lingo, 217

South Eastern Australia, 33, 178

Spain, 251–52, 268–69, 283

  see also Rioja growing regions and
    wines

sparkling wines, 274–79, 282–86

  see also Champagne

sparkling wine stopper, 85

spas and hotels, 149

Spring Valley Vineyard, 158

spumante, 276

Spurrier, Steven, 129

Staglin Family Vineyard, 143

Stags Leap District, Calif., 137–38

Stag's Leap Wine Cellars, 129–30, 138,
    143, 184

Stellenbosch, South Africa, 71, 116

Sterling Joy, 290

Sterling Vineyards, "Vintner's
    Collection," 37, 162

storing and serving wines, 166–69,
    212

structural components, 67–69, 90–91,
    139–40, 240–41

Stuart, Jack, 218

Stuckey, Wendy, 104

stuffed veal chops with white beans,
    228–29

Super Tuscans, 216

Sutter Home, 53, 264

Swanson Vineyards, 57, 162

sweetness levels, 68, 86–88, 91, 98, 241,
    265, 276, 286

sweet potato:

  casserole, 187

  chili and corn bread, 271

Symington, Dominic, 294

Syrah, 170–72, 174–88

  earthy and vibrant, 174–77

  lingo, 172

  pairing food with, 185–86

  recipes, 186–88

rich and fruity, 177–80

shopping guide, 182–85

tacos, fruity fish, 80

Taittinger, Claude, 275

Talus, 53

tannin levels, 68, 139–40

Tasmania, Australia, 33, 196, 283

Tavel, France, 267

Taylor, Fladgate, 296, 302

Tchelistcheff, André, 138

temperatures, serving, 167–69

Tempranillo grape, 251

Tenuto Caparzo, 224

Terra Valentine, 213

terroir, 10, 200–202

Testarossa, "Sleepy Hollow Vineyard,"
    40, 205

Texas, 74–75

Texas Wine Research and Marketing
    Institute, 74

Thelema, 78

Thomas Fogarty, 99

Tiefenbrunner, 56

Tignanello, 216

tomato-blue cheese butter, 146

tomato bruschetta, 228

Torrontes grape, 35

Trefethen Vineyards, 95

Trentino-Alto Adige, Italy, 50, 52

Trimbach, 56, 100, 302

Trimbach, Hubert, 96

Trimbach, Jean, 54, 89

Trinchero, Roger, 265

Trinchero Family Selection, 141

Trinity Oaks, 2421

tuna curry quiche, 60

Turning Leaf, 202

Tuscany, Italy, 150

Tyrrell's Vat 47, 34